The Reiki 1

Incorporating
The Spiritual Healer's Guide
and
The Self-Healing Workbook

From
The Mastership Pathway Collection

Dr Allan Sweeney PhD. (AM)

COPYRIGHT
All Rights Reserved

Published in the UK
by Mastership Pathway UK Ltd
PO Box No. 42424, London, NW10 8WX

ISBN 0-954 3726-0-3

Printed in the UK through Rei On International Ltd

<u>With Special Thanks</u>

With special thanks to Senseis Hiroshi Doi and Fuminori Aoki for their release of true Usui information, to Jeanne Murton who started me on this path 23 years ago and for her openness and brilliant teaching of so many healing, psychic, and spiritual subjects, to Paul Dennis, Margaret Pauffrey and William Rand for starting me on the path to discovering Dr Usui's original reiki methods, to my parents Edward and Betty for struggling to keep me alive during severe childhood illnesses, to my beautiful daughter Angela for her laid-back understanding of my soul need to heal, to Christine Ward for her patient support during the early days of writing, to my ever-helpful P.A. Cheryl Walke for providing a peaceful space for me to write, to Shoshanna Garfield for her intensive help in reformatting the book, to Rosemary Pharo for her gifted editing abilities, to Prashun Dutt for his publishing and marketing expertise, to the anonymous man on the 7th level of Dr Usui's organisation who was kind enough to offer me a limited amount of knowledge of Dr Usui's levels and aims, to the thousands of students who supported me over the years, and to my God and guides and angels.

Allan Sweeney

Medical Disclaimer

The information in this manual should not be used as an alternative to orthodox medicine, nor as an alternative to doctors' or medical consultants' prescriptions, referrals, operations, advice, or treatment.

Rather, reiki should be viewed as a complementary therapy – reiki complements doctors, and is not an alternative to them.

Anyone with any illness whether physical, emotional, mental or on any other level of being should see a doctor first, and accept the doctor's prescriptions, referrals, operations, advice, or treatment. The doctor's opinion about anything in this manual should also be taken, respected and accepted.

Also, no matter how perfect and good something may be, there may be, for someone somewhere, a caveat, danger or contraindication. In particular, if you belong to one of the categories in the section on caveats, you should not use the techniques or exercises in this manual. Please see chapter 24 for more details. You should not use any of these techniques or exercises if you are a UK citizen under the age of 18 or below the age of relevant legality or adulthood in the country in which you live or whilst driving or operating machinery or doing anything potentially hazardous.

<u>Preface</u>

I have put much deep thought into this reiki manual. What should it cover? What should it include? How can it fit in with the teachings of other reiki masters? How could it be useful to both practitioners and people exploring reiki for the first time?

I know it is possible that not everyone will agree with what I have written in this manual, but everything I have done has been with the intention of spreading the most recent revelations about reiki so that all may benefit from them. Most of all I wish to provide knowledge of Dr Usui's 7-level system, to enlighten about rei and spiritual healing and, yes, to tread new ground that may initially provoke some controversy.

Reiki is in essence an unfolding path. Different teachings are needed on different levels. Reiki is like learning a subject through nursery, infants, junior and senior schools, and then on to university degree, masters, and PhD – not everything can be taught on one level. So references are made in this manual to higher-level manuals, and to the learning, techniques, and understanding needed to evolve up to those higher reiki levels.

Evolution and change is a part of all our lives. Dr Usui spent his life searching and developing techniques that would allow himself and his students an ever-greater range of tools to attain physical healing and spiritual enlightenment.

Like any change, this process is not always comfortable, but I hope and trust that it will be the springboard for much creative development in the reiki world.

I look forward to debating and discussing many of the points with you. That is how we discover more, both from other people and from within ourselves.

Dr Allan Sweeney PhD (AM)

NB: For consistency with other healing systems mentioned and stylistic consonance, Reiki has been written in lower case in the body text.

Reiki Unconditionally

If you share all you have with others,
Others may be selfish with you.
Share what you have anyway.
Unconditionally with LOve

If you help others' soul pathways,
They may try to destroy yours.
Help their soul path anyway.
Unconditionally with LOve.

If you're available for others,
No one may be available for you.
Be available anyway.
Unconditionally with LOve.

If you care for others,
They may take no care of you.
Care for others anyway.
Unconditionally with LOve

If you heal others,
They may not always recover.
Heal anyway.
Unconditionally with LOve.

If you reiki others,
They may be ungrateful.
Reiki anyway.
Unconditionally with LOve.

If you LOve others,
They may hate you.
LOve anyway
Unconditionally.

Allan Sweeney - December 1997

TABLE OF CONTENTS

COPYRIGHT... 1
WITH SPECIAL THANKS 2
MEDICAL DISCLAIMER.. 3
PREFACE 4
REIKI UNCONDITIONALLY 5
TABLE OF FIGURES 23

CHAPTER 1 GENERAL INTRODUCTIONS..................................... 25

CAN I LEARN REIKI? 25
STUDENT REASONS FOR TAKING REIKI CLASSES 26
WARNING 27
    1.   *Class Required* 27
    2.   *Attunements* 27
    3.   *7-Level System*... 27
    4.   *Research* 27
    5.   *Specialities*.. 28
    6.   *Biofeedback* 28
    7.   *Special Needs* 28
    8.   *Learning* 29
    9.   *Quality Assurance*... 29
DIFFERENT TYPES OF USERS OF THIS MANUAL.. 30
    1.   *Existing Reiki Masters* 30
    2.   *Existing Reiki 1 Or Above Practitioners* 31
    3.   *A Course Workbook*.. 31
    4.   *Reference Book After the Course* 31
    5.   *Non-Reiki People - Explorers*....................................... 31
    6.   *Those Considering A Reiki 1 Course* 32
    7.   *Those Thirsting for Extra Knowledge* 32
    8.   *The Next Edition*.. 32
LIMITATIONS OF THIS MANUAL IF YOU WISH TO BE A REIKI
PRACTITIONER / TEACHER 33
101 REIKI 1 EXERCISES... 34
WORKBOOK NOTES ON GENERAL INTRODUCTIONS............................. 37

CHAPTER 2 WHAT IS REIKI?..**38**

WHAT DOES 'REIKI' MEAN?..38
1. *Rei = Highest Outer Spiritual Healing Energy*.................*38*
2. *Ki = Various Inner Life Force Healing Energies* *39*
HOW DOES REIKI HEAL?..40
1. *It's All In The Mind – (No It Isn't)*...................................*40*
2. *It's A Placebo Response – (No It Isn't)* *41*
3. *It's Faith – (No It Isn't)*...*42*
4. *It's Magic – (No It Isn't)*..*42*
5. *It's The Last Resort – (No It Isn't)*.................................*42*
6. *So How Does Reiki Heal?* *43*
FREQUENCIES OF REI AND KI...44
1. *Reiki 1 - High Rei Frequency*...*45*
2. *Reiki 2 - Low Ki Frequencies*...*45*
3. *Reiki 2 Sacred Geometric Symbols*.................................*46*
WORKBOOK NOTES ON WHAT IS REIKI 48

CHAPTER 3 DR USUI AND THE HISTORY OF REIKI **49**

INTRODUCTION 49
DR USUI – PERSONAL HISTORY 51
DR USUI, BUDDHISM, SHINTOISM, AND REIKI..............................55
1. *Buddhism*..*57*
2. *Shintoism*..*60*
DR MIKAO USUI'S DISCOVERY OF REIKI.......................................62
1. *Christian* *62*
2. *Sutras* *63*
3. *Buddhist* *63*
4. *The Mountain*..*65*
5. *Beam Of Light After 21 Days*..*65*
6. *Instant Attunement*..*66*
7. *The Reiki Ideals* *66*
8. *The Reiki Lineage*...*66*
HISTORY OF REIKI LINEAGE – ANCIENT 67
1. *Theory One - Tibet*..*67*
2. *Theory Two - Christ*..*67*
HISTORY OF REIKI LINEAGE - MODERN..68
1. *Dr Mikao Usui* *68*
2. *Dr Chijiro Hayashi*...*70*

3. *Mrs Chiyoko Yamaguchi*... 72
4. *Mrs Hawayo Hiromi Takata*.. 73
5. *Mrs Takata's Masters Introduced* 75
6. *Phyllis Lei Furumoto & Barbara Ray*............................ 76
7. *Others Introduced* 77
8. *Dr Allan Sweeney PhD. (AM)*....................................... 78
9. *You*.. 83
WORKBOOK NOTES ON DR USUI AND THE HISTORY OF REIKI 84

CHAPTER 4 DR USUI'S EXPLANATION OF REIKI THERAPY 85

DR USUI'S EXPLANATION OF REIKI THERAPY............................ 85
EXPLANATION OF REIKI THERAPY, BY THE FOUNDER, DR MIKAO USUI .. 88
REACTIONS TO DR USUI'S WRITINGS 101
WORKBOOK NOTES ON DR USUI'S EXPLANATION OF REIKI THERAPY .. 103

CHAPTER 5 DR USUI'S ORIGINAL TEACHINGS........................... 104

FAX ON DR USUI'S TEACHINGS VIA JAPAN............................... 104
AN OVERVIEW OF REIKI AS ORIGINALLY TAUGHT BY DR USUI IN JAPAN
.... 107
1. *Levels Within Levels*.. 107
2. *Progression* 107
3. *Exoteric Subjects*.. 107
4. *Following Dr Usui's Path*.. 108
TRUE USUI REIKI LEVELS INSIDE LEVELS INSIDE LEVELS 109
TOU AND KYŪ_... 110
THE SEVEN LEVELS OF TRUE USUI REIKI................................ 112
REIKI 1 – SHODEN (SPIRITUAL HEALING)............................. 113
REIKI 2 – OKUDEN 114
REIKI 3 – SHINPIDEN... 115
REIKI 4 – SHIHAN-KAKU – REIKI MASTER (BEGINNER TEACHER)........... 121
REIKI 5 – SHIHAN – SENSEI (EXPERT TEACHER) 122
REIKI 6 - BY INVITATION ONLY 123
REIKI 7 - BY INVITATION ONLY 124
USUI REIKI 1 SHODEN TECHNIQUES 125
1. *Rei-ju Attunement*... 125
2. *Byosen Reikan-Ho (The Most Important Reiki 1 Technique)*......... 125
3. *Reiji-Ho* 125
4. *Teate (Practising Hands-On Healing)* 126
5. *Nentatsu-Ho* 127

6. *Jakikiri Joka-Ho* *127*
7. *Shudan Reiki Teate (Shuchu Reiki)* *127*
8. *Renzoku Reiki (Reiki Marathon)* *128*
9. *Reiki Mawashi (Reiki Circle)* *128*
10. *Hand Positions For The Head* *129*
11. *Gokai* *130*
12. *Gyosei Of Emperor Meiji* *130*
13. *Reiki Ryoho Shishin - Hikkei* *130*
14. *Kotodama* *131*
WORKBOOK NOTES ON DR USUI'S ORIGINAL TEACHINGS 132

CHAPTER 6 GOKAI, REIKI IDEALS & WAKA POETRY **133**

GOKAI - THE REIKI IDEALS 134
THE REIKI IDEALS IN DR USUI'S HANDWRITING 135
WAKA (GYOSEI) POEMS 136
WHEN TO USE REIKI IDEALS AND WAKA POEMS 139
1. *At The Day's Start Or End* *139*
2. *Before Or During Self-Healing* *139*
3. *Before Or During Healing Others* *140*
WORKBOOK NOTES ON GOKAI, REIKI IDEALS AND WAKA POETRY ..142

CHAPTER 7 REI AND SPIRITUAL HEALING **143**

REI AND SPIRITUAL HEALING - INTRODUCTION 143
EXPLANATIONS OF SPIRITUAL OR REI HEALING 145
1. *Dr Usui's Spiritual Healing Philosophy* *145*
2. *LOve Versus Love – Why LOve* *145*
3. *Can LOve Heal Everything?* *146*
4. *Can LOve Transform Lower Frequencies?* *146*
DO ALL SPIRITUAL/REI HEALERS CHANNEL LOVE? 148
1. *Capability* *148*
2. *Natural Healing - Frequency* *148*
3. *Natural Healing - Psychic* *149*
4. *Natural Healing - Guides* *150*
5. *Natural Healing – Perfection Intention* *150*
6. *Summary* *151*
HEALING INTO DEATH HELPS TO DIE IN PEACE 152
1. *General – Spiritual Or Rei Energy And The Dying* *152*
2. *Healing Fears of Dying Process, Death Act And After* *152*
3. *Can Rei Healing Cure Someone Close To Death?* *153*

4. Other Options 154
LOVE ASPECTS OF REI AND SPIRITUAL HEALING 155
1. The Enjoyment Of The LOve 155
2. Becoming LOve 155
3. Showing LOve To The World 156
4. Channelling A Piece Of The Peace Of LOve 156
5. The LOve Waterfall 157
6. Intention And LOve 157
7. Scientific Study Of Intention And Unconditional LOve 158
WORKBOOK NOTES ON REI AND SPIRITUAL HEALING 161

CHAPTER 8 RIPPLE EFFECT HEALINGS 162

THE RIPPLE EFFECT 162
1. Time Frames For Ripple Effect Healings 162
2. Ripples Of Rei – Healing Inwards From Spirit Body 165
3. Ripples Of Rei – Healing Outwards From The Soul 166
4. Ripples Of Ki 168
REI SPIRITUAL HEALING MENTAL THERAPY 169
1. Potential Positive Mental Rei Healings 169
2. Genetic Or Chemically Imbalanced Mental Illness 170
3. Other Mental Healing Difficulties With Rei LOve 170
REI SPIRITUAL HEALING – EMOTIONAL REPLACEMENT THERAPY 171
1. Rei Emotional Replacement Therapy 171
2. Adjusting Your Frequency 171
3. Adjusting Your Power 172
4. Emotional Healing Difficulties Using Rei 172
REI SPIRITUAL HEALING FOR PHYSICAL ILLNESS - CHRONICS 173
1. Time Frame For Healing Potential 173
2. If 'Spiritual' Healing Gets Quick Physical Results 173
REI SPIRITUAL HEALING FOR PHYSICAL ILLNESS – ACUTES 174
1. Is There Time To Heal Acutes With Rei? 174
2. The Likely Help Rei Healing Gives To Acutes 174
3. If Quicker Reiki Help Is Needed 174
SUMMARY - WHAT REI MAY OR MAY NOT HELP 175
1. Short-Term – Within 1 - 9 Months 175
2. Medium-Term – Within 9 – 18 Months 176
3. Long-Term – Within 18 - 60 Months 176
4. What Spiritual Rei Healing May Not Help 177
WORKBOOK NOTES ON RIPPLE EFFECT HEALINGS 178

CHAPTER 9 BIOFEEDBACK **179**

REIKI BIOFEEDBACK SENSATION EXPLANATION...179
1. *Explanation To First Time Healees*...*180*
2. *Case History* *180*
3. *Biofeedback During Self-healing*...*181*
4. *Biofeedback Within Healee*..*181*
BIOFEEDBACK THROUGH YOUR SEVEN SENSES..184
1. *Clairsentience - Touch (Or Feeling)*..*184*
2. A. *Clairvoyance – Seeing Through Physical Eyes*.....................*189*
2. B. *Clairvoyant Psychic Vision– Seeing Through Third Eye*..........*189*
3. *Clairaudience - Hearing* *195*
4. *Clairolfaction - Smell* *196*
5. *Clairgustation - Taste*..*196*
6. *Spiritual*...*196*
THE THREE MAIN TYPES OF TEARS..198
1. *Tears Of Desperation* *198*
2. *Tears Of Release*..*199*
3. *Tears Of God Connection* *200*
PRIMAL SCREAM...202
1. *What Is A Primal Scream?*...*202*
2. *How To Help The Healee* *202*
WORKBOOK NOTES ON BIOFEEDBACK 204

CHAPTER 10 DEVELOPING STRENGTHS...**205**

IF YOU EXPERIENCE NOTHING IN ATTUNEMENTS, WHEN SELF-HEALING
OR HEALING OTHERS 205
1. *Why You May Experience Nothing* *206*
2. *If You Experience 'Nothing' Does Nothing Happen?*...................*207*
3. *What To Do If You Experience Nothing* *208*
ACCEPTING AND DEVELOPING YOUR STRENGTHS 210
1. *No Desire* *210*
2. *Acceptance*...*210*
3. *Development* *211*
ARE YOU TOO QUESTIONING? OR TOO ACCEPTING?.............................212
1. *Are You Too Questioning?* *212*
2. *Are You Too Accepting?*..*214*
WORKBOOK NOTES ON DEVELOPING STRENGTHS 216

Table of Contents

CHAPTER 11   ATTUNEMENTS **217**

HISTORY OF ATTUNEMENTS.. 217
1.   *Japan* 217
2.   *Western Attunements*.. 219
3.   *Summary*.. 220
POTENTIAL BENEFITS OF ATTUNEMENTS 221
1.   *Create A Reiki Healer* 221
2.   *Attune To Reiki Symbol Frequencies*....................................... 222
3.   *Channelling Symbols* 223
4.   *Adjustment Of Crown To Higher Spiritual Energy* 223
5.   *Adjust The Third Eye And Psychic Intuition*............................ 224
6.   *Blend The Heart To A Giving Nature*....................................... 224
7.   *Attune The Hands To Let Reiki Flow Through* 225
8.   *Adjust, Open, Or Close Chakras* 225
9.   *Balance The Aura And The Field* 226
10. *Repair Energy Meridians*... 226
11. *Release Negativity*.. 226
12. *Release Energy Blocks*... 226
13. *Harmonise All Energy Bodies* 227
14. *Healing* 227
15. *Past Lives*.. 228
16. *Raising Of Frequency* 228
17. *Create Wholeness Within*... 229
18. *Happiness* 229
19. *Develop Soul Path*.. 229
20. *Reiki Or Other Guides Coming Close To Help You* 230
21. *Provide Protection* 230
22. *Karmic Resolution*... 230
23. *Give A Spiritual Experience* 231
24. *Earthly Enlightenment* 231
25. *God Enlightenment* 231
26. *To Share Only Our Light* 232
27. *Allow Oneness With All* 233
28. *Blessing*... 233
29. *Divine LOve*.. 233
30. *Peace* 234
ATTUNEMENTS ARE FOR THE HIGHEST GOOD OF ALL CONCERNED 235
WORKBOOK NOTES ON ATTUNEMENTS 236

CHAPTER 12 ATTUNEMENT BIOFEEDBACK.................................**237**

STUDENTS' ATTUNEMENT EXPERIENCES 237
CLAIRVOYANTS' ATTUNEMENT EXPERIENCES 240
WORKBOOK NOTES ON BIOFEEDBACK OF REIKI 1.............242
1ST ATTUNEMENT 242
WORKBOOK NOTES ON BIOFEEDBACK OF REIKI 1.............243
2ND ATTUNEMENT..243
WORKBOOK NOTES ON BIOFEEDBACK OF REIKI 1.............244
3RD ATTUNEMENT...244
WORKBOOK NOTES ON BIOFEEDBACK OF REIKI 1.............245
4TH ATTUNEMENT 245

CHAPTER 13 SELF-HEALING NEEDS AND OVERCOMING
DIFFICULTIES...**246**

WHEN I WAS A YOUNG MAN…..246
ON WHAT LEVEL DO YOU NEED SELF-HEALING? 247
  1. *Physical*..*247*
  2. *Past, Present, Future*...*247*
  3. *Emotions* *248*
  4. *Mental* *248*
  5. *Spirituality* *248*
  6. *Soul*..*249*
  7. *Others*..*249*
CAN YOU HEAL OTHERS IF YOU'RE NOT HEALED? 251
  1. *Just Do It*...*251*
  2. *Pre-Healing Alpha*..*251*
  3. *Self-Healing To Create An Excellent Healer* *251*
  4. *Detach From Your Emotions* *252*
  5. *Using Two Consciousnesses At The Same Time*................*252*
  6. *Acceptance Of Impermanent Nature Of Everything* *253*
RELEASING STRESS BEFORE REIKI..254
  1. *Breathing Techniques*...*254*
  2. *Physical Relaxation*..*257*
  3. *Mental Peace Through Meditation* *259*
IF YOU FIND SELF-HEALING DIFFICULT.......................................261
WORKBOOK NOTES ON SELF-HEALING NEEDS AND OVERCOMING
DIFFICULTIES 262

CHAPTER 14 THE INTELLIGENT NATURE OF REIKI ENERGY **263**

How Intelligent Is Healing Energy? 263
Stress Versus Low Energy 265
   1. Is Healing Energy Totally Intelligent? 265
   2. If The Worst Problem Is Stress 266
   3. If The Worst Problem Is Lack Of Energy 266
   4. If Someone Has Stress And Lack Of Energy 266
WORKBOOK NOTES On The Intelligent Nature of Reiki Energy
.... 267

CHAPTER 15 HUI YIN AND KANJI **268**

The Hui Yin 268
   1. Two Main Acupuncture Meridians 268
   2. The Mouth 268
   3. The Hui Yin 269
   4. Result Of Connecting Mouth And Hui Yin 270
   5. When To Connect Mouth And Hui Yin 270
Reiki Kanji (Or Mudra) Hand Positions 272
   1. Unconscious Kanji 272
   2. Kanji Meditation For Focussing The Mind 272
   3. Seven Combinations Of Reiki Kanji / Mudra 273
   4. When And How To Use Kanji 273
   5. Reiki Kanji 1 / Mudra 1 - For Extra Power 274
   6. Reiki Kanji 2 / Mudra 2 - Extra Help From 'Above' .. 275
   7. Reiki Kanji 3 / Mudra 3 - For Extra Understanding .. 276
   8. Kanji Combinations 277
   9. The Thumbs 279
  10. The Ring Fingers (Next To Little Fingers) 280
  11. The Little Fingers 280
  12. Kanji For A Japanese Priest 281
  13. Children's 'Reiki' Kanji 282
WORKBOOK NOTES On Hui Yin And Kanji 283

CHAPTER 16 PROTECTION AND GROUNDING **284**

Protection 284
   1. Origins Of Protection – Spiritualist Healing 284
   2. Is Protection Necessary In Reiki? 284

3. *Is Protection Needed From Others' Negative Energy?* 285
4. *A Simple Protection Method* 285
5. *Potential Healing Conflict Of Gold Protection*..........................286
GROUNDING..287
1. *Origins Of Grounding – Spiritual Healing*................................287
2. *Is Grounding Necessary In Reiki?* 287
3. *Why You Should Customise Your Grounding*.............................288
4. *How To Customise Your Grounding*...288
5. *Grounding During A Treatment*..289
6. *Grounding Options After A Treatment* 289
WORKBOOK NOTES ON PROTECTION AND GROUNDING.....................292

CHAPTER 17 PASSIVE AND ACTIVE REIKI 1 METHODS 293

PASSIVE V ACTIVE REIKI I METHODS..293
ABOUT THE PASSIVE METHOD: ALPHA HEALING.............................295
1. *Reiki As A Passive Method Of Learning Healing* 295
2. *Alpha Brain Waves*..295
3. *Eradicate Egotistical Attachments To Outcome*.........................296
4. *For Beginners: Trust Energy Goes Where Needed*.....................297
5. *Dangers Of Passive Healing For Beginners* 297
ABOUT THE ACTIVE METHOD: FAST BETA HEALING 300
1. *If You Are Unwell, Need A Kick Start, Or If Your Mind Wanders*
   Too Much 300
2. *Fast Beta Brain Waves*...300
3. *Are You A Magnetic Healer?* 301
4. *Dangers Of Active Healing For Beginners* 301
USING THE PASSIVE OR ACTIVE METHOD 302
1. *The Passive Method*...302
2. *The Active Method*...302
WHAT SHOULD HEALERS SAY? 'IT'S NOT ME' OR 'I AM ONLY THE
CHANNEL' OR 'IT'S ME' 304
1. *'It's Not Me' – Spiritualist Healing*..304
2. *'I Am Only The Channel' – Rei And Spiritual Healing* 305
3. *'It's Me' – Ki And Technique Healing*.....................................305
4. *Eventual Healing Mastership*...306
WORKBOOK NOTES ON PASSIVE AND ACTIVE METHODS REIKI 1
METHODS...307

CHAPTER 18 HEALER HAND AND HEALEE BODY POSITIONS
.... 308

WAYS TO HOLD THE HANDS FOR HEALING 308
1. *The 'Normal' Way*.. 308
2. *Thumbs* 308
3. *The Reiki Hand Stack*... 309
4. *Reiki Laser Coning*.. 310
5. *The Reiki Spread* 311
THE BASIC TWELVE HAND POSITIONS FOR SELF-HEALING AND FOR
HEALING OTHERS 312
1. *The Traditional Twelve Hand Positions*................................. 312
2. *If You Cannot Reach A Particular Hand Position*.................. 314
3. *If Some Positions Strain Your Arms* 314
HEALEE BODY POSITIONS ON A CHAIR OR A HEALING COUCH............. 315
1. *Healing On A Chair* 315
2. *Healing On A Healing Couch*.. 318
HEAD HAND POSITION H1 – THE FACE 321
HEAD HAND POSITION H2 – SIDES OF HEAD 322
HEAD HAND POSITION H3 – BACK OF HEAD 323
HEAD HAND POSITION H4 – THROAT 324
FRONT OF BODY HAND POSITION F1 – TOP OF CHEST............................. 325
FRONT OF BODY HAND POSITION F2 – BELOW CHEST............................. 326
FRONT OF BODY HAND POSITION F3 – AROUND NAVEL 327
FRONT OF BODY HAND POSITION F4 – BELOW NAVEL............................. 328
BACK OF BODY HAND POSITION B1 – SHOULDERS 329
BACK OF BODY HAND POSITION B2 – RIB CAGE....................................... 330
BACK OF BODY HAND POSITION B3 – LOWER BACK 331
BACK OF BODY B4 – BASE OF SPINE 332
JOINTS OF ARMS A1 – SHOULDERS 333
JOINTS OF ARMS A2 – ELBOWS 334
JOINTS OF ARMS A3 – WRISTS 335
JOINTS OF ARMS A4 – HANDS 336
JOINTS OF LEGS L1 – HIPS 337
JOINTS OF LEGS L2 – KNEES.. 338
JOINTS OF LEGS L3 – ANKLES 339
JOINTS OF LEGS L4 – FEET... 340
WORKBOOK NOTES ON HEALER HAND AND HEALEE BODY POSITIONS
.... 341

CHAPTER 19 THE COMPLETE REIKI 1 METHOD..........................342

IF YOU CLEAN YOUR TEETH YOU SHOULD ALSO CLEANSE YOUR ENERGY
DAILY..342
HOW TO GIVE YOURSELF A REIKI TREATMENT 343
  1. *How Often Should You Practise Self-Healing*.................................343
  2. *What If You Miss A Treatment* 343
  3. *Falling Asleep During Self-Healing* 343
  4. *The Self-Healing Dosage*..344
  5. *If You Have Little Spare Time*...344
  6. *Should Reiki Be Turned Off*..344
THE COMPLETE REIKI I METHOD...346
  1. *To Touch Or Not To Touch* 346
  2. *Healing From The Head Down Or The Feet Up*...............................347
  3. *For The Highest Good Of All Concerned*.......................................347
  4. *Help From Above*...347
  5. *Kanji* 348
  6. *Place Hands On Or Near First Position* 348
  7. *Eyes Open Or Closed* 348
  8. *Decide Passive Or Active Method* 349
  9. *'Rei On'*...349
  10. *Spend 3 - 5 Minutes In Each Position*...350
  11. *Return To Where Most Energy Was Needed* 350
  12. *Come Around Gently*..350
  13. *Evaluate The Session*...351
  14. *Make Next Appointment* 351
SIMPLE RECORD KEEPING FORM 353
REIKI 1 RECORD KEEPING FORM 355
STUDENTS' COMMENTS ON FIRST SELF-HEALINGS...............................356
WORKBOOK NOTES ON THE COMPLETE REIKI 1 METHOD...................360
WORKBOOK NOTES ON YOUR FIRST SELF-HEALING 361

CHAPTER 20 AURAS AND CHAKRAS..362

AURAS..362
  1. *The Unique Charge Of An Aura* 363
  2. *Feel Your Own Aura*..363
  3. *Filling Your Aura With LOve*...364
  4. *If You Cannot Feel Anything*..365
CHAKRAS 366

WORKBOOK NOTES ON AURAS AND CHAKRAS 368

CHAPTER 21 SCANNING 369

SCANNING WITH HANDS AND EYES: BYOSEN AND HIBIKI 369
1. *Hibiki Sensations* 371
2. *Scanning As A Tool For Diagnosis* 372
3. *Preparation* 373
4. *Thoughts* 373
5. *Which Hand To Scan With* 373
6. *Scanning Method* 374
7. *Young Children And Animals* 377
8. *Self-Healing With Scanning* 378
9. *Scanning With The Eyes* 379
10. *Healing Through The Eyes* 380
SCANNING THE AURA – 1 383
SCANNING THE AURA – 2 384
SCANNING THE AURA – 3 384
WORKBOOK NOTES ON SCANNING 385
WORKBOOK NOTES BIOFEEDBACK OF FIRST SCANNING 386

CHAPTER 22 JAKIKIRI JOKA-HO 387

JAKIKIRI JOKA-HO: CHOPPING AND RELEASING STUBBORN BYOSEN 387
1. *When To Use Jakikiri Joka-ho* 388
2. *When Not To Use Jakikiri Joka-ho* 389
3. *How To Use Jakikiri Joka-ho* 390
WORKBOOK NOTES ON JAKIKIRI JOKA-HO 392

CHAPTER 23 THE 21-DAY CLEANSING OR HEALING PROCESS
.... 393

THE 21-DAY HEALING PROCESS IF … 395
1. *If You Have Had A Very Happy, Healthy Life* 395
2. *If You Have Had A Relatively Good Life* 395
3. *If There Are Current Difficult Areas In Your Life* 395
4. *If You Had A Very Traumatic Or Difficult Life* 395
5. *If You Need Emergency Repairs* 396
6. *There Are No Hard And Fast Rules!* 396
MORE ABOUT 'THE 21-DAY HEALING PROCESS' 397
1. *The First Half Hour* 397
2. *The First Three Days* 397

3. *Healing During The Next Weeks And Months*.................................*398*
4. *Support*..*399*
5. *Acceptance*...*399*
AFTER THE HEALING PERIOD 400
1. *Keeping Up Your Self-Healing*..*400*
2. *Does An Attunement Last Forever?*......................................*401*
3. *Top-Up Attunements - Reiju*..*401*
4. *Reattunements*..*401*
5. *Progression Attunements*..*402*
WORKBOOK NOTES ON THE 21 DAY CLEANSING OR HEALING
PROCESS..403
WORKBOOK NOTES ON 'THE 21-DAY HEALING PROCESS'................404
(IF RELEVANT)..404
WORKBOOK NOTES ON PERSONAL HEALING PROCESS......................405
FIRST 3 DAYS (IF RELEVANT) 405
WORKBOOK NOTES ON PERSONAL HEALING PROCESS......................406
4TH TO 21ST DAY (IF RELEVANT)..406
WORKBOOK NOTES ON PERSONAL HEALING PROCESS......................407
MONTH AFTER 21 DAYS (IF RELEVANT) 407
WORKBOOK NOTES ON PERSONAL HEALING PROCESS......................408
(OTHER TIMESCALE) 408

CHAPTER 24 CAVEATS, CONTRAINDICATIONS, DANGERS 409

SPECIFIC REI SPIRITUAL HEALING – CAVEATS, CONTRAINDICATIONS,
DANGERS 409
1. *Craving For LOve* *409*
2. *Manic Conditions* *410*
3. *Manic-Depressives* *410*
4. *Schizophrenia* *411*
5. *Hallucinatory*..*411*
6. *Grounding*...*411*
GENERAL REIKI – CAVEATS, CONTRAINDICATIONS, DANGERS 412
GENERAL REIKI – CAVEATS, CONTRAINDICATIONS, DANGERS
(CONTINUED)..414
1. *Diabetics Who Are On Insulin* *414*
2. *Pacemakers*...*417*
3. *Hypocortisolism*..*418*
4. *Epilepsy*..*420*
5. *Pain* *421*

6. *Drinking Water Before Or After A Reiki Treatment* 424
7. *Hearing Aids* 425
8. *Using More Than One Frequency At A Time* 426
9. *Healing From The Head Down Or The Feet Up* 426
10. *Chakra Balancing* 427
11. *Reiki Or Chakra Massage* 427
12. *Bones With Plates, Pins, Or Bolts* 428
13. *Third Eye Healing Of A Person With Schizophrenia* 428
14. *Can't Cope With Hot Or Electric Etc. Feelings* 429
WORKBOOK NOTES ON CAVEATS, CONTRAINDICATIONS, DANGERS
.... 430

CHAPTER 25 CODES AND LAWS 431

CODES AND LAWS 433
1. *Psychic Or Clairvoyant Diagnosis* 433
2. *Change Of Intake Of Any Substance* 436
3. *Exploring 'Visions' Of This Or A Previous Life* 439
4. *Counselling* 439
5. *Referring On* 440
6. *Drug / Alcohol Addicts, Clinically Mentally Ill, Hallucinatory Or
    Violent People* 440
7. *Mentally Ill Hospitalised By Their Illness* 442
8. *Notifiable Diseases* 443
9. *The Healing Of Teeth And Gums* 443
10. *Pregnancy And Childbirth* 444
11. *Trance Healing* 445
12. *Giving Healing To Children Under Age of 18* 446
13. *Animals And Pets* 449
14. *Working In Hospitals With Healing* 451
15. *Reikiing Someone With HIV Or AIDS* 452
16. *The Venereal Diseases Act 1917* 453
17. *The Cancer Act 1939* 454
18. *Confidentiality* 454
LAWS OF OTHER COUNTRIES 455
1. *Germany* 455
2. *Austria* 455
3. *France* 455
4. *USA, State Of Florida* 456
5. *Others* 457

How The Codes Of Practice Originated 458
Keeping To The Codes And Laws 460
WORKBOOK NOTES On Codes And Laws 461

CHAPTER 26 FINAL SUMMARIES **462**

The Five Foundation Rei Treatment Options 462
 1. *To Reiki Dis-ease Or All-Over Problems, Give All-Over Treatment And Back To Worst Area* 463
 2. *To Reiki Injury Or Localised Problem, Give Treatment To Injury Or Local Site Only* 463
 3. *Be Guided In Time* 463
 4. *Be Guided In Space* 464
 5. *Scan* 464
Practising Foundation Treatment Options 466
 1. *Teddy Bear* 466
 2. *Self-Healing* 466
 3. *Trusted Friend* 466
 4. *Other Friends And Family Members* 466
Accept Your Fears – Just Do It! 467
 1. *Fear Of Being Laughed At* 467
 2. *Fear Of Having Too Much Ego* 468
 3. *Fear Of The Power Of The Energy* 468
 4. *Fear Of Not Getting Results* 469
 5. *Fear Of Change* 469
 6. *Fear Of Working With Difficult Cases* 470
 7. *Fear Of Not Being Good Enough* 470
 8. *Fear Of Commitment* 471
 9. *Your Reiki Master* 472
Nelson Mandela Let Our Own Light Shine 473
 Further Reading List 474
WORKBOOK NOTES On Final Summaries 476
WORKBOOK NOTES On Further Reading And Courses Needed . 477

REFERENCES **478**

INDEX **481**

OUR INTERNATIONAL REIKI AND HEALING TRAINING CENTRE **492**

Table of Contents

1. *Our Centre's General Aims Are To:* 492
2. *Our Centre's Specific Aim Is To:* 492
ORDER FORM FOR MANUALS AND PRODUCTS 502

Table Of Figures

Figure 1:	Frequency Waves	44
Figure 2:	Dr Usui's Tombstone	53
Figure 3:	Buddha Of Light In Kamakura, Japan	57
Figure 4:	Main Temple On Top Of Mount Kurama	64
Figure 5:	Dr Mikao Usui	68
Figure 6:	Dr Chijiro Hayashi	70
Figure 7:	Chiyoko Yamaguchi	72
Figure 8:	Mrs Hawayo Hiromi Takata	73
Figure 9:	Phyllis Lei Furumoto And Barbara Weber Ray	76
Figure 10:	William Lee Rand And Kathleen Milner	77
Figure 11:	Dr Allan Sweeney	78
Figure 12:	Doi Sensei	81
Figure 13:	Okajima Sensei	82
Figure 14:	Are You Next?	83
Figure 15:	The Reiki Ideals In Dr Usui's Handwriting	135
Figure 16:	Portrait Of The Meiji Emperor	136
Figure 17:	Waka Poetry In Emperor's Calligraphy	138
Figure 18:	Timeline For Manifesting Conditions And Illnesses	164
Figure 19:	Limbic System	222
Figure 20:	Kanji 1	274
Figure 21:	Kanji 2	275
Figure 22:	Kanji 3	276
Figure 23:	Combination Of Kanji 1 & 2	277
Figure 24:	Combination Of Kanji 1 & 3	277
Figure 25:	Combination Of Kanji 2 & 3	278
Figure 26:	Combination Of Kanji 1, 2 & 3	278
Figure 27:	Ring Finger Kanji	280
Figure 28:	Little Finger Kanji	281
Figure 29:	Kanji For Japanese Priests	282
Figure 30:	Reiki Hand Stack	309
Figure 31:	Laser Coning Hand Position, Side And Front Views	310
Figure 32:	Reiki Spread	311
Figure 33:	H1 – The Face	321
Figure 34:	H2 – Sides Of Head	322
Figure 35:	H3 – Back Of Head	323

Figure 36:   H4 – Throat..324
Figure 37:   F1 – Top Of Chest...325
Figure 38:   F2 – Below Chest...326
Figure 39:   F3 – Around Navel..327
Figure 40:   F4 – Below Navel..328
Figure 41:   B1 – Shoulders..329
Figure 42:   B2 – Rib Cage..330
Figure 43:   B3 – Lower Back...331
Figure 44:   B4 – Base Of Spine...332
Figure 45:   A1 – Shoulders...333
Figure 46:   A2 – Elbows...334
Figure 47:   A3 – Wrists..335
Figure 48:   A4 – Hands..336
Figure 49:   L1 – Hips..337
Figure 50:   L2 – Knees..338
Figure 51:   L3 – Ankles...339
Figure 52:   L4 – Feet..340
Figure 53:   Representation Of Rei Flow During A Healing..............349
Figure 54:   Scanning With One Hand..383
Figure 55:   Scanning 2 Negative Energy Spots At The Same Time ..384

CHAPTER 1

GENERAL INTRODUCTIONS

Can I Learn Reiki?

The simple answer is almost certainly, 'Yes!' In the mid-1990s I met a doctor/healer who unofficially explored how many people 'off-the-street' could become healers. He invited them to non-healing 'conferences' in which they would in one particular session, without previously being told, learn healing.[1]

In his conclusions, he found that out of every 100 people, roughly 96 could channel healing energy. When he analysed the remainder, those four in 100 who could not channel healing, he felt that the reason was probably that they were blocked against healing on all levels of their being rather than a complete lack of ability.

So the likelihood of you being able to become a healer is extremely high – you are reading this book, so are almost certainly not blocked against healing on all levels of your being!

So almost all readers of this book could learn reiki successfully. If you take the reiki pathway you will have doubts, as would a beginner gardener, or a beginner plumber. But like gardeners and plumbers you just need to stick at it, to practise, and to study.

The reiki mastership pathway is wonderful – it can be all things to all people. There are many reasons why people take a reiki class. Consider if you fit into one of the following categories (although the list is not exhaustive) of what reiki can help. If you do, perhaps find a quality reiki master soon!

---

[1] As this process was undertaken without the knowledge of participants, the researcher has asked to remain anonymous.

Student Reasons For Taking Reiki Classes

1. Self-healing. (Also, many people who benefit from reiki treatments, but cannot afford the time or money to go to a practitioner, learn reiki to provide their own daily self-healing.)

2. Healing ill family members

3. Healing friends

4. Helping animals or pets

5. Keeping illness at bay – staying in wholeness

6. Increasing existing knowledge

7. Running own Reiki Healing Centre

8. Developing psychic abilities

9. Enhancing spiritual nature

10. Finding soul path

11. Seeking enlightenment

12. Learning distant healing to help our planetary needs

13. Don't know why, it is just a strong feeling inside that reiki must be learned!

14. Teaching reiki on a basic healing, or psychic or spiritual level

15. Becoming an expert teacher with a vast knowledge of reiki and all healing, psychic and spiritual subjects

WARNING

This manual is NOT a substitute for an intensive Reiki 1 course conducted by a suitably qualified and knowledgeable reiki master. Readers should therefore be aware that if they wish to practise reiki, they should attend a quality reiki class for the following reasons:

1. Class Required

There are some exercises that can only be conducted in a class situation. Therefore a quality-assured class should be attended to ensure full knowledge and understanding.

2. Attunements

Although attunements can be given from a distance, it is not advisable for beginners, as the reiki master often needs to be present to advise and help issues arising from attunements easily and quickly.

3. 7-Level System

Dr Usui's original reiki introduced the 7-level system to combine all aspects of human inner nature with all aspects of spiritual and God-nature on a path to wholeness. It is reputed he gave students 84 manuals – but only as course back-up. Until students proved they had mastered each technique, they could not move on to the next. The 7-level system is unique. Unless practice is achieved for each technique on each level, under the guidance of a quality reiki master, it is impossible to understand how good you are on each level.

4. Research

Some reiki courses miss out material in this manual, or include material not in this manual. Therefore, before attending a course, it could be a worthwhile exercise to research and discover exactly what each reiki master teaches. Then, if attracted to the course content and material, attend that course.

5. Specialities

Some reiki masters teach reiki as a special focused, almost religious, path such as a Buddhist, Christian, or other spiritual path, or a path learning only about attunements or self-healing. Specialist forms of reiki are not the subjects of this manual. If this is the form of reiki you are attracted to, seek out a reiki master who teaches in this way.

6. Biofeedback

One of the most valuable aspects of a Reiki 1 class is that of understanding biofeedback. (Biofeedback is defined as experiences received through the senses as one gives or receives reiki.) A knowledgeable reiki master will give you valid interpretations of biofeedback. Chapter 9, *'Biofeedback',* in this manual gives much information. However, biofeedback responses include seeing symbols and symbolism that are so numerous they would need a manual of their own. I have found that, without valid interpretations from a knowledgeable reiki master, it is possible to negatively misunderstand reiki biofeedback. Therefore ensure that you learn with someone who has sufficient knowledge.

7. Special Needs

In a class situation, an experienced reiki master can often spot someone who has a special need. This may mean someone who needs extra support, or healing, or encouragement, or someone who is so naturally brilliant they again need extra support to understand their natural, God-given gift. Time may then be given during breaks or after a class to help anyone seen to be in need. (Or of course, anyone who asks for help.) Thus it is important to learn reiki in a class to receive any extra support you deserve.

8. Learning

Reiki, unlike any other healing method, cannot be learned from a book. Though hand positions, much knowledge, and attunement aspects are in this manual, part of reiki is provided via attunements given to the student by a qualified and knowledgeable reiki master.

The attunement method has been likened to the healing act. If one can pass healing energy to a sick person and potentially cure them, similarly one can pass healing ability to a prospective healer. The student automatically is attuned to 'universal rei-healing' or 'inner ki-healing' energies. These energies can then be used for self-healing, distant healing, and healing other people, animals, or situations.

Due to the complex nature of attunements and their effects (see point 2 above) it is best to receive attunements in the physical presence of a master.

9. Quality Assurance

Many governments around the world are considering integration of Complementary or Alternative Medicine (CAM) with their National Health Services. Some governments are considering voluntary or statutory regulation. If we are to prove our professional worth, it is imperative to provide quality-assured practitioners who have attended quality-certified courses. As indicated above, whilst much may be learned from this manual, aspiring reiki practitioners, or those existing reiki practitioners wishing to expand their knowledge and ability, should attend a suitable reiki course. This manual should be used as a reference work and for extra information over and above the information taught on their Reiki 1 class.

Different Types Of Users Of This Manual

This manual is intended to contain multi-functional tools that can help many people achieve differing worthwhile aims, whilst staying on a 7-level path to Wholeness.

Whilst it is impossible to cater for every need, this book is mainly intended to help the following categories:

1. Existing Reiki Masters

a. Ready-made reiki course manual

Over the years, many reiki masters have said that they do not wish to write their own manual, that they would prefer one to be ready-made, off-the-shelf. Indeed, some reiki masters have not taught, simply because they did not feel knowledgeable enough to produce a worthwhile manual of their own.

This series of reiki manuals can overcome the difficulty of continuous attempts at producing manuals for each individual master. And in so doing, it provides a basic foundation for everyone to feel able to teach. If you are a reiki master, all you need to do then is decide what extra information you wish to include as a personal and individual addendum, to enhance your own unique way of passing on reiki to our world.

Special prices are available for reiki masters who wish to purchase manuals for distribution to their students.

N.B. If you feel that extra information is needed on a certain topic(s), please write and let me know. I may then be able to include it in the next print run of the book.

b. Curriculum

Teaching reiki is a beautiful job. It is a job of LOve. It is work to help us and others progress in so many different ways. Yet this wonderful job, rich with such potential, can always be improved. It is hoped that this manual will allow reiki teachers access to further information that will help their teaching curriculum.

c.   Back-up

Questions from students are many and varied. Because some people teach reiki now in a form that requires little experience from the reiki master, many students' questions are unable to be answered. This series of manuals should provide the answers to many such questions, and enhance the back-up knowledge of all concerned.

2.   Existing Reiki 1 Or Above Practitioners

For many years, I have had comments from some reiki practitioners who previously trained elsewhere who, 'feel there is something missing from their knowledge.' Also that these teachings provided confirmation of things they 'knew deep inside.'

This series of reiki manuals seeks to confirm the inner knowledge and fill in some of the gaps.

3.   A Course Workbook

Various pages have been left blank for your own notes. Use them to record your own experiences and development. Who knows? Maybe these notes will one day find their way into new reiki books.

4.   Reference Book After the Course

Like many of my students you may choose to carry the book around with you and use it as a handy informative reference work.

5.   Non-Reiki People - Explorers

There are many people who are not really interested in reiki, yet are interested in healing or spiritual or other development potentials. Some are 'explorers', seeking new avenues for personal growth. This manual may well provide insights into how these explorers may further their path towards the ultimate discovery of their inner need.

6.   Those Considering A Reiki 1 Course

If you know you have to take a healing or therapeutic course but don't know which one, this manual contains information that should help you decide if reiki is the right path to take.

7.   Those Thirsting for Extra Knowledge

Many students learn reiki because they are on a knowledge path. This in fact was my reason for learning reiki initially. After being given two years to live, I had just been cured in one session by a healer. I then knew that, as most of my previous 12 years of knowledge had come from 'above', I had to spend one year studying as many healing and spiritual courses as I could find. Like many others in this category, I did not know why. I just trusted that knowledge was needed. Similar people may find this manual invaluable.

8.   The Next Edition

I hope that everyone who wishes to further the development of reiki will send some positive and constructive feedback on this manual.

Limitations Of This Manual If You Wish To Be A Reiki Practitioner / Teacher

Rei energy as taught and used on most reiki courses is essentially the same as spiritual healing – a passive, high frequency, God, or LOve energy. Many spiritual healing systems let students practise this spiritual form of energy healing on others after only a two-day class, although most would ensure that the beginner obtains insurance cover, and that mentors are present during the beginner's first healings, even for up to two years. Theoretically, Reiki 1 practitioners could also practise on others after only a two-day class.

As Usui's Japanese reiki is a system of progression of knowledge and ability, this manual aims to provide a broad base of knowledge for the beginner healer, but mainly for self-healing. It does not provide vast knowledge on healing others professionally. Please read the extensive Reiki 2 and 3 Manuals if you wish to heal other people.

The Reiki 2 and 3 Manuals also have many professional subjects such as how to prepare your Reiki Healing Centre and yourself, how to keep records, visual analogue scales, anatomy and many other subjects currently deemed necessary for a professional healing practice. Most of these subjects are likely to become voluntary or statutory law in many countries.

Dr Usui's system is still being discovered; not all knowledge has been released by his organisation, nor translated from discovered manuscripts. Our only hope and prayer is that we do justice to a beautiful system of potential cures and enlightenment, and ensure that we develop reiki in an honourable way to help others and ourselves around our world, always in healing and in peace.

101 Reiki 1 Exercises

Please note the medical disclaimer at the front of this manual and that, whilst all exercises and guidelines are essentially of healing light and goodness, there may be something that disagrees with somebody at some time. If so, first read chapters 9 *'Biofeedback'*, and 24 *'Caveats, Contraindications and Dangers'*, to see if your experience is a standard response to a healing or energy process. If in doubt, seek positive and constructive advice. Or do not use the exercise or guideline again, until greater understanding or ability is achieved.

The exercises are designed to help both the healing progression and also the self-development of Reiki 1 practitioners.

Exercise 1 -   **Feeling Frequency** **46**
Exercise 2 -   **Historical Habits** **50**
Exercise 3 -   **Your Reiki 'Guru' Lineage** **83**
Exercise 4 -   **Increasing Happiness In Self & Others** **106**
Exercise 5 -   **Happy Rain** **106**
Exercise 6 -   **Connecting Microcosm To Macrocosm** **106**
Exercise 7 -   **Search And Research** **116**
Exercise 8 -   **Intuition Notebook** **118**
Exercise 9 -   **Finding Ways To LOve Yourself** **119**
Exercise 10 -   **Finding Ways To Love Others** **119**
Exercise 11 -   **Goal Setting To Improve Weaknesses** **120**
Exercise 12 -   **Specialist Reading Material** **121**
Exercise 13 -   **Guidance Of Healing Hands** **126**
Exercise 14 -   **Guidance Of Healing Hands** **126**
Exercise 15 -   **Nentatsu** **127**
Exercise 16 -   **Shuchu** **127**
Exercise 17 -   **The Reiki Marathon** **128**
Exercise 18 -   **Mawashi – Reiki Circle – Group Sharing** **129**
Exercise 19 -   **Kotodama Before And After Treatment** **131**
Exercise 20 -   **Kotodama During Treatment** **131**
Exercise 21 -   **Having An Ideal Day** **139**
Exercise 22 -   **Programming Self-Healing** **140**
Exercise 23 -   **Inner Mantra** **140**
Exercise 24 -   **Love and LOve** **146**

Exercise 25 -   Rei The Fear Of The Dying Process 152
Exercise 26 -   Rei The Fear Of The Death Moments 153
Exercise 27 -   Rei The Fear Of What May Happen After Death 153
Exercise 28 -   Channelling Pieces Of LOve 156
Exercise 29 -   The LOve Waterfall 157
Exercise 30 -   Double-Checking The Type Of LOve 158
Exercise 31 -   Intentions For Tomatoes 160
Exercise 32 -   Healing The Spirit Body 166
Exercise 33 -   Healing The Soul 167
Exercise 34 -   Emotional Replacement 171
Exercise 35 -   Adjusting Frequency 172
Exercise 36 -   Adjusting Power 172
Exercise 37 -   Developing Gifts 211
Exercise 38 -   Acceptance (if you do not normally accept) 213
Exercise 39 -   Questions (if you do not normally question) 214
Exercise 40 -   The Self-Healing Shopping List 250
Exercise 41 -   Healing With Two Consciousnesses 252
Exercise 42 -   The Impermanent List Of Permanence 253
Exercise 43 -   Mirrored Breathing 255
Exercise 44 -   Breathing By Numbers 256
Exercise 45 -   Timed Breathing 256
Exercise 46 -   Loving Your Body Parts 258
Exercise 47 -   Down The Staircase 258
Exercise 48 -   Candle Gazing 259
Exercise 49 -   Singular Focussing 259
Exercise 50 -   Sparkling Stream 260
Exercise 51 -   Floral Garden 260
Exercise 52 -   Combining Relaxation And Peace 261
Exercise 53 -   Healing Stress – Head Down 266
Exercise 54 -   Healing Low Energy – Feet Up 266
Exercise 55 -   Developing The Hui Yin 269
Exercise 56 -   Reiki With Hui Yin 271
Exercise 57 -   Using Kanji 273
Exercise 58 -   Pre-Healing Fill-Up 285
Exercise 59 -   The Golden Cloak 286
Exercise 60 -   Customised Grounding 288
Exercise 61 -   Physical Post-Healing Grounding 290
Exercise 62 -   Emotional Post-Healing Grounding 290
Exercise 63 -   Mental Post-Healing Grounding 290

Exercise 64 - Spiritual Post-Healing Grounding 290
Exercise 65 - All-Time Favourite Post-Healing Grounding 291
Exercise 66 - Alpha Techniques 296
Exercise 67 - Preparing For Magnetic Attraction 298
Exercise 68 - Feeling Emotional Magnetic Attraction 298
Exercise 69 - Feeling Physical Magnetic Attraction 298
Exercise 70 - The Passive Healing Method 302
Exercise 71 - The Active Healing Method 303
Exercise 72 - Handy Experiments 311
Exercise 73 - Hand Position Practice 314
Exercise 74 - Testing Your Self-Healing 342
Exercise 75 - Remembering The Complete Reiki I Method 351
Exercise 76 - Annotation Of First Self-Healings 352
Exercise 77 - Recording 354
Exercise 78 - Feeling Your Own Aura 363
Exercise 79 - Rei Shower 364
Exercise 80 - Unconscious Chakra Balancing 367
Exercise 81 - Letting Go Of Thoughts 373
Exercise 82 - Which Is Your Dominant Energy Hand? 374
Exercise 83 - Feeling The Closest Layer Of A Person's Aura 374
Exercise 84 - Test For Breathing Hibiki 375
Exercise 85 - Scanning For Byosen 375
Exercise 86 - Treatment Of Byosen 376
Exercise 87 - Scanning Memory Jogger 377
Exercise 88 - Practise Daily Self-Scanning 379
Exercise 89 - Unfocussing 379
Exercise 90 - Scanning With The Eyes 380
Exercise 91 - Healing Through The Eyes 381
Exercise 92 - Jakikiri Joka-ho 390
Exercise 93 - Diary Logs 399
Exercise 94 - Awareness Of Self-Healing Need 400
Exercise 95 - Being in Your Body 410
Exercise 96 - Researching Laws And Codes In Your Country 457
Exercise 97 - The Five Foundation Rei Spiritual Healing
              Treatments 465
Exercise 98 - Advance Anyway 469
Exercise 99 - LOving Your Fear Away 471
Exercise 100 - Releasing Fear 471
Exercise 101 - Let Our Own Light Shine 472

WORKBOOK NOTES
On General Introductions

CHAPTER 2

WHAT IS REIKI?

What Does 'Reiki' Mean?

Reiki has become known in the Western world as a description of the Usui system of healing. Reiki is not a religion, not a cult, not a philosophy. It is not mind over matter, not a belief system, or a placebo. It is simply a natural way for energy to be activated and used for healing the self or other people or animals, potentially from any illness. However, literally, reiki is two words that Dr Usui, the founder of reiki in 1922, combined into the process we now know as reiki.

1.   Rei = Highest Outer Spiritual Healing Energy

Mrs. Takata said rei probably means universal, showing reiki is in all places at once. She also accepted that there are other meanings of the kanji ideograms. These include soul, ghost, and spirit. It can also have more subtle meanings like supernatural power or ethereal.

Many reiki masters now believe that a more correct description is the highest spiritual consciousness, the universal energy outside all living things, God's highest power. Healers channelling this energy often have a profound feeling of LOve. Then, both the healer and the healee will feel LOved. Reiki masters channel this life-giving energy and attune others to it!

There is a widespread practice of spiritual healing, especially in the UK, and it should be noted that the essence of rei is identical to the essence of spiritual healing.

2. Ki = Various Inner Life Force Healing Energies

Ki is non-physical energies animating all living things. In China, this is called chi; in Seneca, orendo; in Sanskrit, akasha; in Hebrew, rueh; in Islam, barraka; in Pueblo, itaki; in India, prana; in Hawaii, mana, ti or ki; in Cherokee, nuwati; most cultures have a name for it.

Scientists, however, cannot call ki 'energy', as the word energy has a specific scientific meaning and reiki energy does not do 'work', as defined by science. In a simplified way 'work' in this case means the ability to exert a force on a physical object that affects movement, such as picking up chocolate. Scientists have called healing forces various words to identify different energies. These include monads, bioplasma, odyle, orgon, bioenergy, od or odic, or orgone, the latter being a special type of universal energy blocked in the body due to emotional problems (Benor v1).

The Chinese use life-force energies in many ways. Martial arts and acupuncture are well-known. Chinese ki studies go back more than 4,000 years, as documented with the discovery of 32 different chi energies in *The Yellow Emperor's Classic of Internal Medicine*.

Ki life-force energies are energies that surround and are in all living things. The healthier a living thing is, the more life-force energies it has. The sicker a living thing is, the less life force energies it has. Ki energies are lower frequency than rei, or spiritual, energies.

In humans, channelling low-frequency ki life force energies can help promote balance in many areas of the being including physical, emotional, and mental rebalance. Ki healing can therefore potentially help return imbalance to 'normal' more quickly than rei healing.

Reiki has spiritual energies to use and ki energies to choose

How Does Reiki Heal?

This is the question everyone interested in reiki wants to find the answer for. However, despite many scientific experiments, most scientists have given up on the question 'how' reiki works. The pharmaceutical industry does not know how many drugs work – they simply accept that they do work. So it is with reiki. But there has been a progression of understanding. So much so, that even professional sportsmen and women, medical professionals and royalty are waking up to the potential of how reiki may help.

So, what are the options?

1. It's All In The Mind – (No It Isn't)

'It's all in the mind' was a popular belief in the 1980s, and is still held by some people today. They believe that the healee's mind wants to be well, so when they meet a healer, the healee creates his or own healing process.

This opinion was all but discounted in the 1980s after many experiments on healing were conducted not on people, nor on animals, but on single-celled organisms, plants, seeds, bacteria - anything in fact where it could not be considered that 'a mind' of the subject was creating its own healing. The results were remarkable, even on seeds. The results of 189 of these experiments were tabulated by Dr Daniel Benor (Benor v1) who proved that 64% were of significant or highly significant value – almost twice the percentage of proof needed for some drugs to be on the market![2]

So reiki is not 'all in the mind.' It works when no mind is present.

---

[2] Proof required for a drug to go to market varies a great deal according to such criteria as toxicity reports, comparison with other available drugs, severity of condition, and therapeutic indication (i.e. what kind of disease it is). The point here is that there are prescription drugs that only needed half the proof of efficacy of these healing studies to become available.

2. It's A Placebo Response – (No It Isn't)

a. What is the placebo response?

A placebo is understood to be a medicinally inactive substance or procedure, such as a sugar pill or a fake healing, given to people who think they are getting something truly medicinal, such as antibiotics or a proper healing from a qualified practitioner. Then, solely because the person thinks it is supposed to work, it does.

As can be seen from section 1 above, seeds or bacteria benefit from healing. Such non-sentient life probably has no expectations that would affect the outcome of a reiki healing and therefore reiki does not work through a placebo response.

As all theories (see below) of how reiki works apply the same way across different life forms, it is again confirmed that reiki therefore does not work by placebo response.

b. Placebo response - current research

It was formerly accepted that the placebo response would be elicited in about 30% to 35% of cases (Beecher, Kienle & Kienle). Recent research has put the 35% figure at the low end (Dodes, Hart).

c. My opinion

I consider the placebo response to be an automatic, naturally occurring self-healing in response not only to a medicinally inactive substance or procedure, such as a sugar pill or a fake healing, but also to any change in thought patterns, or external to internal process, or intake of any kind.

The placebo response is not commonly understood or agreed, and it appears to vary for different conditions and illnesses. Doctors cannot explain why or how someone suddenly gets better, especially when it might appear that they should not. I believe that future research into the placebo for healing will confirm the original figures of an average of 30-35% placebo for all illnesses or conditions.

Dr Michael Dixon is in the public eye as one of the medical doctors who has employed a healer in his surgery. He states: "As a pragmatist, I don't care what makes my patients feel more positive and lessens their symptoms" (Rudebeck). Perhaps the goal of all healing and medical treatment should, through adequate research, ultimately be to understand and foster that currently mysterious self-healing, so that patients are empowered to produce their own good results and a higher success than we can currently achieve.

3. It's Faith – (No It Isn't)

Faith implies that reiki practitioners have such faith in their healing method, it becomes like a religious healing where faith creates a God intention to heal. Again this is not true.

Students are often surprised on courses when they see that, even if they were sceptical previously, they can often cure someone during their first practice session! Such a case was when BBC television filmed an English comedian and healing sceptic on my beginners' course. He says at the end of the film that he admits to being a sceptic when he arrived, but maybe would now call himself a reiki healer. The film shows him curing a lady's throat problem.

4. It's Magic – (No It Isn't)

Magic implies witchcraft. However, reiki is simply something science does not yet understand. It works. It cures. It relieves symptoms of illnesses.

And, almost anyone can do it (roughly 96 out of 100). It is the normal, natural, inner healing ability that almost everyone has providing they learn how to use it!

5. It's The Last Resort – (No It Isn't)

This again implies that because the person is going to a healer, all else has failed, so the healee's desire for cure will create the result.

This is discounted by studies done in doctors' surgeries where healers are given patients the doctors could not help, but who could have been referred to specialists.

These studies show that the healer helps 71% of cases – an incredibly high figure (Dixon; Brown).

Studies were also done on people who received distant healing and did not know they were receiving it; they displayed significant improvement (Astin, Benor v1, Byrd, Harding, Pearsall, Targ).

6. So How Does Reiki Heal?

No one yet knows, but there are very good suggestions. Major options are as follows:

a.   Cancelling out the frequency of the illness

Cancellation of frequencies is explained in the next section, *'Frequencies Of Rei And Ki.'* Due to a progression of understanding, there is also a section on this in the Reiki 2 Manual, and in-depth technique and analysis in the Reiki 3A Healing Mastership Manual.

b.   Replacement of good energy instead of bad

Please see section 'Rei Spiritual Healing - Emotional Replacement Therapy' *in chapter 8.*

c.   Slow healing via ripples

Please see chapter 8, 'Ripple Effect Healings'.

d.   Rebalancing to create wholeness

Please see chapter 7, *'Rei And Spiritual Healing.'* Rebalancing can also include rebalancing of the aura, chakras, meridians, and other energy bodies.

Frequencies Of Rei And Ki

For the more scientifically minded, the reference work for this section is Valerie Hunt's book, Infinite Mind, and her tapes and videos advertised in the book. This brilliant research is cutting edge. One of my student reiki masters who is also a theoretical physicist, read her book three times and considered the information so good, he considered giving up his physics research to concentrate on furthering the frequency work of Valerie Hunt.

For raw beginners, it should be noted that a frequency is simply a wave. The more waves there are in one second, the higher is the frequency.

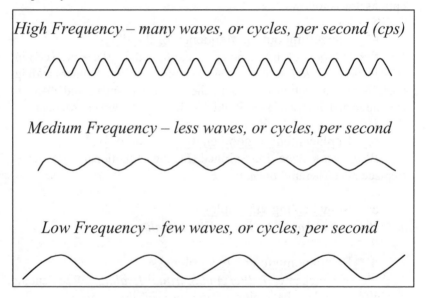

Figure 1:   Frequency Waves

Everything is a frequency of energy. And all these frequencies can be measured. This includes the frequencies of illness. (McTaggart)

Frequencies are explained much more in the Reiki 2 Manual, as it is only after Reiki 2 that practitioners can choose ki energies. The objective here is to explain simply the scientific difference between rei and ki, and to give a basic idea how each may work for healing purposes. One may then see the healing importance of taking Reiki 2.

It should be noted that, in this manual, frequencies given are a guide in order to explain how frequency healing may work. So there are sometimes different frequency readings for different conditions, etc., as there are various internal and external factors that could affect each frequency. For example, Hunt has measured the auric field of those having God-type experiences as ranging upwards from 7200 cps, while Zohar presents data that the brain itself oscillates at 40 cps during these experiences. The latter is an internal measure and the former is a physically external measure, while the next layer of externality, the frequency of God-LOve itself, has not yet been measured to my knowledge. Specificity of frequency use can also be seen as the important difference between spiritual healing and reiki.

1.   Reiki 1 - High Rei Frequency

When the frequency of the field of a person reaches over 7,200 cps, the person will have a God experience, according to a tape by Valerie Hunt at a 1992 conference. This high frequency can be attained via types of yoga, meditation, prayer, and spiritual or rei healing.

If spiritual healers, or reiki healers using rei, strictly use spiritual or rei healing energy and nothing else, they will channel LOve. Then both the healer and the healee will feel the highest LOve as a beautiful experience.

2.   Reiki 2 - Low Ki Frequencies

All illnesses in all living things have their own frequencies. These are much lower frequencies than those of rei. Some of these low ki frequencies are stated in the Reiki 2 Manual. E.g., some cancers are around 380 cps, much, much lower than the 7,200 cps experienced with rei (McTaggart). This is confirmed by Valerie Hunt who states in e-mail correspondence to me that these "statements are from old reductionist correlation concepts".[3]

As scientists or good clairvoyants would agree, if two identical frequencies touch, one of many things that could happen is that the two frequencies cancel each other out - they cannot exist any more.

Similarly, one method to potentially obtain a cure is to channel the same frequency as the illness. This channelled frequency may then cancel out the frequency of the condition and the person may be cured (Greene, Benor v2).

Homeopathy works on this principle of applying a substance of the same frequency as the illness, and then giving a greater or lesser dosage - that is, more or less power. The ki energies of reiki can do the same.

3.   Reiki 2 Sacred Geometric Symbols

Sacred geometric symbols can be scientifically and mathematically proven to have a frequency. On Reiki 2, the first symbol is a low frequency used more to cancel out the frequency of physical problems. The second symbol is a medium frequency for mental and emotional problems.

Exercise 1 - Feeling Frequency
Although reiki uses spiritual energy or frequency symbols, every frequency is also a colour.   To start to be aware of how frequencies can affect you, go into a room decorated in one of the low frequencies of the rainbow such as red or orange. Look at the

---

[3] E-mail dated 29th July 2002.

colours. Imagine the colours entering you. How do they make you feel?

Then do the same in a room decorated in medium rainbow frequency greens. How does that feel?

And in a room with high frequency violets or purples or golds. How do you feel now?

Note: if you find this difficult, try again after a few months. You may well have developed the relevant sense of awareness by then...

WORKBOOK NOTES
On What Is Reiki

CHAPTER 3

DR USUI AND THE HISTORY OF REIKI

Introduction

When relating the history of anything, the one thing that is certain is uncertainty. Every history scholar will choose a perspective of history that fits with his or her philosophical viewpoint. It is even the case that the entire history of a country has been changed with a change of government. Have you considered how, if Hitler had won WW2, historians would have described Nazi concentration camps? Have you considered how many different viewpoints there are on the witch crazes of previous centuries? And have you considered how Jesus would have been viewed if those who condemned him to death had written the gospels?

So it is with reiki history. Some facts have emerged that are indisputable. However, the translation of those facts is usually coloured by the individual writer's response to his or her pre-existing knowledge and lack of knowledge, and a willingness (or lack of it) to research and accept indisputable fact even at the expense of destroying previously held beliefs. Thus some writers on reiki history have, quite naturally, allowed their personal thoughts to prevail to a larger degree than prevailing facts should have allowed. Then myths arise and become accepted as truths.

This is an inherent problem with all history writers, and one that I have seen in all reiki books with the exception of the book by Doi Sensei. In it, even though he does not portray all available reiki information, he attempts to distinguish Dr Usui's known teachings from his own – an honourable trait.

In these history chapters I am not professing perfection of historical truths. However, you may refer to the main books that offer reiki history perspectives and versions of truth that have become accepted myths, and are difficult to prove or disprove.

I also try to explain why some historical passages are now proven to be incorrect; and how certain new reiki history information can be viewed. Dr Usui's levels of teaching described in these reiki history chapters are of the utmost importance to the reiki world, so I additionally offer how I teach each level.

Exercise 2 - Historical habits
Choose an aspect of history that interests you. For example, many reiki people are interested in why reiki was taught in the way it was by Mrs Takata. Go to the source of the information and find a way to research the myths or facts.

Dr Usui – Personal History

Dr Mikao Usui, the founder of reiki, was born on 15th August 1865[4] into a poor family. For a number of years from the age of four, he stayed at a Tendai monastery (Lübeck et al.). However, in 1881 at the age of 16, he met an Englishman, a Dr Phillips, who changed his life.

The Englishman was a doctor, a philosopher, and a Christian. His vast medical and spiritual knowledge contained both a scientific and a philosophical approach. This fascinated Dr Usui. So much so that Dr Usui studied and stayed friends with the Englishman for many years.

The next most relevant and dramatic event in Dr Usui's life came nine years later. In 1890, at the age of 25, he contracted cholera (Ellyard). In Japan in those days, there was no cure. Almost everyone who had cholera, died. If someone recovered – which was not very often – it would be a very long, slow, painful recovery.

One day, Dr Usui was so ill that he overheard the Englishman saying to a friend that he expected Dr Usui to die that day. Instead came Dr Usui's first miracle. He was cured on his own deathbed!

During the night, Dr Usui awoke and saw in front of him a Japanese God. Another arrived, and then another, and Dr Usui felt saddened that he had given up his Buddhist roots for Christianity and science. However, one of the Japanese Gods told him that there was nothing to be saddened about. That it was perfectly acceptable in the eyes of the Gods, and that Dr Usui's path would be to synthesise the two forces of spirituality and physical science. The knowledge that learning Christianity and Western science had not offended the Gods gave Dr Usui a deep peace within.

As he lay there, expecting to die, more Japanese Gods arrived and formed a tier in front of him. Suddenly, a bright blue light shone from the heart of one of the Gods and as it touched him he fell into a deep sleep. When he woke in the morning he was cured!

---

[4] As stated on his tombstone.

The experience of being instantly cured on his deathbed had a profound effect on Dr Usui. For the rest of his life he searched for ways to help or cure others, feeling it was why he had been saved from death. In his writings he mentions 'cure' many times. He wanted to show that cures were potentially feasible for all. The fact that he was cured when he was supposed to die that night may be why he said that reiki practitioners should try to cure until the patient's last breath.

During his travels it seems that he collected information on his favourite hobbies of healing, esoteric, and mystic arts; although it is known that he also paid others to seek out such information. He even discovered the Tantra of the Lightening Flash when he was 34, and many other healing processes (Yeshe).

Dr Usui's reiki enlightenment came on Mount Kurama in March 1922. (There is still much confusion over this date. Some sources that translated some of Dr Usui's diaries say the date was much earlier, in the 1890s. Other sources say 1914.) Whilst on the mountain taking Isyu Gyo, a 21-day life-style training discipline, his 41 years of collected experiences came together into the system he named reiki. If you count the start of his learning from when he was sent to the monastery at the age of four, he had had 53 years of experience and study in the spiritual, intuitive and healing arts.

In Dr Usui's writings he states that he was 'wondrously inspired, and realised purely by chance the spiritual capabilities of therapy'.

It seems that on Mount Kurama at that moment, he suddenly realised how rei and ki could be put into a system to help the world. Also at that moment, all of his previous years of learning came together. This is why on his tombstone it states that he taught many topics under the reiki umbrella – fortune-telling, astral travel, astrology, I Ching, and numerology all became parts of his reiki teachings. Anything, in fact, that could help others.

His first clinic and teaching centre was opened in Harajuku in 1922 when he started Gakkai, the Reiki Society. He was its first president - the current president is Mr Masayoshi Kondo. His second reiki clinic was in Nakano-ku (Nakano district of Tokyo). It was much bigger and built from donations given to him from helping the injured in the Tokyo earthquake of 1923.

Figure 2: Dr Usui's Tombstone - Simon Blythe, one of my students, paying respects at Dr Usui's tombstone in 1999. The highest stone in the background is Dr Usui's tombstone, while the three sticks are memorial sticks. The longest one is for Dr Usui and the smaller ones for his children.

During his reiki teachings he would, like any brilliant master of his craft, tell many stories about how he treated or helped someone or some situation. His stories are wonderful. They show an excellent understanding that some people need to learn by the visual impact stories give. Not many reiki masters in the West tell enough stories.

Dr Usui was a highly intelligent man who was honoured with a medical degree by a decree of the Japanese emperor. He understood and had a deep interest in medical drugs, psychology, incantations, divination, herbalism, ju jitsu, surgery, history, biographies, medical philosophy, physiognomy, I Ching, governmental processes, medical diagnosis and treatment and, according to his tombstone, rose through the ranks of the Japanese navy to become the naval attaché / white-collar secretary to the foreign minister of Japan, a Mr Gotou, who later became Prime Minister. To reach that very high rank of Japanese office, Dr Usui must have been not only very intelligent, but also simultaneously both tough and humble.

On his tombstone it states that in the course of his job he travelled to many countries, including Europe, the USA and China and that he 'sailed for China', perhaps a polite Japanese expression for going to war, as Japan and China were at war at that time.

With Dr Usui's wondrous inspiration, his life was complete. His lifetime's learning was promoted as reiki. It states on Dr Usui's memorial stone at Saihoji Temple at 1-4-56 Umesato, Suginami-Ku, Tokyo that, before he died in 1926 he taught about 2000 people, and that he hoped that reiki would spread around the world.

One of his main students, Eguchi, taught thousands of people. With you reading this book, you are also helping Dr Usui's wish come true.

Dr Usui, Buddhism, Shintoism, And Reiki

Extracts from Dr Usui's diaries have been published. They offer brilliant insights into his understanding that the masses of people needed a non-spiritual philosophy first, in order to create spirituality later.

When he was cured of cholera on his deathbed, he returned to his Buddhist and Shinto roots. After all, Japan was a Buddhist and Shinto country. Christianity was almost unheard of. But we need to remember that Dr Usui never forgot the words he heard on his deathbed from the Japanese God, that it is perfectly alright in the eyes of the Gods to explore other paths such as he had done with Christianity and Western science. If Dr Usui had taught in the USA or Britain for example, he would probably have taught reiki within a Christian philosophy to allow reiki to expand within the Christian path that is most predominant in those countries. On Dr Usui's gravestone it states that he hoped reiki would spread around the world, so if he had taught around the world he may well have taught Muslim reiki, Jewish reiki, Hindu reiki, and so on.

According to Dr Usui's diary and teachings, no one faith or belief should become the only force for reiki.

Also, in Dr Usui's own words he states that,

'The Usui Reiki Therapy is something no-one before has discovered, and bears comparison with no other treatment in the world.'

Note that he uses the words 'therapy' and 'treatment'. He does not use the words Shinto or Buddhism. It seems that, near the end of his life, the reiki therapy and treatment were his main aim.

As Dr Usui believed he was the first to discover reiki, it must have had very little to do with Buddhism that had existed for about 2,500 years. And Dr Usui first taught reiki as a system to help everyone, not just Buddhists – Dr Hayashi is reputed to have been a Christian (although there is no evidence for this).

Dr Usui was an enlightened being, a man who had received enlightenment and understood that true enlightenment comes when religious life is not followed. Although the next statement is controversial, many Buddhists and others would say that seeing oneself exclusively as a Christian, Jew, Hindu, Buddhist, or Muslim, means that ego has not been released. As a Jew, Christian or Buddhist etc., you cannot be enlightened due to the limitations of having one particular point of view. Perhaps this is why Dr Usui tried to introduce a system of healing that could be practised by everyone, from any faith.

It seems that, like most Japanese people, Dr Usui's Shinto and Buddhist practice was an important part of his life. However, it seems that when he had his final realisation, the healing, psychic and spiritual subjects of reiki overtook most of his Buddhist teachings.

Reiki for Dr Usui was first and foremost for healing towards happiness, with the highest realisation of a universal-inner God-enlightenment as the ultimate gift.

1. Buddhism

Buddhism[5] began 2,500 years ago in India and was founded by Gautama Siddhartha, the Buddha, or 'Enlightened One'.

There are many major Buddhist scriptures, and some of the more major ones are: the *Thipitaka, Anguttara-Nikaya, Dhammapada, Sutta-Nipata,* and *Samyutta-Nikaya.* Buddhism is practised by over 300 million people worldwide and is third only to Christianity and Islam in popularity.

Buddhism today is divided into three main sects: Theravada, or Hinayana (Sri Lanka, Thailand, Burma, Cambodia), Mahayana (China, Japan, Vietnam, Korea), and Vajrayana (Tibet, Mongolia and Japan).

Figure 3:   Buddha Of Light In Kamakura, Japan

---

[5] This and next section reproduced with permission from Hinduism Today. You can find them at www.hinduismtoday.com.

a.   Buddhist tenets

Life's goal is nirvana, or enlightenment. Toward that end, Buddha's teachings are encapsulated in the Four Noble Truths:

1. The truth of suffering: Suffering, duhkha, is the central fact of life. Being born is pain, growing old is pain, sickness is pain, death is pain. Union with what we dislike is pain, separation from what we like is pain, not obtaining what we desire is pain.

2. The truth of the origin (samudaya) of suffering: The cause of suffering is the desire (iccha), craving (tanha) or thirst (tishna) for sensual pleasures for existence and experience, for worldly possessions and power. This craving binds one to the wheel of rebirth, samsara.

3. The truth of the cessation (nirodha) of suffering: Suffering can be brought to an end only by the complete cessation of desires – the forsaking, relinquishing and detaching of oneself from desire and craving.

4. The truth of the path (marga) to ending suffering: The means to the end of suffering is the Noble Eightfold Path (arya ashtanga marga), right belief, right thought, right speech, right action, right livelihood, right effort, right mindfulness and right meditation.

An ardent follower of Buddhism might additionally tell you:

1. I believe that the Supreme is completely transcendent and can be described as Sunya, a void or state of non-being.

2. I believe that life's aim is to end suffering through the annihilation of individual existence and absorption into *nirvana,* the Real. It is <u>fully my own responsibility</u> to follow the Noble Eightfold Path to be free of karma and thus attain my own enlightenment. How I follow the Path is entirely up to me.

3.   I believe in the 'Middle Path,' living moderately, avoiding extremes of luxury and asceticism.

4.   I believe in the greatness of self-giving love and compassion toward all creatures that live, for these contain merit exceeding the giving of offerings to the Gods.

5.   I believe in the sanctity of the Buddha and in the sacred scriptures of Buddhism: the Tripitaka (Three Baskets of Wisdom) and/or the Mahayana Sutras.

6.   I believe that man's true nature is divine and eternal, yet his individuality is subject to the change that affects all forms and is therefore transient, dissolving at liberation into *nirvana*.

7.   I believe in dharma (the Way), karma (cause and effect), reincarnation, the sanga (brotherhood of seekers) and the passage on earth as an opportunity to end the cycle of birth and death.

2. Shintoism

Shintoism began approximately 2,500 to 3,000 years ago. There are two main divisions; one is the thirteen ancient sects, all of which are similar yet have their own founders. The second is known as State Shinto, and is a later synthesis finding its highest expression in the worship of the Emperor and loyalty to the State and family. It is estimated that there are 30 million adherents to Shintoism, most of whom are also Buddhists. There are over 100,000 Shinto shrines in Japan. Their major scriptures, which are primary works and not regarded as revealed scripture, are: *Kokiji* (Record of Ancient Things), *Nikong,* (Chronicles of Japan), a later work, *Yengishiki* (Institutes of the period of Yengi), and the *Collection of 10,000 Leaves.*

Shinto, (from the Chinese characters Shin and Tao, signifying the 'Way of the Spirits') is called Kami-no-michi in its native Japan. Kami are the many Gods or nature spirits. In the shrines no images are worshipped, rather it is considered that the Kami themselves are there. Fresh foods, water, incense, etc., are offered daily upon the altar. There is an inward belief in the sacredness of the whole of the universe and that human kind can be in tune with this sacredness. Stress is placed on truthfulness and purification through which the 'dust' concealing each individual's inherently divine nature can be removed, and thus allow reception of the guidance and blessings of Kami.

The Shintoist's ardent love of the motherland has found unique expression in the loyalty and devotion of the Japanese people to their state institutions.

a. Shinto beliefs

Shintoism consists of a combination of beliefs, including nature-worship from various Japanese folk religions, the worship of ancestors, and animism. Shintoism believes that it is important to keep focused on the goodness of the individual and the group of humans interacted with at any moment. A fundamental law is to create moral and physical purity. If someone 'back-slides', gentle purification procedures can be followed to bring the person back to purity. An ardent follower of Shintoism is likely to tell you:

1. I believe in the 'Way of the Gods,' Kami-no-michi, which asserts nature's sacredness and reveals the supernatural.

2. I believe there is not a single Supreme Being, but myriad Gods, superior beings, among all the wonders of the universe that is not inanimate but filled everywhere with sentient life.

3. I believe in scriptural authority of the great books known as the *Record of Ancient Things*, *Chronicles of Japan*, *Institutes of the Period of Yengi* and *Collection of 10,000 Leaves*.

4. I believe in the sanctity of cleanliness and purity—of body and spirit—and that impurity is a religious transgression.

5. I believe the State is a divine institution. Its laws should not be transgressed. Individuals must sacrifice their needs to it.

6. I believe in moral and spiritual uprightness as the cornerstone of religious ethics and in the supreme value of loyalty.

7. I believe that the supernatural reveals itself through all that is natural and beautiful, and value these above philosophical or theological doctrine.

8. I believe that all is Divine Spirit, that the world is a one brotherhood, that all men are capable of deep affinity with the Divine and that there exists no evil in the world whatsoever.

9. I believe in the practical use of ceremony and ritual and in the worship of the Deities that animate nature, including the Sun Goddess, Star God and Storm God.

Dr Mikao Usui's Discovery of Reiki

There are many stories about how Dr Usui discovered reiki. His life-long interest in spiritual and healing subjects included collecting many techniques and methods. He may have learned languages, including Chinese and Sanskrit. As he had befriended the Englishman for most of his teens and twenties he probably also spoke some English. Two of the most popular stories about Dr Usui discovering reiki are:

1. Christian

This story is included, not because it is true, but because it has become folklore. This is the version of history taught by Mrs Takata.

Dr Usui was President of a Japanese Christian school, Doshisha, in Kyoto. Whilst teaching about Jesus, two students asked, 'How did Christ heal?' Dr Usui could not answer. He left the school, starting a ten-year worldwide search for the answer.

Many Japanese hearing this story for the first time laugh loudly. To them it is a funny idea that there could possibly have been a Christian school in Japan in Dr Usui's day! And there is no record of anyone called Usui ever having been at this particular school.

This version continues that Dr Usui studied a theology degree at Chicago University. However, Chicago University has no record of any Usui having been there in any capacity whatsoever.

Perhaps Mrs Takata added Christian aspects to reiki history to make reiki more palatable to the West; especially as war broke out between Japan and America just after Mrs Takata took reiki to the USA in 1938. However, Dr Usui had wanted reiki to spread around the world in a way compatible with each culture. Maybe Mrs Takata intuitively understood this?

Or, as Mrs Takata did not teach her first master until 1970, 32 years after learning reiki, perhaps it was simply her lapse of memory. After all, can you remember everything you have read in this book so far? And could you teach it in 32 years' time? Probably not.

2. Sutras

There are different versions of Dr Usui's search for reiki but most stories merge and say that he found a sutra. Even if true, no one yet knows which sutra this was. If true, perhaps it was the sutra translated into English by Raoul Burnham in his book, 'The Healing Buddha'. This states that a spiritual being, the 'Bodhisattva Supreme Healer' can be called upon for healing.

The formula does not explain how healing is given; but it does show a method of contacting the higher power. This includes meditation, mantra, devotion to helping others, and spiritual/physical cleansing. Perhaps Dr Usui decided to use this formula, and went to Mount Kurama to meditate for 21 days. Perhaps the sutra gave him the impetus to discover his enlightenment and reiki.

Another story states that, after a worldwide search, Dr Usui found and studied original Sanskrit Buddhist sutras with ancient symbols that he believed might be a healing formula to help him contact a higher power that could provide healing.

At present there is no evidence to support the theories that Dr Usui studied sutras. In fact, there is opposite evidence. In Dr Usui's writings in the next chapter, he states

"I did not study in order to understand the spiritual capability of therapy."

However, it is known that he used the Tantra of the Lightening Flash, a tantra for the healing of any illness and it may be possible that this or another sutra helped him meditate in such a way to be able to receive the system of reiki knowledge.

3. Buddhist

Yet another story states that, in his early years, Dr Usui was moved by the Buddha's wealth, desire to help others, and rare metaphysical gifts. The Buddha also seemed to heal physical problems; and followers received healing powers from his doctrines. But Dr Usui found that, in his day, not even Buddhist priests knew the Buddha's healing methods. Realising that many people needed healing, he decided to try to discover how healing is given.

During travels, Dr Usui enquired at various Buddhist temples where priests explained that information about healing physical, emotional, or mental problems was not considered important and so were lost in the distant past, and that priests now only healed the spirit.

Eventually Dr Usui studied at a monastery with an abbot who also was interested in healing. From my researches, it seems that there are truths in many parts of reiki history. The abbot on Mount Kurama in the early 1920s was into 'Love, Light, Power, and universal energy'. The prayer book in the mountain's main temple still uses those words.

Figure 4: Main Temple On Top Of Mount Kurama

In 1946, a Captain Blackwell bought a box of manuscripts from a Buddhist monastery. A year later, his son Richard was born. He grew and later turned to Buddhism and reiki, and called himself Lama Yeshe. It must have been a wondrous surprise when he discovered his father had bought Dr Usui's memoirs! Lama Yeshe is translating them. It seems that in the next few years, much will unfold about reiki history.

4. The Mountain

On the holy Mt Kurama, Dr Usui purified his body with fasting, to follow the formula he had discovered to contact the highest power, and then receive knowledge on how to give healing.

Mt Kurama has an open-air hot spring bath where, in Dr Usui's day, Japanese men and women bathed naked while contemplating their lives and meditating for enlightenment. (Nowadays men and women are separated.) It is possible that this is where Dr Usui received his enlightenment. For in his writings he states,

> *'During a period of fasting, I exposed myself to the atmosphere ...'*

Perhaps this was a polite way of saying he had no clothes on.

5. Beam Of Light After 21 Days

Although there is currently no evidence for this, Dr Usui set out 21 stones, discarding one each day. After discarding the last stone, he saw a beam of light rush towards him. The light seemed to have intelligent consciousness; and struck him in the middle of his forehead.

This is a strange phenomenon. When I learned Karuna Reiki ®, I had no intention of ever teaching reiki. But in the attunement, I also saw a beam of light rush towards me. As it hit me in the forehead, my prayer-positioned hands were taken high above my head, and Dr Usui appeared to me for the first time saying, 'You are worthy enough to teach reiki'. After the course, despite my not wanting to teach, it was as if I had no choice. Some of my students have had similar beam of light experiences.

6.   Instant Attunement

This story says that Dr Usui then saw millions of bubbles. Within each were symbols. He was given the best symbols to use in the reiki system and each time he was attuned to that reiki symbol, receiving the knowledge needed to go with it and to teach others. This seems to be how Dr Usui received his reiki attunements.

As with the previous point 5, there is a strange reality to this - a number of my students have had a similar experience.

7.   The Reiki Ideals

Dr Usui spent the rest of his life in Japan sharing reiki. He continued to meditate in order to regularly contact the highest power. Either during or after his mystical reiki attunements, he felt that the Meiji Emperor's Ideals and poems could be used within reiki. This he knew was to help both practitioner and patient create balance and harmony in their lives; and to give reiki healing the best chance to work positively and permanently. Reiki became not just a healing or spiritual energy; it was also a way of life.

8.   The Reiki Lineage

Of the 2,000 students taught by Dr Usui, only six or seven of these reached the top level of his teachings. These included his great friend Dr Watanabe Itami to whom he entrusted his diary and research papers (Yeshe), and a retired naval commander friend Dr Chijiro Hayashi who eventually ran a reiki clinic in Japan. Amongst many others, Dr Hayashi agreed to pass on reiki knowledge. Through him, Mrs Takata spread reiki outside Japan.

History Of Reiki Lineage – Ancient

Reiki 'lineage' history is pitted with myths. Two of the most common current myths are that reiki derived from Tibet or Christ.

1. Theory One - Tibet

It is often stated that reiki symbols and attunements may have originated in ancient Tibet. The likely source of this story is when 'Tibetan Reiki' was brought to America from Tibet in the 1980s, and people assumed, incorrectly, the Tibetan symbols had a historical tie to Dr Usui. Dr Usui categorically states in his writings that 'reiki is something that no one before has discovered'. However he may well have accessed Tibetan information via the 'universal mind'. It is said that symbols similar to reiki are painted on Tibetan and Japanese temple and monastery wall tapestries, on flags, and on silver plates, and used as a focus for spiritual meditation.

The Tibetan Lama sat on a stool in a bowl of water three inches deep. The silver plated seat was engraved with the master symbol, connecting down silver chair legs to the water. In front, a polished copper mirror reflected a tapestry painted with the symbols and a prayer. Meditation on this reflection helped purify body and spirit, and bring the Lama to oneness with the highest power.

2. Theory Two - Christ

I have often been asked if Jesus Christ was a reiki healer. Quite frankly, there is no evidence in the bible to suggest that Jesus Christ used symbols for physical, mental and emotional healing. Nor is there any evidence that he used a system of progressive attunements, and self-healing. Certainly he was an amazingly effective healer, but there are many ways to heal. Without biblical evidence of him using the three fundamentals of reiki, symbols, attunements and self-healing, it should not be assumed that Jesus Christ used reiki.

History of Reiki Lineage - Modern

Dr Mikao Usui started the reiki lineage by initiating 2,000 students. Many of his reiki masters taught others, who still teach today. For example, one of Dr Usui's masters was a Mrs Hirai who taught Okajima Sensei, who attuned me in Japan.

Another of Dr Usui's students, Dr Chijiro Hayashi started the Western lineage by teaching Mrs Takata from the USA.

1. Dr Mikao Usui

Figure 5:   Dr Mikao Usui

Dr Usui introduced:

i.   Reiki to the world, including symbols.

ii.   The Seven Level System.

iii.   The mission statement for reiki of achieving happiness for all.

iv. Many healing, psychic, self-development and spiritual techniques and methods.

v. Reiki Ideals and use of Gyosei.

vi. Use of reiki to cure physical, mental, and emotional illness.

vii. How to reach enlightenment – wholeness of the microcosm of human love with the macrocosm of God's spirit.

viii. The Inner and Outer circles of teachings.

2. Dr Chijiro Hayashi

Figure 6:   Dr Chijiro Hayashi

Dr Hayashi introduced:

i.   Healing with two healers on a person at the same time.

ii.   Clinical trials.

iii. Record keeping.

Although Dr Usui had introduced his 7-level system of reiki, it is believed that in the early 1930s it was Dr Hayashi, a Christian Methodist who had become a 'master' in 1925, who introduced records on treatments at his reiki clinic in Shinano-machi, Tokyo.

Dr Hayashi had eight healing beds and many healers. So he introduced the method of having two healers on one patient. One healer stayed mainly at the feet, whilst the other started at the head and worked down. Students helped at his clinic without payment in return for learning the next reiki level. A written story from his era said that he taught five days a month, so he must have had many students.

Many years later, Mrs Takata said that, as war had seemed certain, and as Dr Hayashi felt women were more likely to survive the war, he wished to pass reiki on to two women, his wife and herself. After WW2, Mrs Takata said she was the only reiki master left alive, and the only woman attuned into reiki. However, Dr Usui's writings state that women can learn reiki, and it is known that Dr Usui taught a Mrs Hirai and a Mrs Yamaguchi. There were probably many Japanese women reiki masters before Mrs Takata.

Just before war broke out with the USA, in 1940, Dr Hayashi committed suicide. He was a highly gifted psychic, and saw that he would be asked to come out of retirement to command a ship again, and that he and his men would kill many of the enemy before all being killed themselves. This was against his loving, peaceful, reiki beliefs.

In Japan, suicide is an acceptable and honourable way to die, and the account of his suicide is beautiful. He gathered friends, family, and reiki people around him, and told them at what time he would die. Then, with energy control, he stopped the beating of his heart.

3. Mrs Chiyoko Yamaguchi

Figure 7:   Chiyoko Yamaguchi

Dr Hayashi attuned a beautiful lady, Mrs Chiyoko Yamaguchi, who presented herself to the world after one of my lectures in Kyoto, Japan, in December 1999.

Mrs Yamaguchi learned reiki from Dr Hayashi in 1938, the same year Mrs Takata received mastership from him. She says that her brother paid for the lessons at a cost of 50 yen. She said that she learned reiki from Dr Hayashi as a Combined Reiki 1 & 2 class and studied for about two hours a day for five days. She said that since then she used reiki mainly on her family as they were growing up, and to very good effect. Her son, Tadao Yamaguchi now works for Miraigo helping the environment, and was her translator for me in Japan.

When I met Mrs Yamaguchi in Japan she seemed to be a wonderful, happy, balanced and healthy lady. Because of the interest of people wishing to connect almost directly to Hayashi's knowledge, yet not via Takata, she had taught reiki to three people, including a man who said he had been a Buddhist monk for 20 years.

4. Mrs Hawayo Hiromi Takata

Figure 8:   Mrs Hawayo Hiromi Takata

Mrs Takata introduced:

i. The 10,000-dollar fee for reiki mastership. This is still charged by some masters. However, most masters now charge a lower fee structure to allow all who feel the calling to become a reiki master.

ii. The simplified system of three levels.

iii. Teaching without manuals or note taking.

iv. Reiki as being essentially an attunement process followed by hands-on practice in standard hand positions.

v. Very little structured knowledge, as she relied mainly on the intelligent nature of reiki to find its way to heal.

vi. The notion that there has to be an exchange of energy for reiki to work, i.e. payment in money or gift or service. (She says that Dr Usui introduced this notion after being unable to permanently heal beggars. Although respected sources state that Dr Usui asked for donations only if someone could not afford to pay.)

Mrs Takata was born of Japanese immigrants in Hawaii on 24th December 1900. During her early working life, she worked hard helping her father in sugar plantations. She married the plantation bookkeeper; he died in 1930 aged 34.

Mrs Takata then worked even harder to support her two daughters. Within five years she was seriously ill physically, and had a mental breakdown. Soon after, she travelled to Japan to relate her sister's death to her parents; and seek treatments for her ill health.

In a Japanese hospital, she was diagnosed as having gallstones, a tumour and appendicitis. She was already on the operating table when she heard a 'voice' clearly state, 'The operation is not necessary.' This was so forceful she asked the doctor what else could be done. The doctor suggested the reiki clinic run by Dr Chijiro Hayashi.

Mrs Takata received reiki from two practitioners daily. The reiki method gave the same diagnosis as the hospital's method. And the heat she felt from the practitioners' hands was so strong that she at first believed trickery or machinery was being used. But, after four months, she was completely cured.

So impressed was Mrs Takata by her cure, she asked to learn reiki. She was told 'No', because reiki was by and only for the Japanese. But Dr Hayashi relented because of her insistence, and because he wanted to 'initiate another woman apart from his wife'.

Mrs Takata received First Degree Reiki in spring 1936 and Second Degree after working with Dr Hayashi for one year. She then returned to Hawaii. Dr Hayashi followed to promote reiki there. And on 21st February 1938 he initiated her as his thirteenth and last reiki master.

Mrs Takata spent the rest of her life sharing reiki. Her charges were $125 for first degree and $500 for second degree, although it states in a book with someone who met her in a chance encounter (Hammond) that she sometimes taught free-of-charge. In 1970 she moved to California and initiated 22 masters who taught many others, beginning the Western lineages. The cost was $10,000 for each master's class – reputedly the cost of a small house at that time in Hawaii. She passed over on 11th December 1980.

The philosophy of 'waiting times' between degrees has become widespread and varied. But it is known that Mrs Takata did not have long waiting times between degrees. For example, when she taught Reiki 1 at Barbara Brown's house in 1979, seven of the students asked to do the next level, Reiki 2, and she agreed to teach them the following weekend. The previous weekend, Wanja Brown was given her Reiki 3 degree at the same time as others were receiving their Reiki 1.

Mrs Takata named her reiki 'Traditional Usui Reiki' a name we now realise is unfortunate because how she taught was nothing like how Dr Usui taught. Her 'Traditional Usui Reiki' became the main instigator for reiki in the West even though Dr Usui had taught vast knowledge compared to Takata. There are now about 1 million reiki masters worldwide and about 10 million practitioners, although most do not follow the teachings of Mrs Takata.

There is a list in many reiki books of things Mrs Takata 'got wrong'. However, even though Mrs Takata's teachings were almost nothing whatsoever like the teachings of Dr Usui, she should be honoured because, through her, Dr Usui's wish on his tombstone that reiki should spread around the world was fulfilled.

5.   Mrs Takata's Masters Introduced

It was Mrs Takata's masters who introduced the 'waiting times' between degrees. Waiting times have become folklore, with some masters considering them a 'must' for a series of reiki classes, even though there are now many versions of what a waiting time consists of.

Mrs Takata did not have waiting times, and nor did Dr Usui. They had quality times, allowing students to take consecutive classes if they were good enough.

6.   Phyllis Lei Furumoto & Barbara Ray

Figure 9:   Phyllis Lei Furumoto And Barbara Weber Ray

There is a story that Mrs Takata asked her friend and a chief student, Barbara Ray, to be lineage head of Western reiki after her death. This story says that, when Takata died, Furumoto then stated that as she was Takata's granddaughter and had travelled with her, she should be lineage head. The 21 Takata masters left alive decided to vote on the lineage successor. Ray did not go to the meeting. This probably changed reiki's evolution, because Furumoto got the job by default.   She taught a simple 3-level system around the world, allowed nothing to be written during classes, gave no manuals, and like Takata, charged $10,000 for Reiki 3.

If Barbara Ray had been voted lineage head, there would have been 7-levels taught around the world, more like Dr Usui's actual teachings, including lower charges. Whilst Ray apparently did not teach Usui's techniques, at least she would have promoted knowledge and manuals within the 7-levels as did Usui.

In 1981, one year after Mrs Takata died, Phyllis Furumoto set up her 3-level organisation called The Reiki Alliance. In 1982, Dr Barbara Ray started the 7-level system called The Radiance Technique.

7. Others Introduced

Figure 10: William Lee Rand And Kathleen Milner

Many reiki masters have introduced extra reiki methods, techniques, interpretations and healing and spiritual tools. Nothing is forever. New improved ways are regularly tried, tested, and approved.

For example, recent healing systems of Karuna Reiki and Seichem Reiki were introduced by William Rand and Kathleen Milner respectively. Both systems are not connected to Dr Usui or to Japan. But, they both have similar symbols and history, so Rand and Milner agreed to use different names.

Common modern-day techniques introduced by other teachers include psychic surgery, meditations, guides, angels, and most aspects of healing, psychic, spiritual, and self-development arts. All can increase the chance of a healing cure and psychic and spiritual development. However, current teachings are often done in unstructured ways, instead of specialising in subject skills through a 7-level structure that leads to wholeness, as did Dr Usui.

8.   Dr Allan Sweeney PhD. (AM)[6]

Figure 11:   Dr Allan Sweeney

Health and medical issues have been integral to my life. I was first hospitalised at 3 months old with severe eczema and was so ill as a child, I was not expected to 'make old bones'. Too ill at the age of 12 to continue daily travel to the local grammar school, I was sent to a special boarding school for chronic asthmatics. As an adult it was not possible to work because of often being ill or hospitalised.

My current path started about 23 years ago. By that time I was registered as being 80% disabled – and watched someone have a massive heart attack, and then saw him cured in about two and a half minutes. The healer, Jeanne Murton, taught me her curing method.

---

[6] Please note that the title Dr is not a medical doctor, it is an Honorary Doctor of Philosophy in Alternative Medicine from the Indian Board of Alternative Medicines affiliated with the Open International University for Complementary Medicines (Medicina Alternativa) established under World Health Organisation Alma Ata USSR Declaration 1962 and recognised by the United Nations Peace University.

One day, my three-year-old daughter damaged her back. Like most parents I pretended to rub it better. Suddenly, bolts of electricity shot down my arm and her injury was cured. As the saying goes, 'God works in mysterious ways'. Minutes later, her friend who was out of bed for the first time in two weeks due to a torn leg ligament, tried to kick a ball, kicked the ground, and tore the ligament again. The same thing happened – while pretending to rub it better, bolts of electricity ran down the arm, and she was cured. Seeing a cure, then getting two cures affected my view of healing from the outset.

During the next 12 years, I was a secret healer. If someone needed to receive or learn healing, I would help. Cures were often instantaneous. Despite success I did not realise self-healing potential, so still had illness and hospitalisations. Not wanting to be known as a healer, and afraid of being laughed at or thought of as having ego, this healing ability was hidden even from most of the family.

The change came 12 years ago when my adrenals collapsed. Due to needed medication, severe osteoporosis developed, followed by a prognosis of two years to live. Whilst dying, a sudden realisation came that I should have offered healing and teaching much more. A deep promise was made to my soul that, given another chance, I would do it properly. Days later, a healer met and worked on me. Hospital synacthen tests were getting worse, but the next test on my adrenal function showed a cure.

I kept the promise to heal and teach healing publicly. In the subsequent attendance of many courses, including Reiki, I found that the many previous years of practice had taught me most things about this particular complementary therapy. One missing piece of knowledge was that we can all use healing energies for our own self-healing and, through self-healing, I am now cured of life-long disablement. My life is now dedicated to promoting, giving or teaching reiki and complementary medicine, 16 hours a day, 7 days a week, free from disability and fully healthy. Unsolicited invitations have come from 56 countries in all continents to provide, teach, or lecture on healing, including to royalty in Africa and Southeast Asia.

My lineages are via a Western and two Japanese reiki lines. Okajima Sensei gave me the Dr Usui's reiki attunements in 1998.

a.　Western lineage

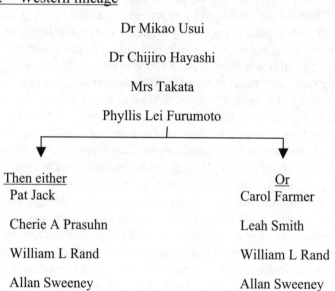

Dr Mikao Usui

Dr Chijiro Hayashi

Mrs Takata

Phyllis Lei Furumoto

Then either	Or
Pat Jack	Carol Farmer
Cherie A Prasuhn	Leah Smith
William L Rand	William L Rand
Allan Sweeney	Allan Sweeney

b.   Japanese lineage 1 – via Doi Sensei

Figure 12: Doi Sensei

Doi Sensei is the Chief Student of Ms Koyama, the 6th President of Dr Usui's organisation, and was responsible for releasing excellent original Usui techniques, and his own material. Although I have not taken his classes, in Osaka, Japan in 1999, Doi Sensei presented me with a pre-publication copy of the information and material taught on his 1999 masters class in Vancouver. In Japan, Doi Sensei gave me attunements, and a Certificate stating that I was the Highly Honoured Teacher of Gendai Reiki (Doi Sensei's school). In a letter dated 6th November 1998, Doi Sensei says that a branch manager of Gakkai attends his meetings. (The Gakkai is Usui's reiki organisation that he founded in April 1922). Via Doi Sensei, my lineage is:

Dr Mikao Usui

Kanichi Taketomi

Ms Koyama

Hiroshi Doi

Allan Sweeney

c.   Japanese lineage 2 – via Okajima Sensei

Figure 13: Okajima Sensei

Okajima Sensei is a brilliant master who has dedicated his life to energy work with reiki and the martial arts. His master was taught directly by Dr Usui. In 1998, in Osaka, Japan he gave me Dr Usui's Reiki 1 attunement and said he would give other attunements. So eventually, my very short lineage could be:

Dr Mikao Usui

Mrs Hirai

Okajima Sensei

Allan Sweeney

9. You

Future
photo of
you?

Figure 14:   Are You Next?

Reiki can progress or develop you as far as you want, hope or need. Although reiki is not for everyone, many reading this manual will, through self-healing and good deeds, find happiness. And some may even rise to prominence. Is one of them you?

Exercise 3 - Your Reiki 'Guru' Lineage

If you are already a rei or spiritual healer, track your own lineage as far back as you can. Ask your teacher/master for the person who trained them, and so on. For those who are presently untrackable, do the research to confirm they exist(ed) if they are not historical figures.

WORKBOOK NOTES
On Dr Usui And The History Of Reiki

CHAPTER 4

DR USUI'S EXPLANATION
OF REIKI THERAPY

Dr Usui's Explanation Of Reiki Therapy

The following highly special document is in original 1920s language and portrays an overview of many of Dr Usui's healing and spiritual philosophies together with an insight that he was an intelligent, articulate, educated, knowledgeable man. He knew his reiki subject in depth, and was a humble but strong character, not afraid to speak his mind if he understood a truth.

It is interesting to note, especially when there appears to be so much confusion about how reiki should be taught, that the teachings of Dr Usui and Mrs Takata were very, very different. In particular note that Dr Usui did not just place hands on and rely on the intelligent nature of reiki to do the work. He taught many techniques, and talked many times about the ability to cure in different ways. And he had extra levels of teachings only available to an inner circle.

Please note:

> *1.   If readers are interested, an article on how Dr Usui's manual was discovered is on my website, www.reiki-healing.com.*
> *2.   Japanese personal names are notoriously difficult so the translator therefore makes an educated guess with a question mark.*
> *3.   The first five paragraphs are written in late 1990s Japanese, as a modern-day introduction to Dr Usui's public explanation of Usui Reiki Therapy.*
> *4.   The subsequent explanation of Reiki Therapy and answers to questions are in the first person and is either Dr Usui's own writing, or by someone who wrote down his words.*

Attention: Mr Allan Sweeney, Reiki International
From: [7]
Re: "Explanation of Reiki Therapy"
Date: 19th January 1999 [8]

---

[7] The translator of Dr Usui's document, who prefers to remain anonymous, was a respected speechwriter for London's Japanese ambassador, and understood classical 1920s Japanese. (Because the Japanese language has evolved so rapidly within the past 100 years, most modern-day people in Japan cannot understand 1920s Japanese language.) It took much time and a series of co-incidences via the Japanese Embassy to find a gifted translator who could deeply understand the now near-obsolete style of handwriting used by Dr Usui.

[8] In 1998, although I was the first reiki master outside Japan to have this information, I felt the time was not right for its release. The Japanese tradition is for the slow release of information and I wished to honour this.

It is possible to get an impression of Dr Mikao Usui that has been traditionally handed down to us, but now a sharper image has been gradually emerging.

We have received articles contributed by Members of this Association who have been delighted to have the opportunity to get closer to the founder of this method of healing, whereas hitherto they had had only vague impressions of the master.

We also received enquiries asking whether only those persons particularly involved in the teaching handed down could familiarise themselves with the records pertaining to Dr Usui's public explanation of the Usui Reiki Therapy.

Therefore, with this special issue, we have decided to make public for the benefit of the Members of this Association the "Explanation of Reiki Therapy" which forms a part of the precious materials published by Dr [?] Yunosuke[9] Yanagihara. He is the direct inheritor of the Usui Reiki Therapy, and his collection is kept by the Human & Trust Research Institute.

As practitioners of Reiki Therapy in this age, we hope that our Members, by getting to know through this text how Dr Usui in his day approached reiki and proclaimed it to the world, will be able to study the origins of reiki, and together, without forgetting any of the essentials, appreciate the principles of reiki even further.

It felt important to me that both the timing and the method of release should be the 'correct' one.

[9] According to the translator, Japanese first names are extremely difficult to translate.

Explanation Of Reiki Therapy, By The Founder, Dr Mikao Usui

From ancient times, each household has discovered its own secret cures,[10] and passed them on only through their children and their grandchildren. In doing so, a family aimed to ensure its stable survival into later ages. It regarded this therapeutic knowledge as something handed down from previous centuries, not to be disclosed to people outside the family. In an age, however, when as present, the basis of human happiness is co-existence and co-prosperity, requiring social advance, this secretive approach to medicine is totally unacceptable.[11]

The Usui Reiki Therapy is something no one before has discovered,[12] and bears comparison with no other treatment in the world.[13] On this understanding, we make known the Reiki Therapy for the benefit of the public in the hope that many people will receive Heaven's blessing, ensuring the unity of body and soul,[14] thereby enjoying natural welfare. From its origins, the Usui Reiki Therapy has been an innovative spiritual therapy,[15] based on universal

---

[10] Similarly, one of Dr Usui's reiki objectives was to cure all ills with different 'secret' techniques.

[11] By analogy, Dr Usui wished the reiki therapy not to be secret, but to be openly available to all.

[12] This statement by Dr Usui contradicts many books that say reiki was 're-discovered'.

[13] Some books suggest that reiki originated in Tibet. In Dr Usui's mind, reiki is unique, and not to be compared with any treatment from any other country.

[14] Wholeness of being, curing and unifying body, mind, and soul is a recurring theme for Dr Usui.

[15] This is an acknowledgment that spiritual powers help reiki, not just one spiritual force.

spiritual powers.[16] First of all, therefore, it makes persons healthy,[17] and at the same time improves their mind,[18] thereby improving mankind's enjoyment of human life.[19]

This is why I,[20] take it upon myself to proclaim the Usui Reiki Therapy to my fellow creatures who require some relief from illnesses that are giving them pain both internally and externally.[21]

Question: What is the nature of the Usui Reiki Therapy?

Answer: I absorbed the last teachings graciously handed down by the late Emperor Meiji [1868~1912], refining my own doctrine.[22] In aiming for the amelioration of both mental and physical exercise and progress upon a righteous way of life, it is first necessary to cure the spirit,[23] and secondly to cure the physical body.[24] If the spirit is healthy, following the path of truth, the body will become healthy of itself.[25]

In this way, it is possible to enjoy a life which brings together the soul and the body and which gives pleasure in the peaceful union

---

[16] Again explaining that the origins of reiki are a unique spiritual innovation.

[17] The initial goal of reiki is to improve health, which in turn helps mankind improve other levels.

[18] Mental healing is part of reiki.

[19] Enjoyment of life is a main goal. See below.

[20] In the first person, so this is either Dr Usui's handwriting or a direct transcription of his words.

[21] Reiki heals all inner and outer aspects of a human being.

[22] Dr Usui uses the Five Ideals and waka poetry of the Meiji Emperor to enhance a righteous way of life in his students.

[23] This corresponds to the common Western Reiki 1 - spiritual rei energy is used to heal a student's soul and spirit.

[24] This is taught on many Western Reiki 2 classes - using the first symbol to help physical problems.

[25] A 'classic' spiritual healing philosophy, showing Dr Usui as a knowledgeable healer who understands spiritual rei healing has eventual automatic knock-on effects for physical healing.

of the soul and the body.[26] This attitude also leads to the cure of other patients.[27] This very increase of happiness in the reiki patient and his or hers fellow patients is the mission of Usui Reiki Therapy.[28]

Q: Is not the Usui Reiki Therapy just another name for saiminjutsu (a form of hypnotism), kiaijutsu (another form of hypnotism), faith healing, or other methods of healing?[29]

A: On no account is the Usui Reiki Therapy practically the same as the techniques you have mentioned. It is a therapy that aims to cure the mind and the body, whereby I have been inspired by esoteric beliefs over a long period of rigorous study and arduous training.[30]

Q: In that case, is it a spiritualistic therapy?

A: The Usui Reiki Therapy may certainly be termed a spiritualistic method of curing,[31] but many of the aspects of the therapy may be called material therapy.[32] The practitioner radiates a spirit and light from every part of his or her body.[33] This spirit and light are manifested mostly in the eyes, the mouth and the hands. For this reason, the practitioner will carefully study the diseased part of the body for two or three minutes,[34] breathe back on the patient,[35] or

---

[26] Classic Reiki 1 & 2 offering the energy options to heal first the soul and then the body.

[27] The first attitude is to self-heal, but others can then be cured.

[28] If someone is healed spiritually, in the soul, physically and mentally, that person will be happy! Therefore Dr Usui's first mission statement is to increase happiness.

[29] No different to today, when reiki practitioners and masters have to defend about what reiki is not instead of being able to concentrate on how effective reiki cures can be.

[30] Dr Usui was inspired by esoteric subjects from four years of age when in a monastery.

[31] Reiki 1 spiritual rei healing.

[32] Reiki 2 material (low frequency physical) methods of curing.

[33] Reiki 2 Hatsurei ho.

[34] Reiki 1 technique of scanning with the eyes.

massage the patient with the hands.[36] By these means, inflammation will recede from the sites of tooth-ache, abdominal pain, gastro-enteritis, neurological pain, mastitis, scars, burns, and other sites of swelling.[37] Chronic illnesses, however, may not be dealt with in this way,[38] but I remember some cases of chronic illnesses which, usually requiring several sessions of treatment, have been successfully treated with just one session of Usui Reiki Therapy.[39]

How to explain this kind of phenomenon to modern medicinal circles? The facts of the account would sound more fantastic than the contents of a novel. However, if those actively interested in the teachings take a real look at the text, I believe they will assent to the assertions of those teachings. No matter how much the wordsmith may use sophistry in his art, he cannot deride the truth.[40]

Q: Cannot illness be cured without believing in the Usui Reiki Therapy?

A: Unlike psychological treatment, hypnotherapy and other mental treatments, the Usui Reiki Therapy does not bring with it empty implications.[41] It does not therefore require an explicit consent

---

[35] Technique to break up a concentrated negative energy

[36] Non-touch massage allows energy from the hands to disperse wider areas of negative energy.

[37] All injuries or localized illnesses may be treated by localized healing.

[38] In this paragraph Dr Usui shows in-depth knowledge of healing, understanding that local injuries and all-over diseases need to be treated differently. He did not passively allow energy to flow through as taught by Mrs. Takata, nor believe that reiki is so intelligent it knows what to do. He had many techniques, therapies and strategies, all under the heading of Usui Reiki Therapy.

[39] This is true for most experienced healers. For example, I have found that arthritis, asthma, and rheumatism that normally take a number of sessions to help, have occasionally been cured in one session.

[40] Dr Usui comes across as a highly educated and humble man.

[41] Highly knowledgeable, Dr Usui was not averse to being blunt and tough to impart his message.

on the part of the patient,[42] or any loyalty to the practitioner concerned. Not only that, we practitioners of the Usui Reiki Therapy do not mind however much our practices are doubted, held in contempt or rejected.[43] For example, the Usui Reiki Therapy is remarkably effective in treating even those who are unconscious of the world around them, such as infants and patients with serious diseases.[44] People who believe in, admire and respect our therapy with only the first treatment would number one in ten, if that.[45] Many such people appreciate for the first time, upon being treated once, the efficacy of the Usui Reiki Therapy, and all at once, they begin to trust it.[46]

Q: What sorts of diseases are cured by the Usui Reiki Therapy?

A: A great deal of diseases, displaying mental or physical symptoms, are cured.[47]

Q: Does the Usui Reiki Therapy concern itself solely with the curing of diseases?

A: No, not at all. The therapy does not involve the treatment of the body's diseases alone. It can remedy a troubled heart or anguish, imbecility or a poor constitution generally, cowardice or timidity, indecision or infirmity of purpose, nervousness, and other unfortunate conditions.[48] Further, by adopting the spirit of the teachings of Shinto

---

[42] Contrary to many books Dr Usui says categorically that patients do not have to give permission

[43] Patients do not have to believe in reiki.

[44] Patients do not even have to know that reiki is being given - for reiki still works effectively.

[45] Showing possibly a similar reaction to present-day patients.

[46] Showing how effective reiki is after just one session.

[47] Once again the word 'cure'. Cures seem a major reason why Dr Usui promoted reiki.

[48] Again showing that Dr Usui's main aim was to remedy all ills

and Buddhism,[49] and with an eye to treating future generations,[50] the results of the Usui Reiki Therapy can be that both oneself and others may be filled with happiness.

Q: What are the reasons for successful cures by means of the Usui Reiki Therapy?

A: This method of therapy was not handed down to me by several people throughout the land of Japan,[51] nor did I study it in order to discover the spiritual capabilities of therapy.[52] During my period of fasting,[53] I exposed myself to the atmosphere.[54] In so doing, I was wondrously inspired, and realised purely by chance[55] that I had discovered the spiritual capabilities of therapy. Therefore, as the founder of the Usui Reiki Therapy, I find it difficult to give a clear account of the therapy myself. Scholars and intellectuals are devoting themselves to the study of the therapy, and although it is difficult to draw conclusions on the basis of modern science, there will naturally

---

[49] As Dr Usui lived in Japan, he promoted Japanese faiths to enhance reiki healing. But, on his deathbed at the age of 27 Japanese Gods told him it is acceptable to follow other paths. So if he had taught in other countries, he may have included the faith of that country as part of reiki.

[50] For Dr Usui, it was not enough to treat those around him – he wanted to ensure reiki would help people long after he had gone.

[51] Dr Usui states clearly that no one taught him reiki.

[52] Here, he categorically states that he did not study to discover that reiki works.

[53] A reference to the fasting often undertaken on Mount Kurama as a spiritual exercise?

[54] Perhaps this is a polite Japanese expression for bathing naked in Mt Kurama's open-air hot spring baths, and contemplating enlightenment. (The next sentence explains that Dr Usui received enlightenment.)

[55] Although it is known from his diaries that he was interested in metaphysical subjects for many years, Dr Usui did not deliberately search for reiki.

come a time when the Usui Reiki Therapy will be consistent with science.[56]

Q: Does Usui Reiki Therapy make use of medications, and are there not bad effects?

A: The therapy never avails itself of medical equipment. A cure is achieved solely by a steady gaze,[57] or breathing,[58] stroking,[59] the laying-on of hands,[60] or light patting.[61, 62]

Q: Does the Usui Reiki Therapy require medical knowledge?

A: Since our therapy is a spiritualistic method of therapy that has transcended modern science,[63] it is not based on medicine. Simply, if the patient suffers pain in the chest, the practitioner of this therapy considers the patient's chest, if the stomach gives pain, then the stomach, and if there is something wrong with the eyes, then the practitioner must be concerned with the patient's eyes themselves.[64]

---

[56] Dr Usui hoped that science would prove reiki. Many properly scientific constructed studies, including my own studies, are fulfilling this prophecy.

[57] Sending reiki through the healer's eyes into the patient's area of need.

[58] The healer blows reiki on an area of the patient's body where energy is blocked in order to disperse the blockage.

[59] Similar to breathing, but stroking the hand in the aura just above the affected area.

[60] The healer places his or her hands on the patient and allows or creates correct reiki energy.

[61] Similar to breathing and stroking, light patting just outside (not touching) a stubborn energy blocked area of the body can break up dense negative energy.

[62] This sentence shows that Dr Usui's techniques are not restricted to Mrs. Takata's system of only the laying on of hands and trusting that reiki energy has its own intelligence.

[63] Dr Usui uses tough language. As shown below, this is based on his belief that reiki can cure.

[64] This shows Dr Usui's deep understanding of archetypal healing. It is classic that when there is a localized pain, or a localized problem such as the

In this way, the therapy achieves its objective of curing solely through a steady gaze on the diseased area, breathing on it, the laying-on of hands or stroking. Therefore, there is no need for the patient to take bitter medicine or be subjected to blisteringly hot moxa cautery,[65] and in a short time the said diseases will be cured. This is the reason for this unique spiritualistic therapy.

Q: How do modern distinguished medical practitioners regard this therapy?

A: As far as we can see, the most distinguished of medical practitioners are giving reasonable regard to the therapy.[66] However, renowned medical practitioners in Europe have expressed their serious misgivings about the therapy because it does not use medications.[67]

Dr Sen Nagai of the Imperial Medical University says, "As a doctor, I diagnose an illness and enter my diagnosis into the records. Although I understand the nature of the illness, I do not know how to cure it."[68]

Dr Kondo says, "One great fault of modern medicine is that, although it has made great strides, it may be described as superstition,[69] and that it gives no place at all to mental function."[70]

---

eyes, the healer should never waste time giving an all-over body treatment, but should heal the localized area directly.

[65] Dr Usui believed deeply that Usui Reiki Therapy is better than 1920s Japanese medicine's.

[66] Top doctors in Japan in the 1920s were accepting reiki.

[67] Showing the difference between eastern and western medicine in the 1920s, with European doctors preferring to use medication as they still do today.

[68] An admission that doctors can often diagnose, but rarely cure most illnesses.

[69] A forceful statement that reverses the common attack against reiki, and implies that some established medical practices are based on tradition, not evidence.

Dr Ei Hara says, "In modern hygiene therapy, the intellect-bearing humanity of the patient is ignored, and that form of therapy has reached the stage at which the human patient is treated in the same fashion as an ordinary animal.[71] This therapy attracts great derision. I believe that in the near future, there will be a great revolution in therapy circles."[72]

Dr Rokuro Kuga says, "It is a fact that, therapies such as psychological therapy at present being practised by non-doctors boast of brilliant achievements, whereas they are inferior to the therapy conducted by doctors,[73] which relies on the type of illness concerned, the individuality of the patient, and the application of operations.[74] However, to blindly resist the work of the psychological therapy of non-doctors, and to strive solely to ostracise this therapy shows a narrow-mindedness on the part of legitimate doctors."[75]

(Quoted from Japan Medical Bulletin)[76]

From these extracts it is indeed clear that doctors and pharmacists are beginning to recognise the efficacy[77] of these alternative forms of therapy.

---

[70] As today, doctors dealt only with physical problems (or separately with mental issues), and did not integrate the two processes into a system of healing the whole person.

[71] Another forceful statement showing that doctors who only treat the patient's physical symptoms are not giving credence to the mental needs or wholeness of a human being.

[72] A prophesy for the current worldwide upswing in the acceptance of complementary and alternative medicine (CAM).

[73] This is an atypical doctor's comment on reiki, stated in the absence of quotable scientific research.

[74] This is still the current medical model.

[75] Even today doctors need to have a more open mind. After all, a true scientist has an open mind to all possibilities.

[76] All the above 'distinguished medical practitioners' quotes were in the respected Japan Medical Bulletin, showing that this therapy was becoming highly regarded.

[77] To doctors and pharmacists, reiki had an acceptable efficacy rate.

Q: How does the Government view the Usui Reiki Therapy?

A: At the Budget Sectional Committee Meeting held in the House of Representatives of the Imperial Diet on 6th February 1922, Teiji Matsushita, a Member of the House of Representatives who was also a doctor of medicine,[78] said, "I would like to know the Government's views on the fact that, recently, non-doctors have been curing many patients with psychological and spiritual therapies." Mr Ushio, a Government delegate, replied, "Therapies such as hypnotherapy had, until ten or twenty years before, been ridiculed. These days, however, after much scholarly research, hypnotherapy may be applied to any mental patient.[79] It is impossible to solve all aspects of the human intellect with medicine.[80] Further, doctors' work relies on what is shown by the various branches of medicine. For example, doctors suggest methods of treatment of a certain illness on the basis of medical findings. It is not, however, doctors' practice to suggest regarding all kinds of diseases that if the root of the illness is electricity, electricity should be applied, and that if it is appropriate to touch the patient, then the doctor should go ahead and do that."[81]

Therefore, the Usui Reiki Therapy does not come under the law relating to doctors, or under the regulations to supervise acupuncture and moxa cautery.[82]

Q: The Usui Reiki Therapy has the reputation that the use of its spiritual power is a natural gift, and as such, is endowed solely to

---

[78] To have questions asked in one of the highest institutions of the land shows governmental acceptance of the grassroots popularity of other therapies.

[79] Perhaps after ten or twenty years of research, reiki will also be an accepted medical model.

[80] This is a governmental admission that medicine cannot help everything. Perhaps today's governments should make similar admissions?

[81] A governmental admission that doctors are limited in ability and technique.

[82] A statement by implication by Dr Usui that reiki should have its own laws.

specific persons. Thus, it is not something that just anybody can study and put into practice. What do you think?

A: No, not at all.[83] Any being who has received the gift of belonging to the Universe is equipped with this therapy's spiritual power as a blessing from Heaven. This is true of all phenomena: grass, trees, and the birds and the beasts. But since Man is the Lord of Creation, this spiritual power is particularly strongly manifest in human beings. This, expressed in concrete terms, has emerged in the form of the Usui Reiki Therapy.[84]

Q: If that is so, can anyone be initiated into the methods of the Usui Reiki Therapy?

A: Of course.[85] From eminent scholars, both male and female,[86] to the illiterate, can, if they are equipped with common sense,[87] impressively cure their own diseases within a short time, and unerringly acquire the spiritual power to cure the diseases of others. Up to today, one thousand and several hundred persons have been initiated into the Usui Reiki Therapy, and not even one of these practitioners' reiki careers has come to nothing.[88] Even those at the beginning of their initiation have been able impressively to exercise the spiritual powers of healing. If you care to think of it, it will seem incomprehensible that within a little time one can be endowed with the spiritual power to cure a disease, which is considered the most difficult task a person can undertake. I think that is an extremely

---

[83] Dr Usui is emphatic - it is not true that one needs a special gift to practise reiki.

[84] This paragraph of beautiful language describes wonderfully the inherent capability of all people to practise reiki.

[85] Once again, Dr Usui is emphatic in his response.

[86] Contradicting Mrs. Takata's claim that she was the only female initiated into reiki.

[87] Intellectual or literacy capability is not needed – common sense is.

[88] A statement that, given the practitioner has common sense to follow reiki correctly, I have found to be true.

natural reaction. However, the ability to accomplish this most difficult task with ease is the special feature of our spiritual therapy.[89]

Q: If it is possible to cure other people's diseases, is it possible to cure one's own disease?
A: Why should a person who cannot cure other people's diseases be able to cure his own disease?[90]

Q: How would one be initiated into the more exoteric dimensions of the therapy?
A: The initiation into the more exoteric[91] side of Usui Reiki Therapy consists of the Therapy of Discovering the Spirit,[92] the Tapping Therapy, the Stroking Therapy, the Therapy of Pressing with the Hands,[93] the Remote Therapy,[94] the Natural Disposition Therapy,[95] and so on.[96] The aspiring practitioner is first initiated into the elementary teachings, and then those who have achieved

---

[89] Beautiful language to describe how easy it is to cure with reiki.

[90] The translator said that he spent much time deciphering this sentence, and that this must be a Japanese conundrum.

[91] 'That is exoteric which is communicable to the outer circle of disciples.' (Fowler's Modern English Usage, Sir Ernest Gowers, Guild Publishing, 1986.)

[92] Understanding one's spiritual nature.

[93] Not allowed by most western Codes of Practice and insurance policies unless the reiki practitioner is adequately qualified in massage or similar because of the dangers of fracturing weak bones.

[94] Distant healing.

[95] Disposition means, 'temperament; personality; a tendency'. Chambers Compact Dictionary, Chambers Harrap Publishers Ltd, 2000. Or 'setting in order, a person's natural qualities of mind and character.' The Oxford Everyday Dictionary, J.M. Hawkins and E.S.C. Weiner, The Leisure Circle Ltd, 1985. Dr Usui is stating that reiki included a specific therapy aimed at improving these human qualities.

[96] Suggesting that Dr Usui introduced many therapies under the umbrella heading of reiki.

outstanding results, deported themselves well, and are enthusiastic, are initiated into the esoteric teachings.[97]

Q: In the Usui Reiki Therapy, are there stages above the exoteric teachings?
A: There are the mystic teachings.[98]

[Ends]

The text dates from 1920s and is beautifully written by a trained calligrapher. Medical quotations are in classical Japanese, which makes it a highly respectable document.[99]

---

[97] Although Mrs. Takata's students introduced 'time gaps' between the reiki levels, Dr Usui had 'quality gaps'. So, providing students proved their ability and understanding of what had already been taught, and behaved well with common sense, and showed enthusiasm, they could automatically move on to the next level. This obviously meant that good students could move on quickly, whereas not-so-good students were not allowed to move on until they portrayed these three qualities.

[98] The translator said that he deliberated for much time before choosing the word 'mystic'. For higher-level reiki practitioners, mystic has 'spiritual or occult or theological implications'. (Fowler's Modern English Usage, Sir Ernest Gowers, Guild Publishing, 1986.) Therefore, by suggestion, if exoteric meant the teachings for the outer circle of disciples, the mystic teachings were for the inner circle only. Therefore Dr Usui cannot describe the mystic teachings openly, and the document ends here.

[99] Comment from the translator.

Reactions To Dr Usui's Writings

I often read this translation to students on my classes. Many of them have had profound encounters while listening to this, and below are a few highlights of their thoughts and experiences:

'His vision had no limit to what can be achieved with reiki – he had complete faith, no doubts whatsoever. The root of reiki. Like telling an oak tree that it's not an oak tree.' R

'Usui entered the classroom, walking back and forth while Allan was reading – at one time he was standing behind Allan. He was a loving and caring man, focused on principles – eager to find cures to everything.' S

'A very strong and powerful man. I felt as though he was saying no matter where you are you can give Reiki. Felt he was in the room looking down on all of us with love.' B

'Usui, the man – eminent brain, very skilled, more than well-educated, had absolutely no doubts about his abilities. Most arrogant. Almost too convinced of his capabilities. Very self-assured. Had some tough fights to convince people about his new ideas. Didn't take 'no' for an answer – probably couldn't even spell the word – not humble.' L

'No nonsense man – with an open mind. Enveloping nature and all things spoken in a very positive, almost authoritarian way with no doubts at all regardless of others' doubts. A man of his time, the now, and the future.' J

'I felt a closeness to Dr Usui. His crystal clear answers to questions asked of him, his honesty and compassion, his total command and insight/knowledge into causes of disease and its cure, he was tuned in to the divine.' P

'Usui, the man was forthright, single-minded with purpose, honourable, not humble but without ego; certain of himself - his understanding of himself within the universe.' L

'A very intelligent, correct man who has methodically thought out all aspects of his therapy. An unwavering believer with great visions for the future. Reiki therapy was open to absolutely everyone from the highest to the lowest and all could have the ability to apply this therapy. Reiki should be correlated with all medical and governmental circles as it could cure all diseases and would in a short time be general policy.' C

'Energetic, determined, knowledgeable, clarity, wise, authoritarian, single-minded, focused with a clear purpose... clear, compassionate, peaceful, confident... Appeared to see his face, very energetic body, walking around. I felt held and protected; safe; and like a precious gift has been given to me.' S

'Obviously a very intelligent and well-educated man, with a caring for the whole being of mankind. A very strong person... He wants reiki to be available to as many people as possible to learn reiki healing.' T

N.B. I find it interesting that many students comment on similar aspects of Dr Usui's character such as his 'unwavering belief', his being 'not humble but without ego', and that he was 'most arrogant. Almost too convinced of his capabilities. Very self-assured. Had some tough fights to convince people about his new ideas.' These are all marks of a true master of knowledge, of a man at the height of his profession, a man who knew his subject in-depth, wishing to let others know of his vast knowledge and ability and the potential of his therapy to help everyone. A true master just says it how it is, even toughly, and yet, at the same time, has no ego.

Workbook Notes
On Dr Usui's Explanation
Of Reiki Therapy

CHAPTER 5

DR USUI'S ORIGINAL TEACHINGS

Fax On Dr Usui's Teachings Via Japan

This fax to myself from Doi Sensei in 1999 is a literal translation.

"What Usui Sensei taught

Mission of reiki is to:

1. First of all heal the emotional, second, heal the body and enjoy peaceful life and besides heal the patient and increase happiness with others. He asked to have <u>unconditional love</u> – a mission of reiki.

2. He (Usui Sensei) wanted us to master the enlightenment that he got. That is what he really wanted to pass on. Especially he taught strictly about:

   *Unifying macrocosm and microcosm - they must be united

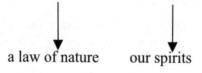

a law of nature   our spirits

   * Universe is oneself, oneself is universe
And also he said

'a whole universe exists within us and I am in the universe.

Light exists within us and I am in the light.
Become one with universe'.

However he wanted to teach reiki to everybody so he didn't say to general students that reiki led to the enlightenment. He said it increased health and happiness, because at that time the standard of living was very very low in Japan and everybody was so poor they couldn't go to a doctor when they were ill and most of their motives were to cure the illnesses. However, what he wanted to teach was to lead them to their enlightenment so he taught that to students who achieved a certain degree. He also said:

'Cultivation of the mind based on truth of universe, earth and nature makes us develop (or grow).'

And also he said

'Reiki can cure any illnesses so devote yourselves to do it <u>with pure soul</u>.
However, there is an illness which can't be cured by reiki and medicine. That is the end of the life.
Our lives are limited, even adult or child. This is providence, we can't change it. But if you know someone is dying, you would do your best to cure the client until last second, and the person even if he/she suffered a lot, she/he can end up the life very very peaceful'."[100]

This fax from Japan is special because it shows the thinking of Dr Usui, with his various aims and goals for reiki of self-healing, cures, and enlightenment to help our world.

---

[100] Unfortunately, I am unable to determine if this is a direct translation or a paraphrase of a translation as the person who provided the text has moved.

Exercise 4 - Increasing Happiness In Self & Others

Smile. Smile at everyone you meet, at any time, anywhere. Smile even if you feel miserable. See the results on your self and others. Try it when you go shopping next. Smile at other shoppers, at the person on the checkout, or at nearby taxi or bus drivers.

After, consider how smiling made you feel inside. And think about the reactions you got from others. Did at least one of your smiles help someone feel a little happier?

Exercise 5 - Happy Rain

Or find another way to make you happy. One lady saw such beauty in appreciating rain and seeing how the drops join and break and reform, she was always happy when it rained! Find your way.

Exercise 6 - Connecting Microcosm To Macrocosm

Take about 5 or 10 minutes to do this.

Relax. Imagine the most loving you have ever felt. Feel the love inside you. Feel the love get bigger. And bigger again.

Then imagine the LOve of your God outside you. Feel the presence of LOve outside you.

Let the love inside you move out, and the LOve outside you move in, until the two merge in a beautiful feeling of love.

Feel that you are the universe and that the universe is you. That you are in the light and that the light is in you.

An Overview Of Reiki As Originally Taught By Dr Usui In Japan

1. Levels Within Levels

As in many Eastern martial arts, Dr Usui taught levels inside levels, inside levels. Students had many different ladders along which they could progress – and some of them went sideways, not up. I understand from an excellent source, that within the first three levels of Dr Usui's teachings there were seven levels. And that within these seven levels were options to develop psychic or spiritual or healing or self-development skills that students could choose if it was right for their individual soul progression. Within these seven levels, I was advised that there were 22 levels and 22 manuals, almost certainly one for each of the 22 levels. And one reputable source has stated that there were a total of 84 levels within those 22.

2. Progression

For Dr Usui, Reiki 1 was first for self-healing with spiritual healing energy, bringing balance to body and soul. Then on Reiki 2, techniques were taught on how to heal others, including using symbols, and many other healing methods. On level 3 he would teach what he called, 'The Reiki Cure' – how to get results - or psychic, or spiritual, or self-development classes. This led to the fulfilment of his mission statement, 'To provide happiness for everyone'. Level 4 was for reiki master beginner teachers; level 5 for reiki sensei expert teachers; and levels 6 and 7 were by invitation only.

3. Exoteric Subjects

Along with 'The Reiki Cure' Dr Usui taught many exoteric subjects – subjects for anyone to learn. Eventually he taught mystic subjects – subjects only for an inner circle – that led to his ultimate reiki goal, to provide enlightenment. Yet all were taught in a scientific framework. For example, according to the man who contacted me from the 7th level of Dr Usui's Gakkai, he taught about frequencies for healing, perhaps gleaned from his technical days in the navy. Science, medicine, and promotion of reiki in Governmental circles were all dear to Dr Usui's heart. Obviously, he had vast knowledge that he readily made available for others.

4.   Following Dr Usui's Path

On discovering how Dr Usui taught, I was most surprised - because I had been teaching reiki in a similar way. Perhaps this is because for about seven years Dr Usui has appeared on courses, sometimes on my face for students to see, sometimes beside me as a guide, and sometimes to students for their own enlightenment. On many of these occasions, direct channelling and teaching has come from Dr Usui and I immediately taught that channelled knowledge on courses.

Develop and progress yourself
towards enlightenment soon.

True Usui Reiki
Levels Inside Levels Inside Levels

There are only ten people in the world on the 7th level of Dr Usui's organisation, and I had the honour of being introduced to one in 1996. He said that the ten meet once a year. For example, in March 1999 they met in Paris. Included in the annual discussions are how and what real, true, original Usui teachings should be released. He explained that what Mrs Takata called 'Traditional Usui Reiki' is nothing like what Usui actually taught. And he then imparted much information about how reiki should be taught.

Here follows what is almost certainly an overview of the strategy of the true and correct Usui teachings.

However, the 7th Level master said that the head of the organisation limited what he was allowed to say. So although the teaching structure is almost certainly correct, the exact nature of each level has been pieced together from meetings with him, comments, books and faxes from Japanese masters such as Doi Sensei and Aoki Sensei, and the original writings of Usui I was given in 1998.

In the Usui Gakkai, masters could do a workshop called Shoyou Kai, now known as Benkyo Kai. Everyone who joined the workshop could have an attunement, although attunements were not always given. They would then receive the Shoden teachings (Reiki 1). Then they could attend levels within Shoden called tou, and levels within tou called kyū.

109

Tou And Kyū

Rather like tai chi, and many forms of martial arts, Dr Usui's true original system had levels inside levels inside levels. This way of structuring progression of knowledge is unfamiliar to most Westerners. An analogy can be made with many martial arts where a white belt can only move to the next colour if various 'sub-level' techniques are passed at white belt level.

This is how Dr Usui taught reiki. Students could progress not only upwards, but also sideways. Thus although the first level was Shoden, there were levels within Shoden called tou and levels within tou called kyū.

There were six levels of tou, with Level 6 being the lowest and Level 1 being the highest.

Similarly there were six levels of kyū, again with level 6 being the lowest.

The following shows how Dr Usui's teachings were almost certainly structured.

The 6th tou of Shoden was about feeling in the hands, hibiki – that is, scanning.

The 6th kyū (first technique) of the 6th tou (first level) of Shoden was how to scan with eyes.

If that was passed students could progress on to the 5th kyū of the 6th tou of Shoden - how to heal, through the eyes, the weakness discovered when scanning with the eyes.

And so on to enable the 6th tou to teach many techniques about scanning.

The 5th tou of Shoden studied dis-ease, with six kyū knowledge levels.

The 4th tou of Shoden taught diagnosis, again with six kyū knowledge levels.

And so on.

If students passed all six tou, complete with all sublevels of kyū, they could progress to Okuden, Reiki 2.

Outside Japan, reiki is taught in many ways. It could be considered in one of the westernised versions of reiki to be like this. Reiki 1, Shoden, may be about spiritual healing. Shoden may include six levels of tou on spiritual dis-ease, another six levels of tou on spiritual healing for the dying etc. And within each of these could be six kyū techniques on how to heal or help the spiritual issue.

Dr Usui issued cards to each student with the list of tou and kyū that had to be passed before moving to the next level. As the students passed each tou or kyū, their card would be marked or holed.

Dr Usui had quality control!

The Seven Levels Of True Usui Reiki

Some people consider that seven levels, with levels inside those, must make reiki complicated. It doesn't. In fact, the opposite is true.

The Western reiki that Takata called 'Traditional Usui Reiki' appears more complicated, as when students discover their specialist healing, psychic or spiritual art, there is often no back-up teaching nor specialist knowledgeable teacher to help develop their gift.

To have seven levels, structured to provide a pathway for the natural development of each individual, is an easy system leading to wholeness of the physical, emotional and mental bio-systems connected to wholeness with the spiritual, soul and enlightenment.

As mentioned, this was pieced together from various sources, including Japanese masters, someone on Usui's seventh level, and Dr Usui's hand-written texts. Not everything is known yet, but it is likely this was at least extremely similar to Dr Usui's reiki structure.

Certainly most reiki masters who have heard of these seven levels agree that they are logical, and that the seven levels provide common sense progression of reiki knowledge and ability.

Especially because the seven level structure helps students develop gradually. They are not held up by their weaknesses, but develop according to their individual natural gifts and strengths.

Some of the techniques taught by Dr Usui on level 1 Shoden and level 2 Okuden are explained in the excellent book by Hiroshi Doi *'Iyashi No Gendai Reiki-ho'*, or 'Modern Reiki Method for Healing'.

As you read the seven levels, feel inside. Begin to realise your path. Perhaps from this realisation your reiki path will unfold. As you read, you may have inner realisation that you need to learn, for example, up to level 3A in order to become a professional healer.

Or maybe it feels right to take levels 3C and 4 so that you can practise and teach the spiritual path.

Or perhaps you would like to be a sensei, an expert practitioner and teacher in all the healing, psychic, and spiritual topics.

Feel within. Then develop your beautiful path to help yourself and others as deeply as you can, in a way relevant to your soul needs.

Reiki 1 – Shoden (Spiritual healing)

Shoden means 'The Entrance'. That is exactly what it is – entrance to the wonderful self-development world of healing, psychic, and spiritual subjects.

There was one main level on Reiki 1 – rei, or spiritual, healing. As it states in Dr Usui's handwriting in the early part of the overview of his teachings, and translated in the chapter above, 'If the spirit is healthy…the body will become healthy of itself.'

Spiritual rei healing allows the body and its functions to slowly be brought into balance.

Also, rei allows the student to learn and awaken to many basic lessons about his or her individual – and often hidden until then – inner healing, psychic, or spiritual nature. There were six tou, and six kyū for each tou, on this level.

(See previous section, *'Tou And Kyū'*)

According to Hiroshi Doi, these include receiving Reiju attunement, **Byosen Reikan-ho (the most important technique on this level)**, Reiji-ho, Teate (hands on healing), Nentatsu-ho, Jaki Kiri Joka-ho, Shudan Reiki, (Shuchu Reiki), Renzoku Reiki, Reiki Mawashi (reiki circle), Head Part Hand Positions, Gokai, Gyosei of Emperor Meiji, and Reiki Ryoho Shishin.

For descriptions of these, please see the following section, *'Usui Reiki 1 Shoden Techniques'*.

Reiki 2 – Okuden

Okuden means 'The Deep Inside', and this is what Reiki 2 does – exploring deep healing needs or healing on deep inner low frequency levels. Hatsurei-ho was taught to allow reiki to cleanse and empower.

On the second level there were a choice of two levels. Students could choose which was relevant to their needs.

a.   Reiki 2A – Okuden Zenki (self-development)

This level was for students who did not wish to heal others and needed to develop or heal the self more. It is beautiful that in the true and correct Usui Reiki there were pathways of levels for those in personal need. Sub-levels of tou and kyū were also taught.

Doi Sensei states that some of the techniques on this level were Hatsurei-ho, Uchite Chiryo-ho, Nadete Chiryo-ho, Oshite Chiryo-ho, **Tanden Chiryo-ho (the most important technique on this level)**, Heso Chiryo-ho, Koki-ho, and Gyoshi-ho.

b.   Reiki 2B – Okuden Koki (ki-healing)

This level studied and used the ki energies and is the common version of Reiki 2 taught outside Japan – except that the Japanese Usui techniques are very rarely taught. On this level, students learn symbols and how to heal conditions with Usui's techniques. As always, there were sub-levels of tou and kyū.

Level 2B techniques attributed to Dr Usui by Doi Sensei include receiving three symbols and kotodama (mantra), Chiryo-ho, Enkaku Chiryo-ho (distant healing), **Ketsueki Kokan-ho (the most important technique on this level)**, Hanshin Koketsu-ho, and Zenshin Koketsu-ho.

Reiki 3 – Shinpiden

Shinpiden means 'God's secret method'. Certainly, according to my contact on the seventh level of Dr Usui's organisation, there were four sub-levels on Reiki 3. Although he did not say this, it seems that students chose which level to take depending on their natural progression. Some students would naturally develop as a healer, some as an intuitive, and some as spiritual beings. Others would need further self-development before evolving their natural gift.

It is likely that Reiki 3 was aimed at becoming a master practitioner (not teacher) of at least one of the four sub-levels of healing, psychic, spiritual, and self-development mastership. This is how I have structured my teaching.

a.   Reiki 3A Healing Mastership

In his writings, Dr Usui mentions how easy it is to accomplish cures 'with ease', and that healers should try to cure until the last breath.

In order to accomplish cures, Dr Usui used and taught many techniques, strategies, methods and modalities. He had huge knowledge about healing, and his 'healing toolkit' was vast. His hope was that techniques could be developed and taught for anyone to use anywhere. At the time of writing, I am setting up research projects in order to scientifically prove, and then promote, many reiki techniques to help Dr Usui's prophesy come true that reiki healing will become consistent with science.

Because he used so many energy processes to try to achieve the desired result, he undoubtedly would have welcomed initiatives and innovative energy healing tools from anywhere in the world and placed them under the heading of Usui Reiki Therapy. For him, probably the quickest, easiest and most permanent solution was the best. Healers should never hold on to any healing technique, strategy, etc, if there is an option for a quicker, easier, and more permanent healing with a higher success rate.

In the Usui documents are various healing skills and therapies, all classed under the umbrella of reiki. To be a healing master means never making an excuse for not getting the result, whilst at the same time working with doctors, not against them. Dr Usui, himself a medical person, urged his students to consider that, if they do not know how to heal a particular illness, they should not treat it until they have researched the illness.

b.   My approach to teaching Reiki 3A

A main aim in the system I teach is to pass on extensive channelled and learned healing knowledge so that students are more likely to obtain a cure as Dr Usui desired. These include many techniques with a high success rate, among which are: a way of using the first symbol (given on the Reiki 2 class) for emotional healing that cures nearly all emotions caused by events in this life in under ten minutes, a way to heal most fractured bones within four days, a way to sometimes return part or all of lost eyesight, a way to cure someone with M.E. or chronic fatigue, perhaps within three sessions, and approaches to use with conditions such as schizophrenia where cure success rates are not high. The aim is also to encourage creative solutions – and then to share options that are quicker, easier and more permanent and with a higher success rate.

(My intention is to prove the above and other techniques through properly conducted clinical trials. The International Reiki & Healing Training Centre actively conducts, and promotes, rigorously supervised trials for the above conditions, plus cancer and many more. For further information please visit www.reiki-healing.com

Exercise 7 - Search And Research
Those wishing to be healing masters should search and research for the quickest, easiest and most permanent technique for every illness guided to them...

c.   Reiki 3B Psychic Mastership

Although it is relatively well-known that Dr Usui taught healing and spiritual mastership, it is not so well-known that he also taught psychic and intuitive subjects. However, anyone who can read the extensive Japanese writing on his Tokyo tombstone can see he taught fortune-telling (nowadays known as clairvoyance or channelling), astral travel, numerology, astrology, etc.   Records have been published of his stories about psychic energy work as diverse as dealing with ghosts and the negative memories of energies in buildings and on land. All were taught under the umbrella of reiki.

d.   My approach to teaching Reiki 3B

After reiki attunements, many students' intuitive psychic side becomes clearer or more powerful. To help students' natural psychic gifts develop, I teach Reiki 3B Psychic Mastership classes to include psychometry, astral travel, clairvoyance (clear visions), clairsentience (clear touch), clairaudience (clear hearing), clairolfaction (clear smelling), clairgustation (clear tasting), how to see auras, healing or communicating with guides, and many other varied psychic gifts. There are also additional specialist classes such as channelling, psychic surgery by seeing inside a healee's body to their internal organs, guides, angels, ascended masters, bi-location, how to access Akashic records (the universe's library of all that was, is, and will be), or animal guides, and the city of healing rays.

It seems that Dr Usui used and taught many such subjects and that his teachings would have included anything that a developed psychic may potentially use to help a person's life.

Rather like people who have a natural gift for playing a musical instrument, some students have a natural gift of intuition, or of accessing one way or another past, present or future knowledge. Others have to work harder at developing their less easily found musical or psychic ability.

Intuition can be tuned, and it again seems that Dr Usui would have been pleased to use and teach any psychic subject if it helped someone.

However, please do not think you can become a psychic master practitioner, nor a teacher of psychic nature, before immense practice and understanding. Intuition can be wrong, even for the best intuitives in the world. It is absolutely essential that psychic intuition develops with gradual understanding, under the guidance of a qualified, intuitive master – a master who not only can teach the wide variety of psychic arts, but also practise them with great and good skill.

For many students who have not developed spiritually it is also essential, before taking the 3B class, to study and develop their inner spirituality on 3C. The LOve of spiritual mastership normally provides a protection for psychic natures that may otherwise be lacking...

Exercise 8 - Intuition Notebook
Start a notebook. Keep records of your intuitive thoughts, and regularly check to see how often they are correct. Include your other potential psychic gifts, such as vision, hearing etc.

The objective is to see if you have strength in one or more areas that can ultimately be developed to help you or others in need.

e.   Reiki 3C Spiritual Mastership
Dr Usui's ultimate goal on the reiki path was that students would achieve enlightenment. This level provides the first real chance for spiritual enlightenment.

Spirituality is left until Reiki 3C because most students need to self-heal first. After all, if someone is not healed of their lower frequency, denser, heavier energy imbalances and blockages, they may be able to experience connection to God-force, but are unlikely to stay there, as their imbalances and blockages would drag them down to earth quickly.

f.   My approach to teaching Reiki 3C

My aim of spiritual development is to find the LOve of your version of God within you, to connect it to be at one with the LOve of your version of God outside you, and then to be able to share that LOve with others. There are many ways to achieve this.

Techniques on this class also include how to create peace permanently within, and how to find and achieve the individual's soul purpose.

There may only be two reasons to incarnate on this planet:

i.   To develop our own soul on its pathway back to God

ii. To help the souls of others

These two reasons for living encompass all others. But it is harder to help others' souls progress if we have not helped our own. There are many ways to do this, for example time-lining, understanding your personal karmic resolution need, rediscovering and using the perfect LOve of God you had before incarnation, using soul frequency energies during healing, etc. But in reiki, the main way is through gradual self-healing.

Enlightenment is beautiful.

Exercise 9 - Finding Ways To LOve Yourself
Make a list of everything that makes you feel loved. Do one from each list every day.

Exercise 10 - Finding Ways To Love Others
Make a second list of ways you can help another person feel loved. Practise one from each list daily.

g.   Reiki 3D Self-Development Mastership

A sub-level Reiki 3D for self-development is included as some students do not develop healing, psychic or spiritual ability, and have a greater need for self-healing. Many techniques may be taught, including goal setting, problem solving, affirmations, life coaching, positive thinking, and further self-healing techniques.

Exercise 11 - Goal Setting To Improve Weaknesses

Concentrate on your main physical, emotional, mental and spiritual weaknesses. For each one, make a list of 22 possible ways to resolve it. Try the quickest easiest and best solution.

Thus students can take the class that is their strength or need. After practising and understanding the teachings of that class subject, they can develop further in another Reiki 3 class, or move on to Reiki 4 where they can teach the strength or strengths they have studied.

In other words, a student may take Reiki 3A because he or she wishes to be a healer. Then the student may study Reiki 3B to enhance their psychic nature. But if teaching healing is an aim, the student could progress to Reiki 4 without the level 3B development, but with the understanding that only healing subjects will be taught.

h.   My approach to teaching Reiki 3D

My approach is to empower the person to regain control of their life path. I've been teaching this for thirty years, and have taught it as a 10-week course. Self-development is achieved via specialist techniques to empower the person to find coping strategies for any aspect of their life regardless of their particular type of being. Normally, it has been my experience that within three sessions their issues are substantially resolved.

Reiki 4 – Shihan-Kaku – Reiki master (Beginner Teacher)

It is interesting that, in the same way that Dr Usui allowed most people to become beginner reiki healers on Reiki 1, it seems that he allowed many students to become beginner reiki teachers on Reiki 4. It appears that Reiki 4 graduates could teach the strength or strengths (their gifts) they had mastered on Reiki 3. I.e., they could teach the healing path, or the psychic, or spiritual, or self-development path.

I remember my first visit to Japan in December 1998. The Japanese masters and senseis presented themselves. First a small slim man in his 60s said his name, 'Doi Sensei', gave me his card, and bowed. Then a stocky man in his 30s said 'Okajima Sensei', gave me his card and bowed. Another sensei did the same.

Then a man presented his card, said his name, but did not include the word sensei. 'Are you sensei?' I asked.

He became extremely embarrassed. 'No, no, no, no, no, no, no, no!' he said. 'I'm no sensei. I'm only reiki master!'

This sums up Reiki 4 exactly. This man had taught reiki, but would not dare call himself sensei as he did not have the knowledge nor the ability, and nor the earned respect of a Reiki 5 sensei.

<u>Exercise 12 - Specialist Reading Material</u>
Some people know that one day they will teach reiki. If you are like this, prepare now. Do not read just any book on reiki. Specialise in the subject of your strength. If healing is your strength, read as many healing books as you can. If spirituality, or psychic matters, or self-development is your strength, read extensively on that subject. Focus on your chosen path.
If in doubt, read generally until you begin to feel which subject is your main path.

Reiki 5 – Shihan – Sensei (Expert Teacher)

Some people think 'sensei' means teacher. It does not, although teacher is the nearest translatable English word.

By the time a student applies for Reiki 5, he or she will probably conform to the four main criteria of a sensei. These criteria exist for all senseis in Japan, even if they are a sensei of martial arts, flower arranging, or the tea ceremony!

a.   Dedication
The sensei will have dedicated at least a part of his or her life to reiki.

b.   Vast knowledge
Huge knowledge about the subject is needed to be classed a sensei – in the case of reiki, huge knowledge of healing, psychic, spiritual and self-development subjects.

c.   Ability to use the knowledge
It is one thing to acquire knowledge and quite another to be able to use it! So a sensei must be able to demonstrate ability to competently practise the healing, psychic, spiritual, and self-development skills.

d.   Respect from students
To be called a sensei, level 5 students must have gained respect from the vast majority of his or her students.

Thus in Japan, a doctor is an automatic sensei because, if the doctor is still practising, the above criteria must be present. But reiki masters and other senseis must earn their title. This should be the same in the West.

Reiki 6 - By Invitation Only

Many people ask how they can be invited into the 6th level. The simple answer is that they can't. This level is what it says – by invitation only! However, there are criteria available to share.

First you have to be noticed by a master already on the 6th or 7th level. You would have become noticeable because by the Reiki 5 level, you as a sensei would have been teaching many subjects and people in a beautiful, knowledgeable, and honourable way. By the 5th level you would also be dedicating part of your life to reiki.

Next, you would be invited to send in a written application. If you decline the invitation, you would never get another chance - unless perhaps you beg: because the refusal would have dishonoured the person who had asked.

In your application you would state your reasons for wishing to take the 6th level. If these reasons were not adequate, you would not be allowed further.

If your application were accepted, you would be invited for an attunement. No words may be spoken. After the attunement you must leave, and not return until you can repeat the attunement exactly how it was done to you; be able to explain and demonstrate the energy force of the attunement; and also to show how the attunement has helped you and therefore how it may help our world.

If you get it wrong, there is no second chance, no second attunement, no questions allowed. You simply have to leave and not return until you think you have it right.

For beginners this process will of course seem a daunting prospect. But for someone on or near the 5th level, or someone naturally talented or with vast inner knowledge, the process would be an interesting challenge and test of their abilities.

I have also heard, but not had it confirmed, that on this level Dr Usui taught anti-satanism, spiritual warfare, and other difficult subjects. One person said that this is stated on his tombstone, but again this has not been confirmed.

Reiki 7 - By Invitation Only

As only ten people in the world are on the 7th level and I am not one of them and have been told very little about it, there is not much to say about this. The only information I have at present is that, like Drs Usui and Hayashi, the person I know who is on the 7th level was in the military, and that the ten meet annually and discuss reiki matters under the guidance of the current President. Also to be invited into the 7th level, the person must have been honoured by the Japanese Emperor.

That probably excludes you and me reaching the 7th level.

Usui Reiki 1 Shoden Techniques

1. Rei-ju Attunement

Reiju means the empowerment and healing process given by a reiki master to a student to enhance their abilities and well-being and to heal and connect them to wholeness.

See section 'Potential Benefits Of Attunements' in chapter 11.

2. Byosen Reikan-Ho (The Most Important Reiki 1 Technique)

Byosen means feeling healing sensations, no matter of what type, in the hand. Where a healing need occurs, more byosen is usually felt in the hands.

Almost all students can feel byosen. However, some students may find this technique takes time to master, whilst others may never feel byosen in the hands because that is how their God has made them.

If you are like this, you must trust more that something is happening, and keep the scores of the symptoms to see logically that your reiki is helping to heal by bring the scores down. See section *'Simple Record Keeping Form'* in chapter 19. Byosen feelings can occur in a body part that is seemingly not relevant to the illness. For example, the knees often store unwanted emotions.

See chapter 9 on 'Biofeedback': and in chapter 21 on 'Scanning' please see 'Scanning With Hands And Eyes: Byosen And Hibiki' further information.

3. Reiji-Ho

This technique allows the practitioner's hands to go to where they feel the right position is (assuming of course that the position is polite.) In other words, very quickly on Reiki 1, Dr Usui taught his

students that they could move away from the 'standard' hand
positions, to hand positions that are 'guided' to what is needed for the
healee.

Exercise 13 - Guidance Of Healing Hands
**Place your hands just outside your own or a
healee's body. Do not touch as, for beginners,
touch could confuse your guidance.**

**Then allow the hands to move, maybe in
different directions, until it feels right to stay
in a certain position.**

**Let energy flow through your hands in that
position until you feel the byosen stop.**

**Continue to allow your hands to move to new
positions until all areas feel balanced.**

Exercise 14 - Guidance Of Healing Hands
**Another way is to do Nentatsu-ho (see 5.
below), using the intention, or prayer, that you
will be guided to where the hands should be
placed.**

**Let reiki flow through the hands until byosen
stops.**

**Repeat as needed, until the entire being feels
balanced.**

**This technique will, for some, take much
practice to master.**

4. Teate (Practising Hands-On Healing)

*See chapter 19, 'The Complete Reiki 1 Method'; chapter 18,
'Healer Hand and Healee Body Positions'; and chapter 17, 'Passive
And Active Reiki 1 Methods', etc.*

5. Nentatsu-Ho

On Reiki 2, there are many special hand positions used by Dr Usui for particular healing needs. This hand position, according to Doi Sensei was taught on Reiki 1.

Exercise 15 - Nentatsu
Place your hands above your or your healee's forehead on the hairline. Then allow reiki to flow with an intention such as the person is healed of a bad habit, or fear, or phobia, or allow one of Dr Usui's Reiki Ideals to flow through. This is considered to heal the unconscious mind's negative pre-programming.

6. Jakikiri Joka-Ho

This is a technique to cut away stubborn energy blocks and lumps in the aura.
See the specialist chapter 22, 'Jakikiri Joka-ho'.

7. Shudan Reiki Teate (Shuchu Reiki)

This is a technique that may not be appropriate now, because of recent scientific and clairvoyant knowledge about using different healers' energies at the same time. Please see point 8 below.

Exercise 16 - Shuchu
Practise this in a group where everyone sends reiki to one healee, at the same time as praying for his or her recovery and happiness. Note that the results of prayer seem to be

**more positive than the potential in the next
technique because prayer instigates an out-of-
phase waveband that is more likely to get a
good result. Explanation is given in the Reiki
2 Manual when out-of-phase theory is
discussed in relation to the use of Reiki 2
symbols.**

8.   Renzoku Reiki (Reiki Marathon)

This is one technique that I apologise to Doi Sensei for
disagreeing with. Although wonderful healings can and do result
from the extra energy generated, the scientific reference (Greene,
Benor v2) and clairvoyant evidence is that, occasionally, the
unpreventable different energies of the healers can clash to become
an energetic mess. When this occurs, healees feel so awful, they will
not tell the healers – they will simply not return again.

This is shown in depth in the Reiki 2 Manual because level two
is when healers have choices of different energies and are therefore
more likely to cause this problem.

Exercise 17 - The Reiki Marathon
**In this method, many healers place their
hands on one person, and if there are too
many healers, the healers place their hands on
the shoulders of those giving reiki.**

9.   Reiki Mawashi (Reiki Circle)

This is an interesting technique and although it has the same
potential for energetic mess as the previous two techniques, there
have not been any reports of an energetic mess so far. Maybe it is
because it is used less often?

Exercise 18 - Mawashi – Reiki Circle – Group Sharing
Hold hands in a circle and create a flow of energy from above the head and let it flow through you to the person in front in a clock-wise direction. (Clock-wise helps the energy turn in towards the group.)
Even beginners normally feel the flow circulating within them and therefore within the circle itself.

Some people suggest that the entire group should hold hands with one particular hand facing up and the other facing down. Scientific evidence disagrees as to which hand your energy flows in, and which hand the energy flows out (Benor v2). On my reiki classes, it seems about 3/4 of the students have the in-flow from the right, and out-flow from the left – but some teachers have found the opposite. However, the majority scientific and experiential opinion is in from the right, out of the left.

So it may be unimportant which hand faces up and which faces down – although the best way may change from group to group depending on the majority.

10. Hand Positions For The Head

On page 198 of Doi Sensei's book, it states that Dr Usui only taught 'head part hand positions' on Reiki 1. In other words, reiki healing would only be given to the parts of the head, i.e., front, back, sides, and throat, whether for self-healing, or the healing of others. However, Doi Sensei, and most reiki teachers in the world teach the 12 hand positions as in this manual. And positions for the body are included in the Hikkei – see point 13 below.

11. Gokai

The Reiki Ideals.
Please see chapter 6, 'Gokai, Reiki Ideals & Waka Poetry'.

12. Gyosei Of Emperor Meiji

These are the poems of the Emperor Meiji that Dr Usui asked his students to meditate on, chant, or sing, to help their spiritual and soul development.
Please see chapter 6, 'Gokai, Reiki Ideals & Waka Poetry'.

13. Reiki Ryoho Shishin - Hikkei

The Usui Healing Guide/handbook is called Usui Reiki Hikkei. There are stories that this guide was given to all Dr Usui's students. However, according to my contact on the 7th Level of Dr Usui's organisation, the Hikkei may not have been in Dr Usui's handwriting, but were probably notes of one of his students. It seems that Ms Koyama, the 6th President of Dr Usui's society handed the Hikkei to her students, including to Hiroshi Doi.

It is a remarkable document that gives a great insight into the teachings and character of the founder of reiki.

Also, there is evidence to suggest that Dr Usui taught Reiki 1 as a very simple system of spiritual energy, and that his levels within levels within levels allowed students to progress slowly but surely to where they needed or wanted to develop. Due to the complicated nature of the Hikkei hand positions, it is probable that it was used for a higher level than Reiki 1.

One source suggested it was only used when a student could not intuitively feel where to place their hands.

As this understanding would have been a slow process for many, the Hikkei is introduced in the Reiki 2 Manual.

14. Kotodama

This is a mantra-like chanting of the chosen reiki energy's name to give a spiritual affirmation and protection of the energy.

Exercise 19 - Kotodama Before And After Treatment
When using rei spiritual healing, say, 'Rei, rei, rei', immediately before or after channelling the energy in order to set your intention.

Exercise 20 - Kotodama During Treatment
Chant the name silently and constantly during the treatment to aid concentration of appropriate energy flow.

WORKBOOK NOTES
On Dr Usui's Original Teachings

CHAPTER 6

GOKAI, REIKI IDEALS & WAKA POETRY

Gokai - The Reiki Ideals

Like most of Japan and much of the world, Dr Usui adored the Meiji Emperor, a highly respected, spiritual, and enlightened being. Even President Roosevelt of the USA sent a message to Japan, "to have such an emperor, you are indeed a lucky people." From the Meiji Emperor's magnificent abilities of writing we have the Reiki Ideals and waka poems.

The Reiki Ideals, or Gokai, were a very small part of the sayings of the Meiji Emperor. But Dr Usui felt that if he incorporated them into reiki, daily repetition by students would help them more quickly become better more balanced humans. It is a way to re-programme the unconscious mind towards harmony and perfection.

Some Christians have called the Ideals the Reiki 10 Commandments – except there are only five. As with the biblical 10 Commandments, Reiki Ideals are designed to enhance all aspects of human life.

The Five Reiki Ideals
(One of the more common translations)

Just for today,
I will give thanks
for my many blessings

Just for today,
I will not worry

Just for today,
I will not hold on to anger

Just for today,
I will do my work honestly

Just for today,
I will be kind to my neighbour
and every living thing

The Reiki Ideals In Dr Usui's Handwriting

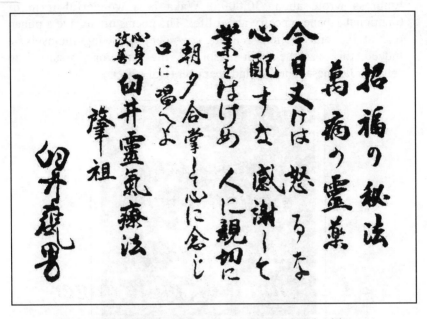

Figure 15: The Reiki Ideals In Dr Usui's Handwriting

The meaning is, reading from right to left:
"The Secret Method of Inviting Happiness,
The Miracle Medicine for all Illnesses,
Just for today. Do not have anger. Do not worry.
Be full of gratitude. Do your work honestly.
Be kind to all people,
Each morning and night time, with your hands held in prayer,
Think these in your mind and chant these with your mouth.
The Usui Reiki method brings cures to your mind and your body.
The founder, Mikao Usui"

Waka (Gyosei) Poems

The Meiji Emperor wrote over 100,000 waka poems, and his Empress wrote about 30,000. Waka is a wonderful form of traditional Japanese poetry about life. The poems often have a punch line at the end to help readers consider improving themselves. Indeed, this was the main reason for the Emperor's poems – to enhance Japanese morality and character (Doi 1999).

Figure 16: Portrait Of The Meiji Emperor

Dr Usui realised how precious the poems were to help create perfections for living humanity, and asked his students to choose daily one of 125 poems relevant to their lives - and then meditate on one poem daily.

Try meditating on one of the following as you channel your reiki (Doi 1999):

i.   'Your soul is perfect if you have nothing to be ashamed of in front of your God who you cannot see yet knows you well. I wish that every human being had such a soul.'

ii.   'If you have a bright shiny precious jewel, you must polish it daily to keep its brightness. So it is with the human heart.'

iii. 'When you look at the sea, you notice that the sea flows easily around every obstacle in its path. Yet one drop of water has the potential to break a huge boulder. Human beings should have such abilities.'

iv.   'I wish my mind and soul was perfect like those of unknown great people of the past who had great minds and souls. For although I am the Emperor, I am not great as a human being.'

v.   'It is evening, and I regret today because I did nothing for my people. But I must not waste time in regret. Tomorrow I must be more perfect.'

vi.   'Our mirrors are untarnished when we look at them each morning. How I wish that each morning's inspection in the mirror, would also see untarnished souls.'

vii. 'Because of the future that has not arrived, and because of meetings that are yet to be, everyone must know how to tread the path of sincerity.'

viii. 'The sun rises perfectly every day. If only we could rise daily in such perfection.'

ix. 'True friendship is when we can show and accept each other's faults'.

x. 'We pray that we will have a peaceful world. Why then do the waves and winds have anger?'

xi. 'Even though the world be full of storms, let us remain like a pine tree, unwavering, with roots sunk deep in virtue.'

xii. 'If you see a towering mountain, inspect it closer. There will be a path to the top.'

The last poem above is shown here in the Emperor Meiji's handwriting. (With thanks to Meiji Jingu.)

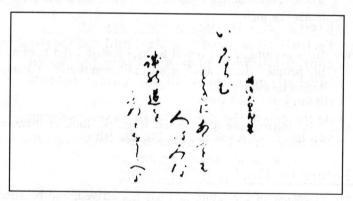

Figure 17:   Waka Poetry In The Meiji Emperor's Calligraphy

When To Use Reiki Ideals And Waka Poems

The Ideals and/or one of the poems should be repeated daily, continuously for a short while, out loud if alone or if you are Buddhist, or silently if you are not a Buddhist, or are 'shy', or are with others. Or repeat three times prior to healing, out loud if the situation permits.

1. At The Day's Start Or End

As the objective of the Ideals and poems is to re-programme the unconscious mind to become a more beautiful force, there is no better time than on just waking or just before sleeping. For at these times the brain's wave pattern is alpha with a little theta, the patterns naturally conducive to unconscious mind programming.

> **Exercise 21 - Having An Ideal Day**
> **Feel what you need that day, and choose the appropriate Ideal or poem. Bring the chosen Ideal or poem to mind at spare moments throughout that day.**
> **At the end of the day, evaluate to see how well you have achieved the goal of the Ideal.**

2. Before Or During Self-Healing

The intelligent nature of reiki energy is programmable. Much more information is given about this in the Reiki 2 Manual when the nature of symbol energy is discussed.

139

<u>**Exercise 22 - Programming Self-Healing**</u>
**The chosen Ideal or poem can be continuously
repeated as reiki energy comes through. Part of
the energy is then likely to take on qualities of
the Ideal or poem, and then be a more relevant
healing along the lines of the chosen Ideal or
poem.**

3. Before Or During Healing Others

As with prayer or mantra, the beautiful force for goodness of an
Ideal or waka poem could become reality for a healee in need.

<u>**Exercise 23 - Inner Mantra**</u>
**If an Ideal or poem is relevant for a healee,
repeat it silently as a prayer or mantra before
or whilst channelling reiki.**

FOR SELF-DEVELOPMENT

MEDITATE DAILY

ON ONE

REIKI IDEAL OR WAKA POEM

OR BEFORE OR AS

YOU DO YOUR HEALING

See The Reiki Ideal

Become The Reiki Ideal

See The Waka Poem

Become The Waka Poem

141

WORKBOOK NOTES
On Gokai, Reiki Ideals And Waka Poetry

CHAPTER 7

REI AND SPIRITUAL HEALING

Rei And Spiritual Healing - Introduction

The exact equivalent of Reiki 1 rei healing is to be found in spiritual healing. Indeed, it is because Reiki 1 and spiritual healers both channel highest God energy, and bring a feeling of LOve into both healer and healee, that many healers believe incorrectly that reiki and spiritual healing are identical healing systems.

They are not.

The problem of misunderstanding is enhanced because many reiki practitioners only learn Reiki 1. Therefore, especially if the person is already a spiritual healer, it is easily thought that reiki is the same as spiritual healing.

It is not.

The two healing systems are only identical when one compares Reiki 1 rei healing with spiritual healing. On the next level of reiki, lower frequency Reiki 2 ki healing is very, very different from the high God-LOve energy feeling of Reiki 1 rei healing and spiritual healing.

So what is rei, or spiritual, healing? Yes it is a feeling of LOve. Yes it makes both healer and healee feel good and feel God. No, it does not normally get quick results for physical problems because the frequency of rei/spiritual healing is too high to affect the physical form.

Before responding to the above statements, please read the next pages for clarification and explanation.

Explanations Of Spiritual Or Rei Healing

1. Dr Usui's Spiritual Healing Philosophy

It seems highly likely that Dr Usui understood the forces of spiritual rei healing. In his writings discovered in 1998 and as noted in Chapter 4, Dr Usui stated,

> *'If the spirit is healthy...the body will become healthy of itself.'*

This statement is classical spiritual healing philosophy. Spiritual or rei healers create a flow of LOve into the spirit and soul of themselves and their healees. This LOve rebalances, re-energises, harmonises, and generally creates an all-over feeling of peace and wholesome well-being. This in turn can have an eventual knock-on effect on the lower frequency issues such as physical, emotional, and mental problems.

So, if we use rei healing to create a healthy spirit, as Dr Usui said, the body may eventually be cured.

2. LOve Versus Love – Why LOve

Many years ago, over a period of a number of weeks, I found it impossible to type the word 'love' on the computer. It always came out 'LOve.' Then I realised that in English, unlike Sanskrit and some other languages, there is only one word to describe every type of love imaginable, including motherly, brotherly, sexual, friendly and so on. And that the word love should be written as LOve when it is to denote the highest universal LOve - the LOve of God - to distinguish the many lowly human and earthly loves with the highest LOve possible.

Capital L – shows the importance of the LOve of God compared to the relatively unimportant human loves.

Capital O – portrays the circular, never-ending, universal nature of God-LOve.

Small v and e highlights the above two points.

Most healers can channel love, but not many can channel LOve.

> **Exercise 24 - Love and LOve**
> **Consider the different loves you have for different people in your life, and the different types of love you have for different possessions, animals, plants, etc. Write them all down, and then try to find another word to describe your human love for these things.**
> **Then compare each with the highest, most perfect LOve of your God.**

3. Can LOve Heal Everything?

Rei energy has an innate intelligence, and in its highest purest form has the potential – not always the reality - to know exactly who needs what type of healing energy, and when and why!

However, this is not the norm. If the healer is truly bringing down highest LOve, and not using some other energy force, it is unlikely that a quick cure can be obtained for lower frequency issues such as physical problems since the experience of 7,200 cps is too high a frequency to cancel out the physical problem's low frequency!

Therefore, even though the answer to this question may be learned in more depth from the sections above and below, it is emphasised here to confirm that LOve cannot quickly heal many mental, emotional, or physical problems.

4. Can LOve Transform Lower Frequencies?

Over the years I have often heard the theory that spiritual LOve healing automatically and immediately transforms down the frequencies to heal lower frequency issues such as physical problems, and that a healer is thus a transformer. Rather like electricity can be extracted from nature, and transformed downwards to a more manageable level via power stations, so it is thought that healers can transmute the high frequency of universal energy to manageable and needed levels.

Is this theory true? Remembering that everything is a frequency, take the example of colour. Gold is high frequency. But if a healer chose to bring in a gold ray for healing, could that gold be transmuted down the frequencies to, for example, red?

Logically and realistically, the answer is, 'no'. If a healer chooses to channel gold, the gold frequency cannot immediately change to red, even if red was the colour needed for that healing. Gold cannot become red!

So it is with spiritual or rei healing which, if channelled, cannot immediately become low frequency.

However, there is the 'ripple effect'. Please see chapter 8, *'Ripple Effect Healings'*.

Do All Spiritual/Rei Healers Channel LOve?

Almost certainly for many 'spiritual' or 'rei' healers, the answer, is 'no', they cannot always channel LOve - for many reasons. The following are classic ways that healers can heal naturally because of their particular 'gift.'

1. Capability

It is logical that not all healers have the capability to create the experience of 7,200 cps. It is not physically, emotionally or mentally possible for many healers to even reach such a high frequency state of LOve themselves.

Therefore many 'spiritual' healers actually heal in various ways that are not strictly spiritual, but are on much lower frequencies. That is why some 'spiritual' healers get quicker results for lower frequency conditions such as mental issues, emotions, and physical problems – because they are unknowingly not channelling rei, but a lower frequency more relevant to the condition.

2. Natural Healing - Frequency

Consider that all illnesses have a unique frequency, and that one way to heal is to transmit the identical frequency so that they cancel each other out.

There is much scientific evidence from researchers such as Valerie Hunt in California who discovered that different healers operate on different frequencies naturally. This enables some healers to just place their hands on a healee and then release their natural frequency that is more likely to heal pain, or to regenerate, or to increase vitality, or to reduce fatigue associated with emotional problems etc.

A classic example is that of healers whose natural frequency is akin to the frequency of pain. Their frequency is sometimes so strong, all they have to do is talk with someone in a shop or in the street or wherever who has a pain, and the person's pain will disappear without any thought on the part of either person. This can even happen when talking on the telephone to someone. A surprisingly high number of healers have said that they were on the phone, when the person on the other end of the line has suddenly said something like, 'Gosh. Since talking to you, my pain's gone!' And the healer did not even know the person had a pain!

In this type of case, healing someone of pain does not make the healer a good practitioner. They are simply allowing their natural energy to work. They now have to go out into the world and learn how to master other energy techniques and processes to be able to heal a wider variety of illnesses.

The energy field spectrograms of natural healers as shown in Hunt's book '*The Infinite Mind*' seem to show that spiritual healers may not always bring down the energy they hope for.

So instead of high frequency spiritual rei energy, natural healing ability in the form of lower frequency or combination of lower frequencies often flows through. This results in some of this type of healer getting quicker results with physical, emotional, or mental problems that other - real - spiritual healers cannot.

However, because they are not channelling spiritual rei, their natural frequency healing is unlikely to have quick effects on the spirit or soul.

3. Natural Healing - Psychic

Psychic healers are different. They use their learned or naturally developed intuition, channelling, clairvoyance (clear-seeing), clairsentience (clear-feeling), or clairaudience (clear-hearing) etc., in order to understand how to heal the presenting energy problem.

Similar to 2 above, this type of healer would be unlikely to channel high frequency spiritual rei God-LOve energy, because the healing energy force would come via their medium frequency clairvoyant vision etc.

Psychic healers have especial potential to more quickly help physical, emotional or mental problems because of the specialist techniques they can consciously – or unconsciously – apply.

4.   Natural Healing - Guides

Many healers become aware of guides coming close to help during a healing. There are many ways that spirit-healing guides may help. For example the guides may heal the healee at the same time as the healer, or channel the appropriate frequency through the healer, or give advice to the healer's or healee's conscious or unconscious mind, or enter the physical body of the healer and work through the healer's hands.

Because guides are rarely of a high spiritual frequency like Christ, Mary or Krishna, and are simply dead people learning more by helping our world, the energy force of the healing guide is likely to be low frequency. Therefore the healer working with guides is not likely to channel high frequency rei that could help the soul or the spirit of the healee. They are also consequently more likely to help physical, emotional and mental problems quicker.

5.   Natural Healing – Perfection Intention

A Christian Scientist healer uses prayerful intention that there is only perfection, and that the illness is not there. This 'perfection intention' creates miracles.

But it is not working on a high spiritual rei frequency. It is working on an out-of-phase frequency, where the frequency becomes out-of-phase with the illness, and therefore creates successful results.

This is discussed in depth in the Reiki 2 Manual when it is relevant to the chapter on symbols. Also see below in this chapter, '*Scientific Study Of Intention And Unconditional LOve.*'

6. Summary

In future, if you attempt to use spiritual or rei healing, try to ensure you really do go high up in the energies. Attune yourself to God-LOve before you start by visualising your version of highest God.

If in doubt, and especially if you are trying to channel spiritual rei yet get quick results for physical problems, check within yourself how healing energy is being transmitted – and whether you are using your natural healing ability.

Healing Into Death Helps To Die In Peace

In the spiritual healing movement, it is taught that spiritual healing (rei) can help someone die in peace. This is realistic for the following reasons.

1. General – Spiritual Or Rei Energy And The Dying

Spiritual or rei healers learn how to heal someone into death. In other words, by the continuous provision of universal LOve energy, the feelings of the dying person and their emotions whilst dying may be healed to make it less traumatic than it may otherwise have been.

2. Healing Fears of Dying Process, Death Act And After

There are three common fears of someone who is dying. The three fears are, the fear of the dying process, the fear of the death moments, and the fear of what may happen after death. (The three exercises below may help these issues.)

Use rei if these fears – or other anxieties, etc. are present. Then the automatic peace from the highest rei or spiritual healing will permeate the healee. That peaceful feeling will often take away their fears, agitations, and anxieties to enable the person to die in peace.

These scenarios are realistic because of the beautiful feelings LOve provides.

Exercise 25 - Rei The Fear Of The Dying Process
Because this is such a common fear, almost certainly it could be an unwanted part of one

of your close friends or family. Give the person rei healing regularly, using the *'Simple Record Keeping Form'* from the section in chapter 19.

Exercise 26 - Rei The Fear Of The Death Moments

Make yourself comfortable sitting in a chair or at a desk. Contemplate the inevitability of your own death. Ask yourself, 'Do I have a fear about death, or any other 'negative' feeling about death?' Self-heal yourself with rei on these issues.

Exercise 27 - Rei The Fear Of What May Happen After Death

Consider your beliefs about what happens to you after death. If you were to pass on tomorrow, would you have any fear or other unwanted emotion? If so, heal yourself with rei spiritual healing.

3. Can Rei Healing Cure Someone Close To Death?

Unfortunately, it is unlikely that rei or spiritual healing will cure a person close to death or put their condition into remission.

Remember that an identical frequency to the illness is needed in order to cancel out and potentially cure the frequency of the illness? Thus the frequency of LOve experienced at 7,200 cycles per second or above is far too high to cancel out and cure the perhaps 380 cycles per second of some cancers. So assuming the healer is channelling the highest God / universal / LOve / spiritual / rei the healee will probably have peace but is likely to die.

It will probably take far too long for the ripple effect to ripple down from the high LOve frequency to heal the low physical frequency. Long before the high frequency has had a chance to ripple down to the physical frequency needed, the person will have died.

This is always assuming the healer does not use his or her own natural healing method.

4.   Other Options

With reiki, we are 'lucky.' On Reiki 2 we have low frequencies that other healers do not normally have. We can choose spiritual healing to facilitate a peaceful death – but we could also choose low frequency symbols that may have better options for a peaceful life!

This is not to say that most dying persons will be cured. Dr Usui said that the only thing that cannot be cured is death! (See section in chapter 5 *'Fax on Dr Usui's Teachings via Japan'.*)

But Reiki 2 healers using low frequency ki energies do have potentials to reach parts that most other energy healing systems perhaps cannot reach.

LOve Aspects Of Rei And Spiritual Healing

Rei or spiritual energy has many beautiful uses, not just for healing a person. Remember to be creative, to enjoy your healing, and look for opportunities to share the beautiful energy of LOve.

1. The Enjoyment Of The LOve

Spiritual rei self-healing may take time to resolve your imbalances, but perseverance with LOve usually wins.

There can be no greater love than the love of LOve. It feels like God, like going Home, or like being in heavenly peace. To rediscover feelings of LOve is one of the finest rediscoveries of your life.

All this and more may arise from healing with rei. To feel the LOve of your creator, to enjoy the highest LOve your soul remembers from before incarnation, these are true blessings to be enjoyed.

This time of your life, when spiritual rei LOve provokes positive vibes on all levels of being is a time to look back on with joy and enjoyment.

2. Becoming LOve

After much self-healing with rei, when LOve has permeated your every atom and molecule, and when you have so much LOve within you that it is seeping outside you, you will then become LOve.

You may find your thoughts changing to idealistic thoughts, your words changing to harmonious words, your actions changing to actions that only occur out of highest motives, and your ideas changing to ideas that can only bring LOve.

You will change, not in a way to make you afraid of change, but in a way so perfectly beautiful that friends and family will love you more than ever.

3. Showing LOve To The World

Once you become LOve, the next steps are to share it with the world around you. Keep LOve flowing from inside you to the outside world. Others will feel it when you shake hands, when you talk to them on the phone, and simply when you are in their presence.

If LOve is everywhere within you, and surrounding you in your aura, ultimately your potential is to become 'like Jesus', where someone near you could touch your clothes and receive the healing LOve.

If each rei or spiritual healer could try to attain this goal, what a wonderful excess of high LOve healing this would share in our world. The universal conscious and unconscious minds, those overlapping forces that connect us all, would exist in higher, Godlier frequencies.

If frequencies of planetary conscious minds were raised, imagine the knock-on effects to all people. Almost certainly, as has been proved effective in over 50 cities in the United States with 'Super Radiance' groups, if you meditate regularly with a group on LOve, your LOve would spread around your town and reduce crime in your area due to extra peace within localised universal minds (McTaggart).

And if more rei healers bring peace from their hearts, souls, and minds, in thoughts, words and deeds, the LOve will reverberate around our globe and peaceful times could befall us all.

4. Channelling A Piece Of The Peace Of LOve

Start now, if you are a Reiki 1 healer. What you choose to channel LOve to is not as important as just doing it. Be creative. Be blessed that you have this ability. Be grateful that you can channel a piece of such beautiful Godly peace.

Exercise 28 - Channelling Pieces Of LOve
Start channelling LOve now. Channel it in pieces to start with – a piece of LOve for you,

a piece of LOve for your family or friends, or a piece of LOve for pets or plants. See chapter 19, *'The Complete Reiki 1 Method.'* Spend 5-10 seconds on each chosen subject, bringing the energy through you and allowing it to go to them. Eventually build up to 30-second bursts of LOve. (A doctor who is also a healer said that as each patient enters his surgery, he pretends to finish paperwork of the previous patient – whereas he actually sends him or her a piece of spiritual healing for 30 seconds. He says that he does not expect many cures, but that he does get some...)

5.   The LOve Waterfall

Eventually, after practising with small pieces of LOve, channel a permanent LOve waterfall pouring into and around you and out of you to our world. Give peace a chance...

Exercise 29 - The LOve Waterfall
Imagine above your head a colour that to you represents the highest, most perfect LOve.
Imagine that colour pouring down, through you and around you.
Practise whilst washing up or watching TV to program your unconscious mind into accepting the permanence of the LOve waterfall.

6.   Intention And LOve

When you channel rei or spiritual healing, your intention as you bring the LOve energy through you should be that the highest universal (or God, or spiritual, or whatever) LOve is pouring through. Never just say that love will channel through you – there are countless versions of lower loves that should not be considered nor used as highest LOve because they are comparatively low frequency.

Exercise 30 - Double-Checking The Type Of LOve

When the LOve comes through you, how does it feel? If it gives a love feeling other than the highest LOve of your God, start again. Try to start with your thoughts higher above your head, and if necessary, higher again, until eventually you feel the beauty of the highest LOve coming through you first.

See below, 'Scientific Study Of Intention And Unconditional LOve.'

7.   Scientific Study Of Intention And Unconditional LOve

The results of the 1992 study by Drs Rein and Laskow in a quantum physics laboratory surprises many healers. See if you can guess the result of the study!

Three different intentions were used whilst healing was channelled separately into three identical flasks of cancer cells to see whether different intentions would have different results. Only one intention was used on each of the three flasks.

Scientists know the normal birth and death rate of cancer cells and checked to see if one intention would have greater success in increasing the death rate of the cancer cells. (There were actually 5 intentions, but only three are paraphrased here and relevant to reiki.)

Don't look at the answer before you guess.

Think... which of these three paraphrased intentions do you believe gained the best success, and increased the death rate of the cancer cells the most?

i. The cancer cells return to their normal and natural harmonious state of being.

ii. To let God's Will flow through these hands.

iii. Unconditional LOve.

Before seeing the answer, what do you think? Which of the above three options increased the death rate of the cancer cells the most?

On courses, most students raise their hands for option c., thinking that unconditional LOve would get the best result and kill a higher percentage of the cancer cells. The results are interesting.

For the first option there was a 39% increase in the normal death rate of the cancer cells. In other words, 39% of the cancer cells that would normally have lived, died (Benor v1).

The second option was only about half as successful. Only 21% of the cancer cells died, that would otherwise have lived.

The result of the third intention, unconditional LOve, surprises many people. Intention of unconditional LOve created no change whatsoever.

The cancer cells stayed as they were!

If your answer was incorrect, consider that if you are using unconditional LOve to the cancer cells, you are in effect saying, 'Dear cancer cells, I love you. Unconditionally. You are wonderful as you are. You can kill the person, I will still love you, unconditionally.'

The living force of the cancer cells responds better to an affirmation that they should not exist, that they should 'return to their normal and natural harmonious state of being.'

In any event, if you have read the previous pages about frequency, you should realise that the experienced frequency of LOve at 7,200 cycles per second or above is far to high to have a chance of cancelling out the 380 cycles per second frequency of some cancers! (McTaggart)

So from a frequency and an intention angle, it can be seen that LOve is the wrong energy to use to have a chance of helping cancer quickly.

When treating cancer or other low frequency illnesses, use Reiki 1 LOve to give peace, and Reiki 2 or above energies to try to heal.

Exercise 31 - Intentions For Tomatoes

Try the above experiment yourself, but instead of three flasks of cancer cells, use three ripe tomatoes. Give rei energy daily for at least half an hour to each tomato, but use a different intention on each. Remember also the intention that reiki is only ever to be used for the highest good of all concerned.

WORKBOOK NOTES
On Rei And Spiritual Healing

CHAPTER 8

RIPPLE EFFECT HEALINGS

The Ripple Effect

The ripple effect is not immediate; it takes time. Imagine the ripples that spread out if you throw a pebble into a pond. Rei healing is rather like throwing a spiritual energy into the energy pond of the healee.

It takes time for close-together-high-frequency-type ripples to spread and become wide-apart-low-frequency-type ripples. Eventually, over time, they will affect the edges of the pond.

Similarly it takes time for high frequency rei energy to ripple down through the various medium-to-low frequencies of mental, emotional, and physical energies and positively affect them.

Dr Usui understood this because he said that outside influences caused disruption within human energy systems. The points below will clarify this.

1. Time Frames For Ripple Effect Healings

Over many years, I have had discussions with various scientists and medical researchers who have considered that trauma can provoke an inherent genetic or this-life created illness. In 1973, Sally Hammond published parts of an interview (Hammond) with the then-chair of the Department of Materials Science at Stanford University, Dr Tillner, who refers to the ripple effect as the 'ratchet effect':

'An illness has its origin in a disharmony between the mind and spirit levels of entity and that of the universal pattern for the entity,' suggests Tillner. In healing, he theorised that there's a 'ratchet effect' as energy transfers take place between these levels of substance. For example, a mind image concerning a physical change in the body creates 'a coherent potential distribution' on the etheric level which in turn causes changes in the energy patterns of the etheric body. This in turn effects the physical level of substance and finally manifests as changes in the energy patterns and atomic reorganisation of the physical substance!'

A common concept is that it takes approximately 18-30 months for a trauma to manifest in illness. In my 20 plus years of experience, many cases fall into this category, but I also have noted that this is mainly for emotional and mental traumas. This is probably confirmed because, for example, it seems to be now generally accepted that cancer can be provoked by a trauma within the standard 18 to 30 month time frame. [101] One of the main cancer charities in the UK, Bacup, states on its website that "regarding emotional aspects, emotional stress and other emotions can be major contributors (to the development of cancer)."[102] Remember that there are many causes for cancer, such as exposure to toxic chemicals, genetic problems, infections, etc. and therefore an emotional cause should never be assumed.

---

[101] As noted in chapter 10 in the section *'Are You Too Questioning?'* it is likely that we just don't have the equipment yet to measure the appropriate phenomena to prove the timeline.
[102] See www.Bacup.org.uk. The full citation is in the reference list.

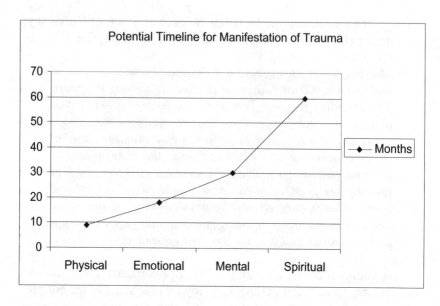

Figure 18:   Timeline For Manifesting Conditions And Illnesses.

a.   Spiritual trauma[103]

It may take about 60 months for a spiritual trauma to manifest as a physical illness, as the frequencies are so far apart.

A spiritual trauma may be a sudden dislike for God after, for example, the loss of a loved one, or the start of a war.

b.   Mental trauma

It may take 30 months for a mental trauma to manifest as a physical illness. Mental traumas could include mental cruelty, mental rejection by a loved one such as being cut out of a Will, or a child or grandchild not wanting to see them any more.

Because this mental frequency is closer to the physical frequency, it takes less time to manifest in the physical body as illness.

---

[103] The information in this and the following three sections is based on unpublished analysis of case records over a 20-year period.

c. Emotional trauma

About 18 months is needed for emotional traumas to ripple down to the physical. Emotional traumas include severe bereavement, or an event that made the person extremely sad or angry.

d. Physical trauma

It may take about 9 months for a physical trauma such as an accident injury to manifest into another physical illness.

e. What does the trauma attack?

If unhealed, any trauma will slowly be attracted in to the physical body by the positive ionic charge of the physical. In the case of spiritual trauma, the negative energy of the trauma will eventually cause mental problems, followed by emotional difficulties, and finally attack the weakness of the physical, either a genetically inherited weakness, or a weakness created in this life.

The closer the trauma is to the physical, the longer it will take for spiritual healing to work because the rei will be further away from the frequency needed to potentially cure quickly.

2. Ripples Of Rei – Healing Inwards From Spirit Body

Healing with spiritual (rei) alone can take a long time; it can take up to 60 months, for example, for rei healing to have a positive effect on a physical illness.

a. The spirit body – a force of this lifetime

The spirit body is your etheric blueprint, the sum total of this lifetime. The spirit body is all you have been in the past, are in the present, and have potential for in the future - in this lifetime.

b. Potential immediate results from healing the spirit

Due to rei's high frequency, one of the quickest positive healing effects that rei is likely to have is on this similarly high frequency spirit body. By bringing harmony to the spirit, rei can bring calm, peace, and a happy sense of wholeness to the entire person.

c.   How to heal the spirit
Because the spirit body exists around each person, it is probably best to heal the spirit by healing the aura with spiritual rei healing.

> **Exercise 32 - Healing The Spirit Body**
> **Start giving the beautiful rei energy to a wide sphere about four metres from the body. Then heal a little closer, then closer, and so on, until spiritual rei energy has been poured into the complete four metre spherical energy force surrounding the person.**
> **Scan to ensure the entire sphere feels smooth. Repeat for as many sessions as are needed for the person to feel and live in peace, harmony, and whole-wellness.**

d.   Inward ripples of rei from the spirit
Ripples from healing the outer spirit body spread from the etheric blueprint inwards and down the frequencies to the physical being.

Some spiritual healers say that (assuming as always that only high frequency LOve is being channelled by a healer) it will take at least 9 months of regular spiritual healing before most physical problems have a chance of being resolved.

3.   Ripples Of Rei – Healing Outwards From The Soul

a.   The soul – a force of all lifetimes
The soul is the part of you that never dies, the complete evolving memory of all that you have been, are, and can be - in all lifetimes.

b. Potential immediate results from healing the soul

The LOve of rei can provide a beautiful LOve healing effect for the soul. Rei helps the soul remember the LOve it was connected to before birth. This reawakened remembrance of perfect God-LOve, can have an incredibly positive loving knock-on effect in the healee. Their human faults may become less problematic, they can become more accepting of others around them, and they could start to understand - perhaps for the first time – what unconditional LOve truly means.

c. How to heal the soul

The soul resides within the body, although where it resides is open to debate. Some organisations like the Brahma Kumaris consider the soul to be within the third eye in the centre of the forehead.

Maybe this is true for all people, or perhaps it is true for only some. Maybe what is believed to be soul travel by some is actually third eye psychic projection.

Certainly for me and for many others I have met, when the soul leaves the body to astral travel, it leaves from the solar plexus – or should it be 'soular' plexus?

Wherever the soul resides, it seems certainly to be within our physical being. Therefore:

Exercise 33 - Healing The Soul

Project spiritual rei healing into the body via an all-over hands-on treatment. Or give an all-over treatment, passing the hands a few centimetres from the healee's physical body. Repeat for as many sessions as needed to help you or the person feel a life-change of thoughts, words, and deeds of LOve, giving love, and being loved. Permanent positive change may take some months.

d.   Outward ripples of rei from the soul

When the soul within the body is healed with LOve, ripples of the LOving soul may spread out to eventually heal others parts of the healee. Often a clairvoyant-type person healing the soul will feel the ripples of warmth or see the Light spreading outwards from inside them.

Eventually there may be an automatic knock-on healing of lower frequency mental, emotional and physical conditions.

4.   Ripples Of Ki

Starting with rei, the highest frequency of LOve, the frequencies gradually become lower through the ki energies of mental, then emotional, then finally the lowest frequency, physical.

Since lower healing energies are not learned until Reiki 2, they are therefore explained in more depth in the Reiki 2 Manual. For now, understand that, the same as rei can eventually ripple down the frequencies to heal low frequency physical, emotional and mental problems, so ki can ripple the other way and eventually have a positive effect on the high frequency spirit and the soul.

Rei Spiritual Healing Mental Therapy

Because mental frequency is the next frequency down from the LOve of rei, then the LOve frequency ripple effect is likely to cancel out the frequency of mental problems relatively sooner than lower frequency emotional or much lower frequency physical issues. Many mental problems have physical causes such as chemical imbalance. So rei ripple effects may take time to affect certain mental illnesses.

1. Potential Positive Mental Rei Healings

The ripple effect of rei may help some healees more quickly with mental issues such as fear, anxiety, or other mental problems caused by an event that occurred during this life.

Then the ripples may flood and push out the event-caused inappropriate mental frequency. And because it was a problem caused by a past event in this life, the event and therefore the condition is unlikely to repeat. The person may be healed.

A classic case that is normally difficult to heal is depression. Providing the depression is induced by a life-event that will not reoccur, if enough spiritual healing rei LOve energy is pushed into the healee, he or she may eventually have the depression energy pushed out. If this happens, often the person will feel warm for the first time since the depression, because depression is cold energy, and LOve is warm! When there is warmth, you know you are on the way to a positive result.

It is not uncommon for this process to work in one session. For more information on healing this type of unwanted mental problem, please see section, 'Rei Emotional Replacement Therapy' below.

2. Genetic Or Chemically Imbalanced Mental Illness

Be aware that if the mental problem is caused by a genetically inherited weakness, or a chemical imbalance, the ripple effect will almost certainly take much longer because the rei ripples must reach not the nearby mental frequency to perhaps effect a healing; it must reach the further physical low frequency genetic issue.

Do not give up. Stay with the healee until you have success, or until the healee gives up. Usually, long-term rei healing is needed if these mental issues are to be helped.

3. Other Mental Healing Difficulties With Rei LOve

Similar to point 2 above, there is also usually a difficulty getting results using rei healing with forms of schizophrenia, or other mental conditions, especially where hormones, glands, neural pathways, or any other physical cause has provoked the mental illness.

Again, continue for as long as possible or needed. It can take a long time for spiritual rei frequency to transmute down the layers to effect a physical healing.

<u>Rei Spiritual Healing – Emotional Replacement Therapy</u>

High frequency rei healing can often help heal relatively low frequency emotions fairly quickly - but not because it cancels out the frequency of the emotion. In the case of emotions, the rei energy of LOve works <u>as a replacement</u> of the unwanted emotions to help give the person the LOve they need.

<u>1. Rei Emotional Replacement Therapy</u>

If enough LOve energy is channelled through to the person with emotional problems, it will push out unwanted energies of sadness, anger, hate, or other negative feeling – a replacement therapy!

Vast energy is often needed to push out and replace unwanted emotion; if this is achieved, rei may help in one session.

It will depend on the healer's ability to channel huge quantities of the highest and genuine LOve frequency into the healee, with such force as to push out emotion that needs to be healed. Many beginners cannot channel such huge amounts of high frequency LOve in enough quantity to obtain one-session results. So keep going.

> <u>Exercise 34 - Emotional Replacement</u>
> **Keep the frequency very high ensuring the energy is of the highest LOve.**
> **Then, instead of letting the rei come through you as a trickle, let it come through and towards the person as a flooding river.**

<u>2. Adjusting Your Frequency</u>

If you are not getting quick results using rei healing with emotions, try to adjust the frequency you bring in to an even higher level. If imbalances of sadness, anger, hate etc. can be replaced by highest LOve, the person will feel happier, calmer and more peaceful.

> **Exercise 35 - Adjusting Frequency**
> **Meditate on your vision of your understanding of the highest God before you start. Then, during the healing, bring in that version of God through you and to your healee.**

3.   Adjusting Your Power

Assuming you believe you are truly bringing in highest God-LOve spiritual rei healing, if success does not occur, it is almost certainly the amount of power you channel that needs to be increased.

Many healers, especially those who are naturally meek in nature, just let the energy trickle through. Other more bullish healers naturally let energy crash through. Healers need to be able to control what is needed for each session.

Be creative in creating the amount of power you need. Keep records and analyse to see which energy power gets the best result.

> **Exercise 36 - Adjusting Power**
> **Imagine a large tap above your head and that you can turn the tap on and off as needed.**
> **Let spiritual rei energy drip through, then let it trickle through, then turn the tap half on and finally on full blast.**
> **Feel the differences and record them.**

4.   Emotional Healing Difficulties Using Rei

These are the same as points 2 and 3 above.

172

Rei Spiritual Healing For Physical Illness - Chronics

1. Time Frame For Healing Potential

The president of a major spiritual healing organisation once told me it takes at least 9 months for spiritual (rei) healing to affect a physical illness. The experience of many spiritual or rei healers is that it takes much longer – up to 60 months! In my own case, it took about 2 years to bring my defective immune system that had caused me disablement since babyhood back into balance.

The main point is to never give up. Harry Edwards was probably the best and most famous healer in England in the 20th century. In his brilliant book, 'A Guide to Spirit Healing', he states that (assuming spiritual healing will work) it takes at least two years to return Downs Syndrome condition to normal. If you did not know that, you would probably give up after a few months...

Remember that physical healings using strictly high frequency spiritual rei healing will often take a long time.

Lastly, remember Dr Usui's words in the fax translated in a previous chapter that you should try to cure until the last breath. That means your last breath or the patient's last breath - whichever comes first!

2. If 'Spiritual' Healing Gets Quick Physical Results

Also remember that, if a spiritual / rei / LOve healer gets quick results with physical illnesses, they are almost certainly not using high frequency rei energy, but their own psychic healing, or colour healing, or healing with the guides, or some other low frequency process.

Students should understand how they are healing.

Rei Spiritual Healing For Physical Illness – Acutes

1. Is There Time To Heal Acutes With Rei?

Sadly, if the healee has been given not long to live, the answer to this question is usually, 'no'. It is unlikely that rei or spiritual healing will cure the person because it will take too long for the high frequency of LOve to transmute down to the low frequency of the physical issue.

2. The Likely Help Rei Healing Gives To Acutes

Peace is the most likely outcome. For example, someone who receives rei healing who has an acute problem, or is awaiting hospitalisation, or is in hospital awaiting an operation is far less likely to be stressed, anxious, or nervous. This is because they will probably receive peace and calmness from the rei energy.

3. If Quicker Reiki Help Is Needed

Take the Reiki 2 class and use more relevant Reiki 2 low frequency energies that may have a higher success rate.

Summary - What Rei May Or May Not Help

The following is a likely list of what rei may or not heal. The list assumes the healer only channels spiritual rei LOve - not his or her psychic, spiritualist, guided, intention or other personal natural healing method.

This list is not definitive. Use your personal experience to add more potential to each of the following sections.

And understand that, whilst the following is the likely scenario outcome of rei healing, due to the 'order-within-chaos' nature of universal influence, some items from each list may occasionally overlap, whilst others may be found in any of the three lists. Indeed, your experience on some issues may have completely different results or interpretations.

Definitive research is needed to confirm the average time spans for different conditions' healing results.

1.   Short-Term – Within 1 - 9 Months

   i.   Relaxation of body

   ii.   Peace of mind

   iii. Happiness of spirit

   iv. May help a cold person feel warm

   v.   Spiritual issues about relationship to the person's God

   vi. LOve may permeate the spirit and soul

   vii. Anger, if it is this-life-created (replacement therapy)

   viii. Sadness, if it is this-life-created (replacement therapy)

   ix. Hate, if it is this-life-created (replacement therapy)

   x.   Calmness of other emotions (replacement therapy)

   xi. Rebalance on LOve levels

   xii. Re-energise on LOve levels

xiii. Harmonise on LOve levels

xiv. Create an all-over feeling of peace

xv. Someone with short time to live may die in peace

2. Medium-Term – Within 9 – 18 Months

i.   Ripple effect

ii.   Eventual knock-on effect on the lower frequency issues

iii.   Eventual healing of mental, emotional or physical problems

iv.   Wholesome well-being

v.   Healing of soul's past life memories

vi.   Friends and family may love you more than ever

vii.   Ability to share LOve with the world around you

viii. Keep LOve flowing from inside you to the outside world

ix.   Raise Love in the universal conscious and unconscious minds

x.   LOve may reduce crime with peace in localised universal minds

xi.   Someone with medium time to live may die in peace

3. Long-Term – Within 18 - 60 Months

i.   Ripple effect

ii.   Eventual knock-on effect on the lower frequency issues

iii.   Eventual healing of mental, emotional or physical problems

iv.   Genetically inherited conditions

v.   Thoughts may change to idealistic thoughts

vi.   Words may change to harmonious words

vii.   Actions may change to those of the highest motives

viii. Ideas may change to ideas that can only bring LOve

ix. Someone with long time to live may die in peace

x. Become LOve

xi. Let others feel LOve just by talking or being with you.

xii. And if more rei healers bring peace from their hearts, souls, and minds, in thoughts, words and deeds, the LOve will reverberate around our globe and peaceful times could befall us all.

4. What Spiritual Rei Healing May Not Help

i. Manics who are already too high in their frequency

ii. Manic-depressives in the manic phase

iii. Some types of schizophrenia

iv. Someone who hallucinates

v. People who find it impossible to ground themselves

vi. Those who cannot cope with the biofeedback

vii. A person who uses LOve as a drug

WORKBOOK NOTES
On Ripple Effect Healings

CHAPTER 9

BIOFEEDBACK

Reiki Biofeedback Sensation Explanation

Reiki energy is <u>not</u> electromagnetism, as science understands, as proven with a chamber that excludes all electromagnetic energy entering it: yet from outside, a healer was able to turn cancer cells inside to normal (Benor v1). However, reiki energy has many electromagnetic type properties such as heat, cold, electric, vibration, or pushing or pulling sensations.

Please explain to your healee some of the potential experiences before you start healing. Also explain biofeedback to members of your family or friends before healing.

Then, if they feel the energy in an extreme form, they are less likely to be afraid.

I have lost count of the numbers of healees who say they had healing elsewhere, but did not go back because 'the healer burned my scalp' or 'the healer took my energy away.' I explain that the healer was probably doing a good job, but simply did not explain the potential biofeedback responses of reiki energy.

1. Explanation To First Time Healees

Explain potential biofeedback responses, along the following lines. You have permission to freely use or add to the below as part of your printed leaflet if you wish, providing you include on the leaflet:

"© Universal Copyright 2001,
Dr Allan Sweeney www.reiki-healing.com
You may feel reiki energy in a form such as heat, cold, electrical tingling, a breeze outside, energy movement inside, or muscles twitching. Some healees, especially those with bone or ligament problems, may feel pain for up to 3 days; but sometimes, when the pain goes away, some of the problem goes as well.

You may also experience unusual colours, sounds, or smells, or some sensation from one of your other senses.

It is not important to understand what each experience means as it is simply one of your senses becoming aware of reiki energy and how it works within you. Just accept whatever occurs passively, with the understanding that not everyone will experience all, or even one sensation. Whether you experience a lot, or nothing, is not the relevant point. The relevant point is whether the scores of the symptoms come down over a period of seven sessions."

2. Case History

One of my students phoned a few days after her beginner course. She said, 'Allan, I gave reiki to my mum and she hates reiki now.' When I asked why, she said, 'Well, my mum did not feel anything.'

I asked whether she had explained to her mother that you do not have to feel a thing for reiki to work. She said, 'No, I thought that my mother would understand, so I just did it.'

Unfortunately, human ego means that if a healee experiences nothing, they will think it did not work.   Try to help the understanding that it can still work, by using the forms at the back of this manual, and emphasising the reduction in the scores of the condition.

In fact, unless the reiki treatment is of impromptu necessity, please always use the *'Simple Record Keeping Form'* in that section in chapter 19, because when healees can see logically in writing something has indeed happened, they are very likely to believe in reiki.

3.   Biofeedback During Self-healing

Biofeedback experiences can occur during your self-healing. Simply accept that the energy is working in the ways outlined in the following section, *'Biofeedback Through Your Seven Senses'*

Some practitioners feel as if their self-healing biofeedback is not as strong as when healing others.   Do not question too deeply. Simply keep the scores of your symptoms and conditions before self-healing and see whether the scores come down.

Some healers find it difficult to rise above their own emotional or mental attachment to their problems. If necessary, read the section *'Releasing Stress Before Reiki'* in chapter 13. Relaxing deeper prior to self-healing can detach the mind from the biofeedback or healing issues and eventually allow a better flow of reiki.

Remember that some people may experience little or nothing and that some energies are less likely to be felt.

4.   Biofeedback Within Healee

As stated, it will help healees feel comfortable about reiki if you mention a little about biofeedback possibilities prior to the treatment.

181

However, here is a word of warning. After the treatment, do NOT try to interpret everything the person feels, sees, or experiences. It is easy to fall into the trap of explaining too much, and then confuse the healee.

And it is especially easy for some healers to try to interpret healees' visions and fall into the trap of clairvoyance that would not be covered by reiki insurance.

a.   Give as little explanation as possible

As simply as possible help healees feel comfortable about their positive biofeedback. Doctors do the same about the 'negative biofeedback' from drugs, and only talk about the issues relevant to the patient.

b.   Use healees' biofeedback for own purposes

After a reiki treatment, annotate your healees' biofeedback experiences on the forms at the back of the manual. Then analyse their comments to ascertain your healing approach for the next session.

You will find that a database of experiences will be built up, and information gained will help you know how to heal similar conditions.

Often there are standard biofeedback responses for specific illnesses, e.g. injured bones becoming cold or numb, then the area swelling, then pain as bones return to their normal state. Collate your findings and present them as your reiki research project.

c.   The healer's biofeedback

Whilst you are giving a reiki treatment to others, you will experience many, many energy feedbacks. These may be understood in the context of the following pages, 'Biofeedback Through Your Seven Senses.'

However, for reiki beginners, see section, 'Are You Too Questioning? Or Too Accepting?' in chapter 10.

d.   Distant healing biofeedback

Although distant healing is not covered until the Reiki 2 Manual, it should be noted that it is possible for both the healer and the healee to receive biofeedback from a distant healing session.

e.   Beaming, scanning et al.

Biofeedback may be experienced whilst beaming energy across a room (beaming is in the Reiki 2 Manual because most reiki masters teach beaming as a Reiki 2 subject) when scanning, or at any other time reiki energy is used. Heal the worst areas. In all circumstances, refer to these biofeedback pages for relevant information.

Biofeedback Through Your Seven Senses

Please read previous section in this chapter, *Reiki Biofeedback Sensation Explanation*, before reading this section. The following explains some of the more common biofeedback responses, and will give reasons why some of them are experienced. These are often standard archetypal responses.

1. Clairsentience - Touch (Or Feeling)

The first three, heat, cold, and electrical tingling are the most common biofeedback experience of the sense of touch/feeling.

Please note that all biofeedback sensations vary from very slight up to extremely intense.

a. Heat

Heat can be gentle warmth, or a severe burning sensation. Note that the energy cannot burn skin because the heat is perhaps a spiritual heat. According to Dr Daniel Benor,

> *"Heat from healing energy cannot be measured on even a sensitive thermometer, despite the subjective sensations of energy and heat often (but not invariably) experienced by healers and healees."*[104]

b. Cold

Cold can be a little coolness, or as freezing as a block of ice. I will never forget how my back felt like a block of ice when I was cured of my lack of adrenal function. Cold energy is needed (and comes naturally with natural healers) for some conditions such as bones, tumours, and bacterial infection.

---

[104] From private e-mail correspondence, with permission.

c. Electrical tingling

The electrical sensation can be like slight pins and needles, or like a giant electric shock. The shock re-energizes a depleted bio-system. Whenever I saw one of my healees in Germany, soon after the start of each first session he received a huge electric shock. The first time this happened, he almost shot off his chair! But I had previously explained the potential experience so he stayed sitting, even during the minor 'post-earthquake-like' shocks. After, he felt incredibly better. And his hair was not even standing on end!

d. Vibration/shaking

This may be due to various factors, e.g. not being adjusted to the energy frequency. Vibration – or even violent shaking – also happens to some people who practise meditation, yoga, or prayer.

If the reiki energy comes up against an energy block, there may be vibration as that block is pushed against and eventually cleared.

e. Pushing or pulling

This is the magnetic nature of the energy at work.

Pushing is usually due to the positive and sometimes intelligent nature of reiki energy pushing into negative energy to disperse it.

Pulling is usually due to the positive and intelligent reiki energy pulling away, and often taking negative energy from the body.

f. Circular or spiralling motion

This is normally due to one of two reasons: It may be due to the natural spiralling nature of energy as it flows from above into or out of your being – rather similar to water spiralling down from a sink.

Some sensitive, potentially clairsentient, students or healees move in a circular or spiral motion as they become in tune with the circular or spiral motion of one particular Reiki 2 symbol.

g. Feeling as if falling over

This can be either an etheric or a physical issue. Etheric falling over is when it seems as if you are falling to one side. Occasionally

185

this falling feeling is so much that you may even put one leg out to stop yourself falling. But, when you look, you notice that you did not move.

This is due to the etheric body, or aura, having been out-of-balance, or off-centre. Reiki healing energy can automatically return your etheric body into the correct position, and whilst it is coming in for example from the right, you will feel yourself being pushed over to the left. This normally has wonderful healing after-effects.

Physical falling over is more an opening or closing of energies. For example, the head going backwards opens the throat chakra to make communication issues easier.

h.   Movement of energy outside the body
This can be a gentle breeze, or a huge wind. I remember the first time I gave healing to a lady in Ramsgate. I was not touching her, and when I came to her lower legs, her skirt started flapping. She opened her eyes and exclaimed, "What are you doing?"

But she was accepting of the experience as I had explained the possibility before starting.

i.   Movement of energy inside the body
This can mean various things. The twitch of a muscle denotes an energising of that area.

Rippling of muscles, e.g. up and down a leg, does not happen often, but is spectacular to watch. It represents muscle revitalisation.

A rod of energy building up inside is a reconnection to get something going again. E.g. if a rod of energy is experienced building up behind the eye, and if it also extends to the back of the head, 80% of the eyesight may return.

j.   Light-headed or dizzy or sick
This is very important to understand, because it is relatively common, and you may need to explain it to your healee to prevent unnecessary worry. Also see the section on 'Grounding' in chapter 16.

This biofeedback response is a progression where someone may first feel light-headed. If reiki energy gets stronger, the feeling progresses to dizziness. Then, if reiki is extremely intense, sickness.

First, even if the person feels violently sick, try not to let her/him go to the toilet! Instead, ask her/him to put the thoughts inside to where the sick feeling is, and ask, 'Does it feel like a real physical sickness feeling, or does it feel like energy movement?' Almost certainly, the answer will be 'Energy movement'.

Then, whether your healee feels light-headed, dizzy, or sick, ask, 'Have you been low in energy for a long time?' The answer will almost certainly be: 'Yes!'

You can then explain that the feeling is due to a very large amount of positive energy coming into the body.

Then ask the person to sit for up to half an hour. And explain that it usually takes less than half an hour for the majority of the new, positive energy to integrate with the person's natural energy body.

If possible, ask the person to let you know how they feel one hour after the initial half hour. Almost certainly, they will feel better than they have felt for a very long time.

k.   Loss of energy

This is due to stressed energy being taken away. Ask the healee, 'Have you been stressed for a long time?' Almost certainly the answer will be, 'Yes!'

Then explain that the body's stressed electrical energy can be grounded or earthed during reiki, leaving a correct feeling that energy has been taken away.

However, it also leaves the healee with the natural energy body to build on, so that he/she will not live 'on the nerves', and be able to return to a normal way of life.

l.   Pain

During reiki, pain may occur for various reasons, but is usually a sign of excellent healing. The main issue will be to reassure your healee that the pain is there for a positive reason!

Pain may suddenly occur from a healing on an injury site, whether recent, old, or even forgotten. On the site of a fracture, or broken bone, for example, pain could take up to 3 days before it ceases. But after, any old problem is usually healed. It seems that the pain is the bone going back into the correct position. Reassure the healee that healing is occurring. Extra reassurance is needed if the pain is excruciating for 2 or 3 days!

A single sharp pain, like a needle going in, is usually the intelligent nature of the energy finding its way to a weak acupuncture meridian point. Often, the healee will be healed of something elsewhere in the body. For example, I have had many healees experience a needle-like pain in the left elbow, and then their back problem has been healed.

The meaning of head pain depends on where it is in the head. Pain at the back of the head is a healing of the unconscious mind. Within two months, a deep mental or emotional healing will become apparent.

Pain on the top of the head is a closed crown chakra opening to allow a new energy through. Then the person will be able to channel reiki easier.

Pain in the third eye is psychic or intuitive development. After, psychic intuition will become stronger or more accurate. If deeper psychic development occurs, pain can progress to the temples. This is rather like someone wearing glasses and hooking them over the ears. Except this is for the third eye and the 'monocle' glasses' are hooked around energy hooks at the temples. This is a protection against too sudden psychic development, and when the pain goes, psychic intuition is usually more powerful or more accurate. For the same reasons, this psychic pain may go all around the head like a tight bandage. However, this 'bandage' should be discerned from pain all around the head caused by the guides honouring the stage you have reached in your life by placing on your head a hat or cap or crown etc. of honour. Each headwear will have a different honouring meaning.

Pain in the healer's hands is due to some of the myriad of hand chakras being activated to allow healing energy through. However, if painful, the hand chakras are still too small to allow through the large amount of reiki being channelled. Hence pain is felt as reiki forces its way out. If this happens in an extreme form, with much pain, the person is likely to be able to be an excellent reiki healer.

m. Important note on clairsentience
Many healees will think that some of the clairsentient feelings above are negative and mean that something has gone wrong. After all, as children, we are told that pain, sickness, and loss of energy mean we are ill!

Do reassure your healee before and after the treatment that if Reiki healing has been done correctly, it can only have good lasting effects.

2.A. Clairvoyance – Seeing Through Physical Eyes

The biofeedback potentials are almost identical for the physical eyes as they are for the third eye – the difference being that vision from the third eye can be achieved with the normal eyes closed.

2.B. Clairvoyant Psychic Vision – Seeing Through Third Eye

As stated above, the biofeedback of sight and vision can be from the two normal eyes, or the third eye.

a. Colours
The physical and psychic visions of colour are common and important because during a reiki treatment or attunement it is normal for the more clairvoyant-type people to see blobs or clouds or a blanket of colour or colours:

Beginners usually want to know the meaning of the colour seen. This is not to be encouraged on this Reiki level as colour interpretation is an extremely complex subject. For example, most people believe there are seven colours in a rainbow. But scientists would explain that because the colours overlap, a rainbow has about 1,500,000 shades of colour; that each colour is a frequency; and that each frequency has a different interpretational meaning and therefore use. As shown in Exercise 73 different people interpret colours differently. So if you cannot interpret a colour identically to other people, how can you know the shade you are seeing and give an interpreted meaning?

It is better for beginner healers to understand the meaning of colours in the following general ways. It is not necessary to consciously understand the healing issues. Reiki will help dissolve the problem naturally and unconsciously.

i.   Darker, dirtier colours represent 'negative' energy being healed.

ii.   Earthly colours represent the actual physical or other problem to be healed.

iii. A bright fluorescent colour represents one of the healing rays.

iv.   Colours moving or pulsing away usually mean a healing is occurring by negative energy being taken from the person.

v.   Colours moving or pulsing closer commonly shows that reiki energy is healing the energy or illness issue.

vi.   Fluorescent colours around a dirty or earthly colour almost always represents healing process of negative energy or an illness.

b.   The past in this life or a previous life

If a past life arises in a vision it is not to be explored, unless you have a quality-assured certificate in counselling, psychotherapy, hypnotherapy etc.

It is not necessary to explore past life as reiki heals naturally and gently, and because you never know what happened next. For example:

i. This life vision. I remember one case of a lady who, during her reiki treatment, saw herself aged 5 years old, sitting at the table waiting for dinner. I explained that the vision had come to the surface to be healed, but that she does not have to explore it, because reiki heals gently.

    She took no notice, and saw a hypnotherapist who regressed her to that age. She discovered that, aged 5, if she did not eat all her dinner up, her parents would push her face in the plate.

    She was so traumatised by the conscious knowledge of her parents maltreatment of her she needed long-term counselling - whereas reiki should have healed it naturally and *un*consciously.

ii. Past life visions are similar. I heard of one lady who was told 'by her guides' during a treatment that she was a bishop in a past life. This pleased her, because she was devoutly religious in this life. So, despite being warned not to regress, when someone offered to regress her, she jumped at the chance.

    She discovered she was a bishop. But she was a bishop in the Spanish Inquisition. And she saw herself tearing bits of flesh off terrified people, and heard the cries of torment. She went into shock, and needed psychiatric help afterwards.

So this is a word of warning. If during reiki, some healees regress, please do not take them further into a past life experience. Even if you are qualified in regression, unless you know very specialist past life healing techniques, beware.

Whenever I give a lecture on past life healing at a Mind Body Spirit exhibition, I warn of the dangers, and that many people are damaged because the therapist did not know appropriate healing techniques. And I always have a small queue of people after, asking me to help them because they were damaged by a past life regression.

Thus if you are a Reiki I healer, and your healee automatically regresses to a past life, ignore it. If you are a Reiki 2 healer, use the third symbol to connect back in time, and add the first symbol if you feel the main need is physical healing or the second symbol if you feel mental or emotional help is needed.

Or, if past lives rear their heads regularly, attend one of the few courses to learn past life healing (not past life regression as that can be dangerous). A good past life healing course will teach many techniques to perhaps cure physical, emotional, mental and other issues as they arise, not just how to evoke a past life experience.

c. Archetypal images

'Archetypal' images are the inner meaning, not the cultural interpretation of an image. Thus the Star of David archetypally means balance, but Israelis and Palestinians would give it their own cultural ideas.

Images coming from the reiki experience should not be considered as being the same as the images from dreams.

There are four main types of dreams – problem solving, warning, prophetic, and creative. Each type of dream has its own standard, yet different archetypal interpretation. And all are very different to interpretations of images arising from reiki practise.

Images from a reiki treatment almost always give important information about the healee's soul or reiki pathway or his or her healing progress. Examples of archetypal images are:

i.   A baby or a sunrise means the start of the new.

ii. A skeleton or sunset means death of the old.

iii. A river, path, road, or staircase means soul pathway (the shorter, straighter, and narrower the better.)

iv. An ocean or a fish means unconditional LOve.

v.   A wolf means teacher. Almost all students who have had a vision of a wolf have become a reiki teacher. Those who have a vision of many wolves usually become great teachers.

vi. Etc. There are innumerable such images that have standard healing meanings.

d.   Recognisable symbol shapes

These are shapes that have names. Each has a standard healing meaning. Thus, during a reiki treatment, shapes seen may give clues as to how the healing is going. For example:

i.   A vision of a square means physical healing.

ii.   A triangle means spiritual.

iii. A circle means the universal God Force.

iv.   A five-pointed star means healing for Man.

v.   A six-pointed star means balance of Heaven and Earth energies.

vi.   A seven-pointed star means God energy.

vii. An eight-pointed star means God plus the master.

viii. A pyramid is spiritual energy to the physical being.

ix.   Etc.

During a reiki treatment, if your healee sees a recognisable symbol shape, it means the healing is working on that level. It gives an idea of where your healee is at developmentally.

e.   Unrecognisable symbol shapes

These are shapes you have never seen before. They are reiki symbols! But please do not say, 'Alleluia, I've found a new symbol!' and like some reiki masters try to organise a conference on it!

I first channelled shapes for reiki-type healing in the early 1980's. And I was given with the channellings that most new shapes are there for just that moment of time, for that illness, in that person.

They are specific forces for the needs of the individual at that moment only.

Assuming that the energy of the symbol worked, in the next reiki session, a different symbol shape would be needed because the person would have moved on!

Please note that this is taught in-depth on the Grecian Reiki course. This course shows how to channel unlimited symbols for any good healing purpose. Grecian Reiki students often have remarkable instant healings with this method.

f.   Psychic visions

There are many, many possible psychic visions. Most are relevant to a reality that the person is just starting to discover. However, remember that reiki insurance does not cover you for clairvoyance, psychic visions, or psychic interpretations.

The following suggestions are given only to help the healer's understanding, and should not be conveyed to the healee. For example:

i.   Some healees see an eye, a tunnel, or a door. The eye is usually their own third eye, and they go through it or through the door or tunnel if possible.

ii.   At the other side of the eye, tunnel etc, will usually be something beautiful such as the hall of healing colours, the tower for guides, the crystal city, or Akashic records.

iii.   Many other wonderful experiences await exploration in the same way that people have explored them for thousands of years. Simply ask the healee to accept the experience.

iv.   If you or your healees start having many such experiences, perhaps join a psychic development group, preferably run by someone who has attained spirituality and higher realm knowledge. Or, if your reiki master runs a psychic development workshop, attend that.

v.   To protect the psychic seeker, psychic development should usually be undertaken only after spirituality has been achieved.

g.   Guides

'Guides' are a specialist subject and are dealt with on higher-level classes because by then reiki practitioners will probably understand whether their guides are helping.

3.   Clairaudience - Hearing

During a reiki treatment, sounds may be heard. Some potentials are as follows:

a.   Tinnitis – Or Not

i.   Someone with a real physical tinnitis problem will probably hear the same sound all the time. This is a problem and needs healing.

ii.   Someone with 'tinnitis' who hears many different sounds is probably hearing different energies. This is not a problem and needs developing!

iii. To check whether it is a physical problem or if the person has a gift to be developed, simply ask the healee to go into different buildings and note whether they hear different sounds. A spiritual building will have a higher pitched sound than the average pub!

b.   Bell

Do not confuse hearing single notes with hearing a bell. A one-tone tinkling bell is normally a Tibetan monk guide coming to say, 'Hello. I am with you!'

c.   Hearing words

It is common and normal to hear your own higher consciousness or your guides, speak to you. If you believe it is your guides trying to communicate, seek advice from a qualified medium, clairvoyant organisation, or spiritualist church. Or ask if your reiki master runs a specialist course on guides.

Do not expect to hear your guides speak as clearly as a friend in the room. Often, you will hear the guides more as an inner knowing.

4.   Clairolfaction - Smell

Smelling energy is similar to hearing energy.

A good aromatherapist may smell individual illnesses. Also, due to aromatherapists' highly developed sense of smell, they may know what smell to use to heal the smell of the illness!

Guides have their 'signature smells.' A High Being such as Christ, Mary, or an Indian Chief may smell of frankincense, roses or beech wood. Many students have smelt Dr Usui as lemon grass.

A dead friend or relative may come in with a smell you would know them for if you thought about it, such as sour milk if they were known for always leaving the milk to go off, or a particular brand of tobacco or perfume.

5.   Clairgustation - Taste

As above. But it is relatively rare to taste illnesses, guides, etc.

6.   Spiritual

Spiritual biofeedback can come in many different ways. Such as:

a.   Seeing or experiencing a God being

There are many God beings such as Christ, Krishna, Mary, Quan Yin, Aesclepius, or a high-ranking person such as a Saint. Often the God beings are from one of the world's religions.

b.   Angels

Angels may also appear. Angels exist for one main purpose, e.g. the Angel of Truth, or Justice, or Mercy, or Abundance, or Clarity, or whatever. So if you know the name of the angel, you may know the energy of the angel that is now with you.

Some people who have developed spiritually may even have the beautiful and deeply emotional experience of themselves as an angel.

c.   Seeing a white light

If you see a spiritual white light, it will be so bright that it would feel that if it were any brighter it would burn your retinas out.

In Catholicism and other religions, it is stated that it is not possible for God to show himself, so he may come as a brilliant white light.

It is also possible for some angels and God beings to appear in an extremely bright light.

d.   Uncontrollable giggling or laughter

This is a result of connecting in to the ecstasy of God nature. Occasionally giggling or laughter is because the healee inwardly understands that a most profound healing has occurred.

e.   Feeling of ecstasy

A healee having an ecstatically beautiful God biofeedback experience may not understand it. It will be so different to anything previously experienced. To help the understanding, ask, 'Does it feel like all of the most positive emotions you could ever have all happening at the same time?'

The answer will almost certainly be, 'Yes!'

The Three Main Types Of Tears

There are three main types of tears – tears of desperation, tears of release and tears of God-connection. Each type can be confusing for the healee because they usually do not understand why they are crying, nor the feelings they are experiencing with the tears.

As each of the three tear-types is quite common, try to remember the following so that you can help a healee understand and progress.

1. Tears Of Desperation

a. What are tears of desperation?

Some healees will sob uncontrollably during or after reiki. Sobbing may even occur before the treatment.

Often the person's face will be furrowed with anxiety, and their body language will huddle showing need for a cuddle. Although the need may be genuine and you may be the type of person comfortable with cuddles, the professional healer/healee relationship prohibits such contact.

The reason for this type of tears is that there is a deep inner realisation, often spontaneously produced by reiki, that there is a huge amount of healing needed.

b.   How to help the healee

i.   First ask about the feeling with the tears. Ask, 'Does it feel like a recognition of how much healing is needed to be done?'

ii.   If the answer is 'yes', explain that reiki can help people realise deep within them just how many problems they have, or how difficult the problem is. Explain that this realisation is one of the beautiful things with reiki. And explain that you and reiki will help them for as long as is needed to resolve the issues.

iii. Ongoing help is needed. Never give up. Give reiki regularly. A Japanese sensei sent me a fax (see chapter 5) stating Dr Usui said we should try to cure until the last breath. Do so.

iv. Keep records of each session. Use the '*Simple Record Keeping Form*' in chapter 19. Score each symptom before and after a treatment, where ten is the worst a symptom could be, and one is nothing. Some scores may come down relatively quickly, and some may be stubborn. There may be a vast amount of healing to be done over a period of time. Just keep going.

v. Refer on to medical professionals or other experts if necessary.

2. Tears Of Release

a. What are tears of release?

If this type of tears occurs, it is usually at some point during a reiki treatment. They flood or trickle out to release pent-up negative energy. Usually this energy will have been built up over a long period of time.

The tears may relate to energy release of a very recent problem.

b. How to help the healee

i. First ask the question, 'Do the tears feel mainly happy tears, with some sadness attached?'

If the answer is 'Yes', explain that the feeling is because a healing has occurred of a long-standing problem. The negative energy has gone so the healee feels happy!

ii. However, explain to the healee that, because the problem had been there for a very long time, it had become like an old friend who is not very nice. When you decide not to see this 'not very nice friend' any more, although you are happy that they have gone, sadness will be there as well because you had become used to their bad ways. Explain that it is rarely easy to lose a long-term friend, no matter how bad!

Usually the healee will smile with understanding.

iii. Give listening, caring, gentle support until the healee understands or accepts the healing release. Refer on to a professional if needed.

iv. On rare occasions one of my healees has tears that are mainly sadness with a little happiness attached. It is likely that they need some support for a period of time to help them adjust to their new healed self and potential new way of life.

3. Tears Of God Connection

a. What are tears of God connection?

These tears are for possibly a human's most beautiful experience. Sometimes during a treatment, the rei energies will take a person so high up in frequency that he or she will connect in to the energy of whatever God means to them. If this is the first time connecting to the God-force, they almost certainly will not understand the experience.

Because to be at one with the Divine, with God, with the Highest universal intelligence, to be at one with the microcosm of God within and the macrocosm of God without, is an incredibly unusual and mind-blowing experience.

The experience often lasts for only a few seconds. But the memory of the amazing loving energy connection will last a lifetime.

Often the tears will be accompanied by a huge smile, giggles, or laughter.

b. How to help the healee

i. First ask the healee a similar question as mentioned in the section in chapter 9, '*Biofeedback Through Your Seven Senses*', 'Does it feel like all the most positive and beautiful emotions you could ever have, all happening at the same time?'

ii. If the answer is 'yes', just give the healee time to absorb the beauty from the experience.

iii. Do not talk. Create space for wonderful energy to take effect.

iv. Afterwards, the healee often changes for the better. He or she will find their soul's reason for existence in this lifetime, find a beautiful way to help our world, or find peace within.

Primal Scream

Although the occurrence of a primal scream is relatively rare compared to other ways healees release their negativity, it is of such profound nature when it does occur, that it is worthy of a special section.

1. What Is A Primal Scream?

In psychology, an entire therapy has been developed called Primal Scream Therapy, to try to ensure that a primal scream is released. It is a release of torment, of trauma, of longstanding desperation.

The scream comes from deep within the being, maybe even from the soul. It is often a final release of the deepest issues, allowing healing to be undertaken on other, sometimes hidden problems.

As with many things in reiki, this process may, albeit very occasionally, occur naturally.

Primal screams, in my experience, always sound the same. They are high-pitched, extremely loud, and longer than you would have previously thought possible.

They are usually quite frightening when being heard for the first time.

However, primal screams are actually the manifestation of a very wonderful and beautiful healing.

2. How To Help The Healee

First, and most importantly, if in any doubt, refer to a psychologist or similar specialist immediately. Many will have had training to help the healee understand and progress the issues.

Only if you have counselling, psychology, psychotherapy or other relevant knowledge skills, should you reassure the healee that it is perfectly all right to scream. Empower them to keep screaming with the understanding that it is normal.

Your calmness in the situation, that is almost certainly new for the healee, will usually give them the inner calm to release the pent-up scream without fear. Keep encouraging the scream to be released until nothing is left.

After, the healee usually feels at peace within, and understands that a huge healing has occurred.

WORKBOOK NOTES
On Biofeedback

CHAPTER 10

DEVELOPING STRENGTHS

If You Experience Nothing In Attunements, When Self-Healing Or Healing Others

One of my most difficult problems as a teacher is a student who experiences little or nothing. Their ego says that they should experience at least what others have seen or felt.

Egos can be terribly destructive forces. If students desire the experiences of others too much, and cannot have the same experience, they will destroy their own confidence.

Everyone is built differently. For example, some people are more left brained and therefore naturally good at logic. Whereas others are more right brained and therefore naturally good at creativity.

It is the same with reiki. Some students will be naturally able to see auras, or visions. Others will naturally be able to feel energy. Others will naturally experience little or nothing.

1. Why You May Experience Nothing

There are many reasons why little or nothing is experienced.

a.   Nothing happened

It should be accepted that there would be occasions when nothing happens. This should not be denigrated, but accepted on the basis that we are all human beings and cannot be expected to create perfect ability every time. When the excellent healer, Matthew Manning, repeated an experiment 30 times to heal cancer cells in a flask, he had highly significant results in 28 out of the 30 tests. Yet on two of the 30, nothing happened (Benor v1).[105] He did not give in, and nor should you if sometimes nothing happens. Rather, you should simply ask yourself the possible causes, attempt to resolve them, and try to do better next time.

b.   Nothing was 'meant' to happen

If 'nothing' is perceived to be improved in any way, healers sometimes believe that the person has their 'need' for the illness, or a lesson must be learned from the illness, or whatever other reason the cure cannot be obtained. However, these 'reasons' are not strictly correct, because if there is a reason why an illness should not be cured, this reason should be explored adequately until it is understood and accepted. Then the healing can progress. However, this is a subject fraught with difficulty. The medical professions are understandably extremely wary of healers talking about this issue. There is danger that the patient could take offence at you exploring the issue, or even being made to feel worse when being told they are the reason the cure is not being achieved. If you are not a professional counsellor, psychotherapist or in another similar profession, it is safer not to discuss this potential.

---

[105] The number of flasks was obtained through conversation with Matthew Manning.

c.   Healer has too many energy blocks

It is common for beginner healers to have many blockages in their body that prevent the free flow of energy. And as we go through our lives, difficult family, work, and other situations may cause even experienced healers to have blockages.

Blockages are especially common in the lower arms, making it difficult, or in severe cases impossible, for reiki healing energy to flow from above, down the arms and out of the hands. Then neither the healer nor the healee will experience much biofeedback.

You will know if this is the problem because you will feel energy in your head or shoulders, but nothing will be felt beyond the point in your arms where there is a blockage.

Regular self-healing will resolve this problem. Keep at it. Perseverance will eventually break the blockages, and good healing will become reality.

d.   Mind not yet focussed enough

Reiki 1 practitioners often say that they cannot stop their thoughts wandering. After what may for some people have been a lifetime of never having to think about thought, nor having to concentrate hard on something, it is difficult to suddenly be asked to focus, or to concentrate, or to only let a particular energy come through.

If this is the case, relax prior to healing as explained in the section 'Releasing Stress Before Reiki' in chapter 13.

2.   If You Experience 'Nothing' Does Nothing Happen?

Some energies are very subtle, and it is very unlikely that nothing whatsoever ever occurs. For example,

a.   A very high frequency spiritual energy

If there is a very high frequency from the attunement, with very little amplitude, it is almost certain that you will feel nothing. The frequency is too high, and there may not be enough amplitude for you to consciously be aware of it. However, you may find that, within a number of months after the course, you have a very deep spiritual or soul development, and that will be due to the high frequency healing.

b.   Release of negativity in the aura

You may also feel nothing if the release is on the auric levels. But wonderful healings can still occur. If your aura has been healed, within weeks, often within one week, you should feel amazingly better.

c.   Low amplitude

Amplitude means the amount of power needed for a particular condition. A lot of power is not always needed - there are many illnesses that need much less power in order to obtain the healing result.

So, if you do not feel much, question whether a lot or a little amplitude is needed. Maybe the healee does not need the powerful energies you normally use, and the energy is trickling in almost undetected because that is the amplitude needed.

3.   What To Do If You Experience Nothing

a.   Keeping records

Sometimes you will experience 'nothing' because, although something happened in the attunement, your God has built you in such a way that you cannot experience energy. If you are built like this, you have one main option. To accept that you are different from others! If you desire others' experiences, you will demoralise yourself when you do not get similar visions or feelings etc.

Over the years, less than ten of my students have experienced nothing. They experience nothing when they do self-healing, and nothing when they give reiki to others. These students must accept the way they are made, and trust implicitly that reiki will work.

The only way to prove that reiki will work is to keep records. Give each symptom and illness a score out of 10 as described in chapter 19, '*Simple Record Keeping Form*'. Your objective is to bring the scores down.

Do you see that someone may have the greatest visions or feelings in the world but when treating healees, if the scores of the illness do not improve, it is a waste of time and energy?

b.   Student cases

There were nine students that I can remember who experienced nothing. Of these, two gave up reiki. Their ego could not accept that they were built differently to others.

The other seven accepted, and trusted that the energy can flow in the best possible way without them feeling a thing. Three found that after some time, they slowly developed their gifts. Four still experience nothing. All seven are now wonderful healers getting excellent results.

One who still experiences nothing is now a well-respected reiki master, loving to and loved by her many students in her area. Yet after many years she has still not felt even a tiny energy tingle or a glimpse of a vision.

c.   Trust

If you have no experience from attunements or from your self-healing, or from healing others, simply trust the energy is working.

Trust is the issue. Trust that it does not matter if you experience nothing; trust that some people will naturally and automatically develop gifts over their reiki lifetime; trust that reiki will work; trust that you can do it; and trust that the scores of the illness will reduce.

d.   Support

Only if the scores of most illnesses do not have at least 5% better success rate than the probable 30% average placebo response (i.e. 35%) should you consider you have a problem. Then you need support and you should phone your reiki master for help.

Accepting And Developing Your Strengths

Whilst giving reiki, some practitioners experience very little from most of their senses, yet can receive biofeedback via, for example, just the sense of touch, or hearing, or sight, or smell, or taste, or spiritual awareness, or psychic vision. It is perfectly acceptable to accept a natural sense gift.

However, a major problem that can occur is when a practitioner desires not their own natural gift, but the gift of someone else.

1. No Desire

Do not desire the natural gift of another. If others you know can see auras and you cannot, or if others can hear energies and you cannot, or whatever others can do that you cannot, please accept that this is their path of learning and not yours! It may seem strange to you but if, for example, you feel energy with your hand and not see auras, and another person can see auras and not feel energy with the hands, that person may well desire your gift, not theirs!

One of the easiest ways for a beginner to become demoralised is to ignore his or her personal gift, and to try to develop something that is not natural. Then, because others have the natural gift, when it is found to be difficult to learn, disillusionment occurs. Often, a potentially good practitioner will then give up reiki for good.

2. Acceptance

Simply accept however your God has allowed you to experience reiki. Understand that although, perhaps, you can feel physical objects with your hands, it is very different to feeling reiki energy. So some people may not feel reiki. Similarly, some people may see reiki, or hear, smell, taste, have psychic reiki visions or spiritual reiki experiences – whilst others may not.

If you accept your gift with peace within – even if you do not believe you have a gift yet - then peace from reiki will flow.

3. Development

a. Your natural gift should be developed first

If natural biofeedback strength or strengths are worked on, you will feel more confident that reiki is working. You will also gain greater understanding of your particular reiki response.

> **Exercise 37 - Developing Gifts**
> **Keep records of your biofeedback responses when healing self or others. It will usually be apparent which of the seven senses is your main strength. Try to understand everything about that one sense. Ask your reiki master, other practitioners, those in a reiki circle. Do not worry about things that can't be understood. Just understand as much as possible about your particular healing gift.**

b. Non-natural gifts can be learned after

Only when you have learned, practised, developed and understood your individual biofeedback gift, should you move on to developing something that you are not natural at.

It should be understood that almost all ways to experience and use reiki energy can be, for most people, either a natural gift or a learned process. But although it is usually easy to learn for example how to see an aura, if this is not your natural gift, you should develop seeing auras after you are totally comfortable with your own gift.

Are You Too Questioning? Or Too Accepting?

Thank goodness most beginner healers are more or less balanced in their approach to trying to understand biofeedback of the reiki energy. They will question their experiences just enough to create an inner understanding or acceptance of the issue, and then move on to the next part of their learning curve. However, if someone is too questioning or too accepting, his or her reiki growth could be inhibited.

1. Are You Too Questioning?

Why should some people <u>always</u> try to analyse things they do not understand? This is a standard, yet potentially negative trait. In reiki it is far better to understand one's own logical, analytical nature and adjust the mind attitude accordingly.

Are you the type of person who analyses <u>everything</u>? Do you continuously ask questions about every, and any, subject?

Typically this type of person uses their logic left-brain to a high degree in their daily life. Computer programmers, accountants, small business owners, managers and lawyers are commonly of this type. These persons are less accepting of outcomes, always needing to question, to understand, to make logical decisions.

However, reiki biofeedback is often illogical! For example, even a sensitive thermometer cannot measure the heat.

So if your natural attitude is to question too deeply, to analyse even if there is no answer, then you may have a problem with reiki. Because you may try to see if the window is open if there is a breeze from the energy, look to see if the sun has come out if heat is felt, and try to work out why numbness is in the hands if pins and needles sting the hands. And, because no answers can be found, disillusionment may occur.

Too much questioning and looking for earthly answers can create energy blocks, especially on a mental level. Self-created mental blocks will then slow reiki flow. The ultimate problem is that the ability to give reiki is destroyed because no answer will satisfy enough. So there must be different answers for these overly logical questioners.

Answer a. Acceptance

The main answer for this type of person is to accept reiki.

Accept that many reiki questions cannot be answered by science.

Accept that if scientists cannot, for example, yet measure the heat from a healer's hand or discover where reiki energy comes from, it is also probably impossible for reiki practitioners to measure heat from their hands or discover where reiki energy comes from! Science is full of examples where measurable phenomena were hypothesised decades before the proper instruments to measure these things were invented. A current example is in the USA where millions of dollars a year is spent on nanotechnology even though it is currently the stuff of Star Trek type science fiction. A historical example is that bacteria, implied by their effects on people, were considered fantasies by many until we had microscopes to see them. In the case of reiki, reiki's existence is implied by the healing results we get. So, not only do we have the evidence of its existence with people's biofeedback and healing results, we also know that scientific instruments are likely one day to be able to document reiki more thoroughly.

Acceptance that they cannot understand will allow this type of person to release their questioning mind. Reiki energy can then flow without mental restrictions. Not to question anything, simply to practise with reiki and share its energy, will eventually lead to a deep, peaceful, inner understanding.

Exercise 38 - Acceptance (if you do not normally accept)

For the next two months, every time there is a reiki question that you cannot answer, simply

213

accept. Try not to even think about the question.
Accept with love that it is OK to continue reiki without knowing the answer.

Answer b. Keep records

Keeping records as suggested in chapter 19 will satisfy the logical mind that reiki works. Records will show that reiki energy can indeed reduce the scores of illnesses. This will provide the logical answer that reiki is a reality.

Also, records will eventually show that some different illnesses will have standard, not yet scientifically proven, biofeedback responses.

2. Are You Too Accepting?

The natural tendency for some people is to accept everything in their lives without thought, without a question. These types of people are often meek, mild-natured, lacking in confidence, or insecure.

Problems occur because this type of person will not learn reiki lessons through questioning whilst giving or receiving treatments. Eventually, bewilderment or disillusionment may set in because of the lack of understanding. Sadly, many then give up reiki.

a. Think of one question each session

As this type of person accepts so easily, he or she will not have a problem if there is no answer – or different answers. They need to question. Abilities will progress with confidence as answers come.

Exercise 39 - Questions (if you do not normally question)
Ask one question after each reiki session. Ask the reiki master, others in a reiki sharing group, or on a reiki Internet chat room.

Keep a book where you write down your questions and answers, and refer to it every few months to see how much you have learned.
If you truly cannot think of a question, talk to your colleagues about the questions they have.
If you cannot answer a question, take that query on as your own. You will eventually develop the ability to question.

b.   Keep records

For those who are too accepting, it is essential that adequate records be kept. Records will provide answers to questions that have not been asked, and knowledge and confidence can slowly be built. See the beginner's '*Simple Record Keeping Form*' in chapter 19.

WORKBOOK NOTES
On Developing Strengths

CHAPTER 11

ATTUNEMENTS

History Of Attunements

Attunements are universal processes, but not widely understood in the West. In Japan where reiki originated, attunements are much more understood.

This section will describe some of the ways attunements have been used historically in both Japan and in the West. And to show that perhaps many countries could open their hearts and minds more to the beauty and healing and spiritual enlightenment that can come from an appropriate attunement.

1. Japan

a.   Temple attunements
Anyone can go to a temple at almost any time to receive an attunement.

On New Year's Eve people pay £100s for a temple attunement.

When I was at an Osaka temple on New Year's Eve 1998/9, the fee was £700, and bookings had been made years in advance.

b.   Japanese Emperor's attunements
In Japan, attunements are a way of life. For example, when the Japanese Emperor is crowned, he has two attunements, one by the head of Buddhism, and one by the head of the Shinto movement.

Each attunement is watched by millions of Japanese people on television. Dr Usui would have been brought up with this knowledge and perhaps out of respect for the Meiji Emperor, he made attunements a part of reiki.

c. Dr Usui's four meetings with Tokyo students

One story states that, because students could get attunements easily from temples, Dr Usui did not give any attunements unless he felt they were needed. This story states that Dr Usui would arrange to meet and teach his beginner students on four evenings if they lived within the Tokyo area, and only once if they lived outside Tokyo. Therefore the four attunement system for Reiki 1 as introduced to the West by Mrs Takata may have been due to a memory issue where she remembered Dr Usui just meeting and teaching his students four times.

Or perhaps she believed that, because Westerners do not have such easy access to attunements as the Japanese, and that attunements may help with the practitioner's healing ability or self-development, she would make attunements a major part of her courses. Another story says that some students (obviously not all 2000 he taught) stayed with Dr Usui in his home, or were regularly invited for dinner and questions. Again, in both these versions, there is no mention of attunements.

Yet another story says only one symbol was used at a time by Dr Hayashi for attunements, and that in this system, no one has a 21-day cleansing period as in the 'Western' attunement traditions.

d. Course attunements versus taught knowledge

Japanese masters I have spoken with are against reiki being taught as simply an attunement process.

Rather, they believe that the crux of reiki should revolve around vast knowledge and techniques, and that this should be learned on structured courses. Attunements then become a minor part of reiki courses compared to knowledge.

2. Western Attunements

a. Christianity

Perhaps the nearest we get to attunements in Christianity is when children are baptised and older persons are confirmed. Both are special ways to help the person evolve on a pathway to God.

b. Ordination to priesthood

When I was ordained as a priest, the Bishop of the Liberal Catholic Church, whose lineage goes back to 1566, touched my crown, brow, and hands – very similar to a reiki attunement.

The Bishop knew my calling in life was to teach healing, psychic and spiritual subjects. After, he took me to one side and explained that he saw my third eye open too much at the beginning, trying to see what he was doing. He was right! But he said it quickly adjusted, and he felt my heart open and the LOve flow out. Then he explained about the colours of my aura and how they raised in vibration. He finished by describing my spirit guides that came to help, and the beautiful angel that appeared.

It is not much different from many reiki attunements!

c. Old Roman Catholic

In 1999, a group of Danish students visited my Reiki Healing Centre in England. For Sunday prayers, we visited the best-preserved Benedictine Monastery in England. Unknowingly we chose the moment when a new Bishop and Archbishop were being created. The service was read and enacted from an ancient script. After, we were surprised to discover that the document showed that, in the Benedictine branch of the Old Roman Catholic Church, parts of the process have been the same for hundreds of years! The crown is touched and anointed as Aaron in the Bible's Old Testament, and the hands are touched and anointed as Samuel did to King David in the Old Testament. This is very similar to some reiki attunements.

219

It is especially surprising that something that has been around for thousands of years in other parts of the world can have a similar substance to something that came from Japan in the 1920s.

d. Moslem
Moslems have their Sibhud, a secret attunement ceremony where the initiate is attuned to the Moslem version of God energy.

3. Summary

It can be seen that attunements are historically universal, wonderful, beautiful, and natural processes to potentially help an individual progress on any path – regardless of nationality or religion.

I pray that soon, via reiki, nations worldwide will have a greater understanding of the marvellous possible results, on every aspect of being, of receiving quality, unconditional, energy attunements.

Potential Benefits Of Attunements

Good attunements are one of the component parts of reiki that make reiki different - and better - than most healing methods. A knowledgeable and qualified reiki master gives attunements to the student. They are not given from the master's ego, wants, or desires. Instead, the master releases his or her conscious thought, and utilises a process where the attunement is allowed to help the needs of each individual student unconditionally.

Thus it is possible that each student may receive exactly what is needed to help him or her at the moment the attunement takes place. All is done for 'The Highest Good of All Concerned'.

There are many potential benefits of receiving attunements. What benefit you experience will often depend on your state of being at that time. For example, if you are already spiritually evolved, you may have a 'higher' experience than someone who has never thought of God; if you are in need of healing, the attunement may work on that level; and if you have clairvoyant potential, you may get more psychic visions than others.

The following are a few of the many potential benefits of receiving attunements. **As you read the following, remember that many (but certainly not all) potential benefits of an attunement may also be potential benefits of a reiki treatment during your own self-healing, or when you give reiki to others.** So enjoy the process, and be glad that you have discovered this valuable tool to help your life.

1. Create A Reiki Healer

A reiki attunement can help students create an energy flow within them so that they can become good healers.

One morning, on a Reiki 1 course in Denmark, one of my students, a nurse, said that she was not looking forward to practising how to channel reiki energy through her for self-healing. She had tried many times with other non-reiki healing systems and nothing had ever worked.

But she was most amazed and pleased when we practised self-healing because, for the first time in her life, she had incredibly massive energies flowing through her and out of her hands. The attunements had created the energy she needed to help her become a healer.

2.   Attune To Reiki Symbol Frequencies

The reiki symbols are frequencies of energies that can be attuned to via various connections.

a.   Unconscious mind

The unconscious mind is believed to physically reside in the Limbic System (Coleman) and can be accessed via the rear base of the brain. There are researchers who also locate the energetic unconscious mind throughout the body (Hunt, Pert); the limbic system, in particular the interaction between the thalamus and the amygdale, is the physical interface. Attunements create an energy process where, after the symbols enter the unconscious mind, the attunee will be more likely to be able to use the energies when appropriate.

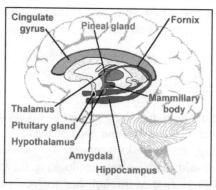

Figure 19: Limbic System

b.   The field

The manifestation of the unconscious mind also exists outside the body in the field (Pert, Hunt). The field should not be confused with the aura, which is a different energy. If reiki symbols are placed in the field, the unconscious mind will absorb them. Then it becomes easier to let the correct energy flow through. Theoretically, better healing results can be obtained.

3.   Channelling Symbols

Some students after the attunements discover they have an ability to channel symbols. These symbols are universal sacred geometry that can be used for good and positive purposes to heal and help the channeller, or people or things or situations around the channeller. Channelled symbols should not be considered as being relevant to everyone in our world. For beginners, channelled symbols should be thought of as being channelled for that moment of time, for that person, for that condition only. If you truly channel symbols, the channelled symbol will help the person move on, and so if you give the person another session of reiki, a different symbol with a different energy may need to be channelled.

4.   Adjustment Of Crown To Higher Spiritual Energy

Reiki, especially the higher spiritual rei energy, needs to come through the crown of the head first to make it easier for higher frequencies to be brought through. Also via the crown, the healer is filled and healed before passing reiki to others. In this way, the healer cannot lose energy. A constant flow of energy from above will always replenish, and a healer should never be energetically tired.

Some students have little or no open connection to 'above.' To achieve this, the crown chakra may need to be adjusted as a natural and unconscious part of the attunement.

For many less spiritually developed individuals, this natural process will mean opening the crown chakra.

For others, especially those already too high in their frequency such as a manic-depressive in the manic phase, or for those with some types of schizophrenia, it will mean the crown chakra must be cleansed, repaired, or even closed.

The important point is that the crown chakra will be adjusted in a way that is right for the individual student to channel energies.

5. Adjust The Third Eye And Psychic Intuition

Many students have an inadequate or inappropriate psychic nature. It is possible that the third eye can adjust in one of three main ways.

a. Third eye becomes more perceptive
Often, an attunement will provide many extra visions and insights. Many students see auras or their guides, or angels or their God, for the first time.

b. Third eye becomes less perceptive
A much-needed option if a person has been confused or hospitalised due to the third eye allowing too many visions.

c. Third eye more accurate
Almost all people do not get 100% correct accuracy via the third eye. Attunements can allow the third eye to adjust so that there will be less 'rubbish' and more correct 'intuitions.'

6. Blend The Heart To A Giving Nature

Healers should be able to share reiki from the LOve in their hearts. An attunement may facilitate this.

In Japan, I gave an attunement to about 30 Japanese reiki masters and senseis. One lady said that she had tried to open her heart for many years, with many techniques, and never succeeded. The individual nature of my attunement opened her heart to allow her to experience highest God-LOve for the first time in her life.

7.   Attune The Hands To Let Reiki Flow Through

Some healers' hand energies are very blocked. In the attunement process, many feel a ball of energy forming in the hands, or their hands being pulled together or pushed apart by the magnetic energy, or sudden heat, or electric, or some other sensation in the hands.

After, reiki will be able to flow through the hand chakras much more easily to heal.

8.   Adjust, Open, Or Close Chakras

It is important to understand that chakras should not be automatically opened. Although many reiki books write about how to open chakras, there is often the case that a chakra should be closed!

A classic example of a need to close a chakra is the third eye of a person with schizophrenia.

On the Reiki 3A Healing Mastership training course, I teach about seven of the main medical and energetic causes of schizophrenia, and how to potentially heal them. One major cause is that the third eye chakra is already too open, and all the good or rubbish things of the universe can enter whether the person wants it or not. If a healer opened the third eye even more, the person might be hospitalised the next day. Psychiatric workers have confirmed this potential.[106]

It may be that the third eye of a person with schizophrenia needs to be closed. However, this would usually be done over a period of time, not in one session, because the person would probably find it too difficult to adjust quickly.

---

[106] This is from many psychiatric workers on classes over the years.

So it is with all chakras – they should be adjusted for the need of the individual!

9. Balance The Aura And The Field

There may be many irregularities in both the aura and the field. For example, trauma may manifest first in the aura before being attracted in to become a physical illness. It is of utmost importance therefore that to stay healthy, the aura and field are regularly balanced.

10. Repair Energy Meridians

Injury, disease or energy blocks often damage acupuncture-type meridians. Attunements may repair these problems, and in so doing a healing often occurs. For example, an injured meridian may cause sciatica. When the meridian from the lower back down to the toe is repaired naturally in an attunement, the sciatica may be healed.

11. Release Negativity

In one Reiki 1 class, in the first attunement, a lady singer felt something release and leave from her. In the next attunement she realised that she felt better about taking a certain action in her life. The attunement had released her negativity towards taking this action.

Negativity may be released on all levels. It is common for tears to flow as the release occurs. After the release, the student usually feels better than for a very long time.

12. Release Energy Blocks

It is common that energy blocks within the body create barriers that positive healing energies cannot pass through. If these blocks are released, so are many illnesses.

For example, a low energy illness like chronic fatigue often needs blocks to be released from the lower legs. Then low frequency earth energy may enter through the feet and re-energise the person.

13. Harmonise All Energy Bodies

Our being consists of many types of energy. These are constantly changing to a form appropriate to our life-style at each moment of the day. Attunements may cleanse to allow greater harmony of our energy bodies as we go about our varied lives.

14. Healing

Many different types of healings may occur from an attunement.

a. Physical
The most dramatic physical healing I have had in attunements was a lady in her 50s.

When she was seven, she was knocked over by a car, and ever since had walked extremely lopsidedly, and with terrible pain. After each of the Reiki 1 attunements, she was able to stand straighter and with less pain, until the end of the day when she could walk almost upright with no pain for the first time in about 40 years. She was overjoyed and let the entire class know it with her surprised delight.

There have been many lesser examples of healings.

b. Emotional
Emotional healings are equally countless. Often there are floods of tears. This is usually followed by calmness within, a peace that is there for the first time since the bad emotion occurred.

c. Mental
It is very common that there is a healing of a wrong mental attitude, a bad habit like smoking, a fear or phobia. Even drug or alcohol addicts have been relieved.

227

Some people cannot eat meat after the attunements. But I have also had a few vegetarians who found that after their attunement they had to eat meat. They found it empowering to do so.

One Chinese lady was a reluctant vegetarian, often craving meat. During four reiki attunements she saw pictures of first chicken, then pork, then lamb, and finally beef! That night she went to a restaurant and 'pigged' herself on meat of all kinds. After, she felt wonderful. Her craving for meat disappeared because she now knew she could eat it if she wished. She is now a contented vegetarian.

Peace is also a very common effect.

d. Spiritual
See below.

15. Past Lives

Occasionally a student has a vision of a past life that needs to heal. Usually it is healed, naturally, by the attunement, with a wonderfully positive knock-on benefit for some connected issue in this life.

Remember that it is not needed to <u>consciously</u> understand the past life. See the section '*Biofeedback Through Your Seven Senses*' in chapter 9.

Healing of any past life problem can occur in many ways naturally – for example through colour, vision, feeling, auditory, or inner knowing. Simply accept the energy work is occurring for your highest good.

16. Raising Of Frequency

Most people regularly get 'stuck in a hole' they have dug for their life. They are comfortable with a certain way of life, even if they realise it is not really the best thing to be doing. And it is difficult for them to dig themselves out.

The general frequency of their energy body will reflect this. If the attunement can raise the frequency of that person slightly, they will be able to see above the hole, and be able to move on to a better, more appropriate way of life.

Frequencies of individual energy bodies should not be raised too much, as this could create a frequency that is too high for the person to easily adjust to. This could even lead to fear of the new energy field.

And remember that many energy bodies, e.g. manic, will need to be lowered in frequency.

17. Create Wholeness Within

For some people, it is not enough to heal or adjust single problems. It is more needed to become a 'whole person.' Attunements may create that beautiful wholeness feeling, connecting all energies within to a complete being.

It may then be easier for other single problems to be healed, or to raise the energies higher.

18. Happiness

Happiness was the first main mission statement of Dr Usui. He hoped that the attunements and their subsequent self-healing would provide happiness to all.

It is one of my greatest joys as a reiki master to see students change from negativity or sadness or depression or whatever, to complete happiness.

Happiness arises from wholeness.

19. Develop Soul Path

Have you ever wondered what your soul path was? Attunements have a wonderfully regular habit of guiding students towards a better relationship, job, house, or hobby, etc.

These are life changes that are more relevant, not to the student's ego or desires, but to the needs of the soul and the development of the individual's soul path.

20. Reiki Or Other Guides Coming Close To Help You

It is possible that during an attunement a student may become aware of his or her guide or guides for the first time. Or they may show themselves partially or fully, or communicate in some way relevant to the attunee.

21. Provide Protection

Protection may be provided for two completely different reasons.

a. 'Bad' energies around you
These 'bad' energies may come from beings that may have disturbed you. And the attunement may provide releases from them or protection against them. Or you may get protections from 'bad' energies coming from the air or earth or geopathic stress, or even computers and electrical equipment.

b. Good reiki energies
This type of protection is to try to ensure that reiki energies only ever work for goodness in your life, and the lives of those you meet, so that all will work energetically for beauty and goodness.

22. Karmic Resolution

Some students are 'given' by the attunement that their 'karma is now resolved'. Healing or LOve or other effects of the attunement can heal karma <u>unconsciously</u>.

It is rarely important – except to satisfy ego – to understand karmic resolution in the conscious mind.

23. Give A Spiritual Experience

It is sad that many people exist on such a low vibration that they cannot understand a spiritual experience. Attunements can give this wonderful feeling or inner understanding of what it means to be a spiritual being. After, some such students will automatically tread a more spiritual path, and try to gain the beautiful forces of ultimate enlightenment.

24. Earthly Enlightenment

There are many things we do in our lives that we do not truly understand. During an attunement, some students may receive an earthly enlightenment, a truth about something in their normal daily life. This could be about anything, but especially about a relationship or a job. Usually this truth is a cataclysmic realisation, and can change that particular aspect of life to extreme positivism.

25. God Enlightenment

This is always an amazingly powerful and beautiful experience. When God enlightenment comes, it comes, for example, in a flash of brilliant light, or a vision of splendour, or a feeling of ecstasy, or a melody of music, that is perfect. These few seconds of enlightenment will become a memory that will last a lifetime. And the entire life of that student will often change forever - beautifully.

It is not the job of the reiki master to make students become any particular faith. I have had students who are strict Moslems or Jews who have suddenly seen Jesus Christ. And Christians who have seen an Indian God such as Ganesh or Krishna or the Buddha. Or lapsed Moslems who have seen Mecca. Or lapsed Catholics who have seen Mary.

It seems that attunees have God enlightenment relevant to the needs of their soul.

And that it is the energy of the God-being that is needed, not the God-being him or her or it self.

To understand your soul-energy need version of God – not necessarily what your upbringing says is God – is extremely empowering for the true meaning of your existence.

26. To Share Only Our Light

Although many people do not want to recognise it, we all have a dark side – our shadow self. Of course, we should try to heal any darkness of any persuasion. But some things are more difficult than others.

So if we can understand and accept our darkness, it means that we will be more likely only ever to share our Light.

The Old Roman Catholic instructions and affirmations made by a new Bishop include to:[107]

> 'never pass off light for darkness, nor darkness for light'.
> and
> 'Lay hands lightly on no man'.[108]

Many centuries later, this is still true. In fact, these words of truth about our inner Light and darkness may be more needed today than at any other time in our history.

After the attunements, a reiki practitioner should remember those words of wisdom as they start on the light path of helping themselves and others in the world.

---

[107] I was very fortunate to one day be present at the ordination of a new Bishop and Archbishop at a Benedictine monastery. The ceremony was being read from a copy of an ancient manuscript. After the ceremony, I was kindly presented with a copy of the translation.

[108] According to the warning of the Apostle Paul.

27. Allow Oneness With All

Occasionally in the attunement, students may suddenly feel as if they are connected into everything in the entire universe. They realise that they are not separate entities, alone and detached as a tiny microcosm in the universe. Instead, they have a realisation that they are at one with everything, connected to all in the universal macrocosm.

Dr Usui in his writings stated that this connected oneness of the microcosm of our God-nature within to the macrocosm of God's nature outside is one of the ultimate purposes of reiki.

It can bring a feeling of ecstasy.

28. Blessing

Many attunements include a blessing for the student. Often the attuning reiki master will also receive a blessing as part of the process.

At the moment of blessing, students and masters can feel as if their guides, their God, or the highest universal intelligent energy has blessed them. It is a beautiful feeling that will usually last for a very, very long time.

29. Divine LOve

God energy equals the highest force of LOve that is possible to exist in our Universe. If students feel this incredible divine LOve in an attunement for the first time, they will understand it is very different to any earthly love they have ever had in their normal life.

Divine LOve is a perfect LOve, a LOve that is impossible to repeat for long periods because there is a normal, low frequency life to lead. But it is a LOve that most people should strive for, re-experience, and eventually passed on to others. For some, it will have an incredibly positive LOving, life-changing effect.

30. Peace

There is too much stress in the average daily life.

Peace is becoming more and more difficult to experience.

Attunements may give some students this much-needed feeling within.

It is wonderful to watch the relaxed faces of the students when peace arrives.

The first time I taught at a particular hotel, it was a course for reiki masters. At lunchtime, the hotel receptionist called me over and asked what was I teaching. I asked why. She said that she had never seen such a peaceful-looking group. I explained that they were reiki masters and had done their self-healing and attunements. Some of the hotel staff asked to book the course!

The following week, I taught a beginners class. The hotel staff called me over and cancelled their booking. When I asked why, they said that they had never seen a group that looked so little at peace and much in need of healing! I explained that this was a beginners group! They had not had attunements nor done their self-healing yet...

Reiki may give you the inner peace you need.

Remember: you may have to make peace with yourself before you can make peace with others.

Attunements Are For The Highest Good Of All Concerned

It is important to remember that it is NOT the job of a reiki master in an attunement to try to create some particular experience for a student.

And students should NOT crave someone else's experience.

The truth of attunements is that the process should be allowed to work in a way that is right for each individual's path at that moment of time.

It should also be understood that it is completely unimportant what experience the attunee receives. Even if 'nothing' is perceived to be experienced in any way, it could mean that nothing was meant to happen, or that what happened was not consciously noticeable.

As can be seen from the previous section, there are many possible benefits of attunements. All are wonderful and perfect.

It is assumed that the reiki master has received proper attunement training and does not include his or her own ideas; as seen from the previous section, individual needs vary considerably. If so, reiki masters and students should simply accept that the attunement WILL work in the most appropriate way for the highest good of all concerned – and the highest good of everybody, and everything, everywhere!

WORKBOOK NOTES
On Attunements

CHAPTER 12

ATTUNEMENT BIOFEEDBACK

Students' Attunement Experiences

The following experiences of attunements are included here not because they are particularly special. Rather, of the many thousands of attunements I have given, they are simply a broad cross-section to demonstrate the potentials of an attunement. Also, although all the ones chosen include immediate healing benefits gained this may not always occur, and are included mainly to show the attunement potentials.

It should be noted that, if you have an attunement, it might be nothing like any of these. Every student should receive the energetic process in a way that is right for him or her at that moment.

'I felt very calm, energised, and in the present within my body – often I do not feel this! Also, on opening my eyes, there seems to be more light and definition, a sense of seeing more deeply.

'Before the attunement I felt slight anxiety, inclination to paranoia, and self blame. After, I felt calm, clarity, a sharpening and greater depth of vision.' NE

'This was a most beautiful experience that I find very hard to put into words. I suppose floating in a pool of colour from magenta to white to pink, all bright and beautiful, with exploding flowers of colour all around. I was coughing, but so happy.

'Before the attunement I could feel my heart beating very fast, and hear my breathing. Then it all went peaceful.' DN

'I saw a blue background colour, in the middle yellow and some kind of shape covered in purple. Then I saw one eye with lots of eyelashes.

'Before the attunement I had a knee pain and backache. Now I feel 99% better.' SN

'When my turn was near, I saw dark purple and white and questions about myself and my aims and intentions.

'Before I was confused, stressed, under pressure, very tired physically and emotionally. After I was more peaceful, relaxed.' SL

'I felt energy going through me from the head through the body. I saw purple, red, orange colours. I also had a vision of a diamond and pendulum shape.

'Beforehand I was emotionally traumatised because of going through divorce, separation (my husband went off with another woman) and shock. Now, I feel peace, free, ready to let go.' KT

'Colours, greens and purples, making way for magenta, gold and violet.

'Before had backache, tension and sadness, problems with colon. After, backache better, warmth around head, shoulders and lower back, sense of calm remained.' MZ

'Feeling in crown of head. Orange to whitish colour changed, when I thought of it, back to orangey. My neck felt very crooked to begin with, but straightened out after the final touch. Aware of a pleasant smell.

'Before the attunement, problem with neck and lower back, twisted and lopsided feeling. Emotional problem coping with partner and feeling inadequate to do right things about it.

'After, neck straightened – lower back and left groin area relaxed. Feel very light and positive – sinuses seemed to clear.' BT

'Intense prickly heat up back. I felt a sadness and grief about my two children who died, and visualised (an unknown) violet symbol and felt I was being healed.

'Before I had grief because I'd been talking about my two children who had died. After, I felt love and acceptance. Belief I can help others with bereavement.' FO

'Lots of red colour to start. Pain coming up in back / neck / head. Remember at one stage as Allan touching me, feeling there was someone else – "a friend" – with me.

'Before I felt major distress and despair emotionally. After, no improvement. Physical pain through head and neck.' BC

'Intense heat all over, burning and pins and needles in hands – light-headed – coloured balls of light – intense feeling of peace, relaxation. The words 'love, light, give' were the only words I could think of. At the end I felt trembling from my shoulders to fingers. A feeling of being 'miles away' after!

'Before I had no aches or pains. I am pregnant – I was excited about the course. Now I am very relaxed and at peace with myself.' PF

'Tremendous heat all over, a sense of floating, general feeling of well-being, felt as if a weight had been lifted. My guide St Teresa was very close in fact closer than I'd ever felt her before. I could see lovely shades of pink, lilac, very bright light. I could see in the distance Our Lady and Brother Jesus, but everything was so very bright.

'Before the attunement I had pains in the left knee, arms, shoulders and neck and a depression feeling. After, the pain in my left leg has ceased, stress levels have lessened, arms feel better, feel very floaty and high. Depression feeling has gone, feel very happy.' VP

Clairvoyants' Attunement Experiences

This section is included because it is how things are. Many things in this world are not taught in school, and are little understood, or completely unaccepted, until one has the experience personally. So it is with this section. At one time I was an atheist and would have scoffed at things people see clairvoyantly. But as thinking human beings, as life progresses we sometimes have no choice but to accept things as real that we previously would have turned our backs on. So it is with these following comments, and I hope that anyone with atheistic thoughts will just keep an open mind and accept the old saying 'there are many more things in heaven and earth than you will ever know'.

Most clairvoyants watching attunements have seen similar things, especially how each student's energy body changes to a better, brighter or higher frequency colour as the process progresses. Also regularly seen are the reiki energies entering the room and being dispersed to the students in the colour form each individual needs. If the reiki master treats it as such, it is indeed an individual process.

'Energy built up in the room rapidly, even before the attunement commenced physically. At the very start there was a guide or angel standing behind each person waiting to be attuned. As Allan/Dr Usui drew reiki symbols in the air they took form. Also, he 'breathed' reiki during the attunement – I saw this as clear energy like a heat haze. Dr Usui was with Allan during the attunement (but also with the other observer). Just before he was with Allan, Usui Sensei followed immediately behind him.'

'The heat was very intense emanating both from and around Allan. The students became as one in a vast flame. Sweet smells of flowers that I felt were of Japanese nature. Dr Usui was present at all times. Many other guides and masters attended, and worked radiating love. Dr Usui was with and through Allan and also myself at the same time.'

'Allan's attunements are beautiful, very moving to observe. Although each one is the same in structure, each one is unique – individually tailored to the students' needs. For each student the same basic method is used for the attunement. However, how long Allan spends with each student; the speed of his hand movements (as well as how smooth or choppy they are); how hard he breathes and for how long for – and how the energies appear as he breathes; whether or not he returns to the student afterwards – these are different with each student. After each attunement, Allan checks the student like a master craftsman examining his work before moving on.'

'Great feeling of magnificence and power. Allan was surrounded by a brightness not of this plane, pure white 'essence' light. Angelic forms surrounded the students. Felt the floor was radiating heat. Also Tibetan-type guide around Allan, very high and ascended, almost to say that this guide/master/teacher was near to the reiki-healing source, that is to say, the highest point. The whole room became translucent.'

'Before attunement a guide or angel was behind each student. During the attunement, a beam of energy extended upwards from each student's head. The attunements altered this energy. Allan asked those receiving attunements to think of issues for self-healing. As he did so, symbols dropped into their crown chakras like keys into a lock.'

'The Christ conscience emanated around and through. Many, many light beings, angelic forms, surrounded all. Beams of reiki energy surrounded the students. The room was very warm.'

WORKBOOK NOTES
On Biofeedback Of Reiki 1

1<u>ST</u> ATTUNEMENT

WORKBOOK NOTES
On Biofeedback Of Reiki 1

2ND ATTUNEMENT

(If given)

WORKBOOK NOTES
On Biofeedback Of Reiki 1

3RD ATTUNEMENT

(If given)

WORKBOOK NOTES
On Biofeedback Of Reiki 1

4TH ATTUNEMENT

(If given)

CHAPTER 13

SELF-HEALING NEEDS AND OVERCOMING DIFFICULTIES

When I Was A Young Man...

When I was a young man, I wanted to change the world.

I found it was too difficult to change the world so I tried to change my nation. When I found I couldn't change the nation, I began to focus on my town and as an older man I tried to change my family.

Now, as an old man, I realise the only thing I can change is myself, and suddenly I realise that if long ago I had changed myself, I could have made an impact on my family. My family and I could have made an impact on our town.

Their impact could have changed the nation and I could indeed have changed the world.

Author unknown

This classic writing is also classic reiki. It shows the importance of progressing from self-healing, to healing family, to healing in your hometown centre, to healing our world. It shows that self-healing first, wins. And it shows how people can get it wrong...

On What Level Do You Need Self-Healing?

There are not many people on this planet who don't need healing. In the late 1990s, I gave a reiki lecture in Denmark. The terrier of Danish politics was there. When I asked, 'Is there anyone here who does not need healing?' she put her hand up. She was the first, and so far, only person to do so, and I said, 'It's nice to meet God!' People often respect being treated how they treat others, and she respected this. She took me to dinner, and afterwards gave me a personally conducted midnight tour of the Danish Houses of Parliament! She agreed later that she really needed healing! As of course we all do until we become God.

1. Physical

Many healers have a majority of healees with physical problems, because it is physical problems that limit most in the world. There are very few physically perfect people because even failing eyesight or bad breath need healing! When teaching the special breathing technique for asthmatics on the Stress Management CD, I have not yet found anyone with perfect lung capacity, even athletes or singers. We are all in need of more physical healing than many would admit.

2. Past, Present, Future

Most people have problems from the past, stress in the present or fears for the future. Some of these issues are buried in the unconscious mind. They pass unnoticed in the hustle and bustle of normal life. Therefore they would not be healed until perhaps you are given another chance in another life…

These deep issues, unrecognised in the conscious mind, may only be released with regular self-healing. Only then can your blocks to true recovery be dissolved, and deep healing be achieved.

3. Emotions

Emotions are feelings. Hands up those who have not had emotional hang-ups! Most people have feelings of anger, guilt, sadness, fear, jealousy, irritability, frustration, loneliness, or accusations against others - or many other emotional issues.

These emotions are not pure LOve. Therefore none are perfect. Therefore all emotions need to be healed.

After self-healing, see how reiki may gradually dissolve items on the list in exercise 40 over the next weeks and months.

4. Mental

Mental means thoughts. There are many negative aspects to almost everyone's mentality. Most people will at some time in their life have thoughts of insecurity, lack of confidence, addiction, bad attitude, anxiety, inappropriate belief pattern, lack of purpose, phobia, depression, fear, or simply an inappropriate thought.

Also, the ideal state of mental being is peace. Unless your mind is peaceful at all times, you will need mental healing. Self-healing after the attunements should gradually bring you back into balance.

5. Spirituality

Most people are guilty of letting spiritual aspects of their being become stagnant. And so most people should continuously be aware of how to improve their spirituality.

It may be good to remember here that spirituality does not necessarily mean religion – or even your version of God. Spirituality may be more to do with how you interact with your place in this world.

Whatever happens within your job, your relationships, your health, or anything else, if you are spiritual you will be at peace.

Whenever I try to describe this ideal spiritual and peaceful way to be, my thoughts go to families I have seen being interviewed on television after a disaster. For example, a bomb-blast, or murder, or plane hijack where their children have been killed. Over the years, I have noticed two types of people.

There are the families being interviewed who use terribly hateful language against the perpetrators of the bad deed, vowing revenge.

Then there are other families who say, peacefully and lovingly, that the perpetrators must have had their own personal good reasons for the deeds, and that they must be LOved and prayed for. Some even go to the extreme of caring for them in prison.

Which one of these two families will have the most spiritually peaceful life?

Perhaps our hardest lesson in life is when our closest loved ones are terribly hurt. Would you have peace if your nearest and dearest were being tortured? If not, regular reiki self-healing will slowly bring you to an inner understanding that there should be peace under every possible circumstance.

6. Soul

Out of all your healing needs, the most important need is for your soul. It is the least understood, because the soul has the least impact in most people's conscious mind.

However, the soul is the one true and permanent force. It lives on after death. And therefore the soul must be the most important part of you to be healed.

Self-healing can reach our deepest levels, and give us a greater chance of achieving a 'perfect pure soul'.

7. Others

There are many other self-healing needs. Apart from the following, please also see section *'Potential Benefits Of Attunements'* in chapter 11, as most benefits of attunements can also occur in self-healing.

a.   Aura

Ensuring our aura is cleansed so that illnesses are less likely to manifest.

b.   Chakras

Adjusting chakras so that more, or less, energy flow can occur, and harmony can reign in the chakra system.

c.   Miasms

Healing miasms or past life problems, or other issues from before birth.

d.   Meridians

Mending a damaged meridian system, for example sciatic pain that also goes down one leg.

e.   Intuition

Adjusting psychic intuition to allow more perception or more accuracy.

The reiki way is to keep self-healing. Even if you feel perfect now, you are probably quite imperfect on some deep level of being. And continuous self-healing may help keep illness at bay…

Exercise 40 - The Self-Healing Shopping List
Make a 'shopping list' of all your healing needs. Decide what is a 'want-to-be-healed' issue, and what is a 'need-to-be-healed.' Then seek answers and healing for your most important needs.

Can You Heal Others If You're Not Healed?

It is often said that you cannot be a good healer until you are healed. However, consider this.

1. Just Do It

Most people agree - if we waited for healers to be perfectly healed on all levels there would be no healers! So you should 'just do it!' In the process of healing, you will receive healing, and become cleansed.

2. Pre-Healing Alpha

If you find your ill-health gets in the way of obtaining results, find a way to rise above your ill-health problem. For example, relax deeply for up to 10 minutes before starting reiki.

This should put your brain in alpha wave band that should allow reiki to flow more easily.

See the section 'Releasing Stress Before Reiki' in chapter 13.

3. Self-Healing To Create An Excellent Healer

You owe it to yourself and your future patients to practise self-healing before healing others. The more you practise, the healthier you will become. And the purer and better channel you will be for others.

You should aim to heal all your emotional issues, and your negative mental attitudes.

Ultimately, you may become more spiritual and God-like in your etheric energies. This will have a positive effect on future healees who should feel wonderful energy coming from you.

The more you self-heal, the greater will be your understanding of healing energies. By the time self-healing becomes a natural and effective part of your life you should have become an excellent healer.

4. Detach From Your Emotions

As taught on a beginner reiki course, you need to detach from your emotions and attitudes. If you see a car crash where people are injured, you may have bad feelings about what happened, or even been injured yourself. Regardless of what happened, you should train your abilities to rise above any negativity, and under any circumstance, be able to channel pure reiki energy to heal the people or the situation.

Some people say that you cannot heal your friends or family because you are too emotionally involved. However, it is your responsibility to detach from those emotions, to rise above the emotions, to your higher consciousness and to allow the appropriate energy for the healing need to flow through.

5. Using Two Consciousnesses At The Same Time

It is possible to develop the use of two consciousnesses at the same time so that you can do your 'normal' job and yet also concentrate on the appropriate reiki flow. This is taught in more depth in the Reiki 2 Manual because of the different energies then available. Until then, practise the exercise below.

Exercise 41 - Healing With Two
Consciousnesses
When watching television, reading, or doing some other passive activity, try to concentrate on both allowing the flow of appropriate

**healing energy and the other passive activity
at the same time.**

6. Acceptance Of Impermanent Nature Of Everything

It is interesting that Dr Usui, through his enlightenment, understood how nothing is permanent – including illness. Deepak Chopra, M.D.[109] relies on the fact that 98% of your body regenerates itself in under a year. After all, people are mainly made of water. People eat, drink and then release. In so doing, the entire body changes substantially from day-to-day.

Accept that, as your body will change daily, you cannot be the same person at night as when you woke in the morning. Therefore, if you can give that process some help, from daily reiki self-healing, you have a chance to change in more positive ways.

Exercise 42 - The Impermanent List Of Permanence
Make a list of everything you can think of that is permanent and will last forever. Then meditate on the impermanent nature of everything, including ill health.

---

[109] Private communication, with permission to publish.

Releasing Stress Before Reiki

For Reiki I students, it is important to control stress before a reiki treatment. If you are stressed, or if you have a cold, flu, or any other illness, it is more difficult to allow the flow of reiki energy. This means that even your self-healing could be adversely affected. So much so, that there may not even be a reiki flow. It is rather like trying to turn on the bathroom tap when the pipes have rusted.

If you have been ill for a long time, almost certainly a stressful physical condition will also have been created. Reiki will help you relax. But if we do not release the stress condition first, reiki energy may naturally be used to help the stress, not the illness you hoped would be helped.

One option to relieve stress is to meditate to create a peaceful mind. However, for most people, it is not enough just to meditate. To have a peaceful mind, the healee must release stress via a three-stage process:

1.   Control the breathing
2.   Relax the physical body
3.   Create peace of mind

If done in that order, all-over physical and mental ideal states of being should be achieved; energy blocks will probably be cleared; and reiki healing energy will more likely have a 'free passage' to work effectively to restore good health.

The following pages on 1, 2, and 3, above should help your reiki self-treatments to be much more effective.

1. Breathing Techniques

When you are stressed, it is the breathing that is first affected. In order to control stress, it is the breathing that should be controlled first.

a.   Healer's breathing

If you breathe in a tense way, the reiki energy may not flow as freely and as forcefully as it could.   In any case, it does not inspire confidence if a healee hears you gasping erratically!   Do practise breathing correctly, both for your own benefit, and for the benefit of others.

b.   Healee's breathing

This is, perhaps, even more important.   Do check their breathing pattern on the first appointment.   If it is erratic, or not as it should be, ask if the person has ongoing stress.

Exercise 43 - Mirrored Breathing

To discover if your healee – or you – is affected by stress, use the simple test of Mirrored Breathing. Ask the healee to close the eyes, and take a few very, very deep breaths in and out.

As they do so, watch their shoulders and head. There are no lungs in the head or shoulders, so they should not move!

But you will soon discover that, the more stressed a person is, the more the head and/or the shoulders will move up and down as they breathe deeply in and out.

You can do this for yourself whilst looking in a mirror.

Then use a breathing technique. Do the technique in front a mirror, and try to control the shoulders and head movement to zero.

This should eventually regain control over the stressed breathing, and relax the general stress. This will in turn increase the chances

of a quicker and more permanent recovery from their illness.

Exercise 44 - Breathing By Numbers

Take a slow, deep breath in, counting to four.
Hold for a count of four.
Breathe slowly and deeply out for the count of four.
Hold for a count of four.
Continue until you feel able to repeat whilst counting to five.
When comfortable counting to five, try counting to six.
Repeat, increasing numbers until you reach your capacity.
Do not over-stretch your lung capacity – just breath as deeply as possible in a way that remains comfortable.

Exercise 45 - Timed Breathing

a. Breathe in and out with very short, fast breaths for 15 seconds.
b. Breathe normally for 30 seconds.
Continue until this feels comfortable, and then repeat a. for 20 seconds.
Repeat b. for 40 seconds.
Continue until this feels comfortable, and then repeat a. for 25 seconds.
Repeat b. for 50 seconds.
Continue until this feels comfortable, and then repeat a. for 30 seconds.
Repeat b. for 60 seconds.

2. Physical Relaxation

The physical being should be relaxed next. If a healee has neck or shoulder pain, of course it could be due to a physical problem. However, stress in the physical body should be explored first.

Look in a mirror. Take a deep breath in. See the height of your shoulders. Now drop them downwards.

How far did the shoulders drop? A few millimetres or a few centimetres? Either is too much!

Many of your healees will have neck and shoulder pains, regardless of their presenting illness. This is usually due to moving their stressed head, neck, and shoulders too much as they breathe. These pains are often released by relaxation.

Indeed, you may be able to relieve the symptoms of the neck or shoulder pain, but if the pains are produced by stress, unless you heal the stress, the pains will return.

Apart from healing stress-induced pain, physical relaxation is also an essential part of freeing yourself to allow reiki to flow. It is an essential part of the healing process.

Physical relaxation means being unblocked. To be unblocked means many conditions have a greater chance of recovery.

a. Relaxation for the healer
Certainly you should relax before each reiki session. Your relaxed state of being will be 'picked up' unconsciously by the healee. This will help relax you both.

b. Relaxation for the healee
In extreme cases, consider giving your healee a relaxation method on their first session (assuming you have appropriate insurance). The healee has probably had the condition for some time; and this has usually meant a build-up of stress and tension. Relaxation will help them considerably in their attempt to return to a natural and harmonious state of being.

c.   Loving your body parts

You may be surprised, not only at the relaxed feeling, but also at how good you feel about yourself with the following exercises.

Exercise 46 - Loving Your Body Parts
Become in tune with your toes and feet. Feel how they feel.
Then, as you breathe out, breathe pure LOve into them. Let it be total LOve, the LOve of God, unconditional LOve. Feel how different and LOved your feet become.
Move up to the ankles and repeat.
Repeat for the shins, knees, upper legs, hips and thighs, lower body, middle body, upper body, shoulders and neck, face and head.
Remember to give each body area that total unconditional LOve.

Exercise 47 - Down The Staircase
Imagine in front of you a flight of ten beautiful, non-slip stairs going down.
Each time you breathe out you descend a stair and are more relaxed.
Let tension go from you more and more on each step until, just before you reach the last step, you say to yourself that when you descend the last step, you are completely relaxed on all physical levels.

d.   When you or your healee are stressed

Practise physical relaxation each morning before getting up, and each night before going to sleep. Add a third session during the day

258

if you are having a difficult time. Or, perhaps use the techniques after arriving home from stressful work.

3. Mental Peace Through Meditation

Mental peace techniques are specially designed to create a peaceful state of mind. This is achieved by clearing the mind of unnecessary or unwanted thoughts. The healer will benefit because the mind will be less cluttered and concentration can be upon the reiki task in hand instead of thinking about trivia; and the healee will benefit because they will be less inclined to worry about their problems.

If you need mental peace, there are two main types of meditation.

a.   Eastern mental peace meditation
This type of meditation, in general, blanks the mind.

Exercise 48 - Candle Gazing
You may use a lighted candle, or the 'gazing' can be on a light that falls on any object.
Stare at the light without blinking for as long as possible.
See the differences that you would not have noticed normally - the shape(s) of light, the surrounding aura, and the various colours.
Become those differences!

Exercise 49 - Singular Focussing
Think of a single number, or letter, or shape.
Or one word such as 'PEACE' or 'CALM' or 'GOD' can be used.

Concentrate on that single image. Allow nothing else to enter your thoughts. Discover its deeper meaning.

b.   Western mental peace visualisation meditation

In general, this type of meditation creates a peace visualisation in the mind.

Exercise 50 - Sparkling Stream
Imagine you are standing beside a beautiful sparkling stream.
Crystal droplets of water splash gently.
The sun shines down, and you can feel its heat.
A rainbow forms over the stream.
The crystal droplets sparkle in the sun.
Allow the crystal droplets to enter you where you need healing the most.
Absorb the healing, refreshing atmosphere.

Exercise 51 - Floral Garden
Imagine a beautiful garden. See flowers in vivid colours.
Walk in the garden and reflect on its beauty.
Breathe in the peaceful and healing atmosphere.
Also, breathe in the colours of the flowers if they feel healing.
Be happy knowing you can visit this place for peace.

If You Find Self-Healing Difficult

As mentioned previously, most people have coughs, colds, flu, and other illnesses during their life. After all, we are human, and it is part of the chaos theory of life that we will catch 'bugs'. It is at these times that self-healing is most needed.

It is also at these times many practitioners find self-healing most difficult because, when we are ill, it is harder for reiki to flow freely, due to build-up of energy blocks within. It becomes more difficult to rise above our problem, illness, or mental attitude to channel positive reiki energy. So, if you become ill, and reiki flow seems difficult, go back to basics.

This process is also useful prior to treating others if you are unwell, or if you have a personal emotional crisis to deal with and rise above, or if you feel you are too emotionally involved with your healee and need to detach.

Exercise 52 - Combining Relaxation And Peace
Try different combinations of techniques in this chapter. Or one of many other different breathing, physical relaxation and mental peace techniques that are available. Or, try the 'Stress Management CD'.

Spend 10 minutes preparing prior to self-healing, i.e. about 3-4 minutes on breathing control, 3-4 minutes on physical relaxation, and another 3-4 minutes on creating peace of mind. If self-healing is done immediately after this 3-stage relaxation procedure, most practitioners find that reiki energy flows through adequately.

WORKBOOK NOTES
On Self-healing Needs And Overcoming Difficulties

CHAPTER 14

THE INTELLIGENT NATURE OF REIKI ENERGY

How Intelligent Is Healing Energy?

Reiki healing energies have intelligent capability. You will soon realise this when, one day, the energy finds its own way to a weak point in your or your healee's body. I have often found that the energy will travel to the site of an old injury that I was not near. Sometimes the healee has completely forgotten about the old injury, and it is only after deep thought, or even asking a relative, that the person remembers that he or she was, for example, in an accident as a child. It is wonderful that, via the intelligent nature of reiki energy, we can facilitate healing in this unsought-for way.

However, there is a philosophy that says reiki energy is so intelligent you have to do very little. All you have to do is put your hands on, and the right energy will flow through.

If this is so, why is it that so many healers have trouble healing low energy problems like chronic fatigue? Is it that reiki is inefficient in this type of issue? Or, do our assumptions about reiki prevent us from using it to better effect?

Because symbols have a bearing on healing results, this is discussed in a higher-level reiki manual. In the meanwhile, the following should be considered to ascertain the truth of these philosophies.

Stress Versus Low Energy

'To start healing from the head, or not to start healing from the head?' That is a good question!

1. Is Healing Energy Totally Intelligent?

A basic but much needed to be understood aspect of healing is to understand that if you start to heal at the head, and finish at the feet, it relaxes someone who is stressed - because your hands will collect and earth the negative stressed electrical charge.

Many healers feel this stressed energy being collected in the hands as they move down the healee, and then feel that stressed electrical charge being released into the ground as they touch the feet.

Certainly a stressed healee will feel more relaxed after this simple head-to-toe treatment.

But it does not mean the healer is brilliant. Relaxation comes from the simple act of starting at the head and finishing at the feet and grounding and earthing the stressed electrical charge. Relaxation is a natural effect of head-to-toe healing!

A two-year old child could do it. Ask a young child to put their hands on your head, and take all day to slowly move their hands to your feet. That will probably mean about two minutes!

After, you will feel relaxed.

But if you heal head-to-feet with someone who is very low in energy, e.g. chronic fatigue, or someone who is dying, you will not only earth and ground some of their stressed energy - you will also earth and ground some of the little energy they have left.

This is why most people whose worst problem is very low energy levels usually feel even worse lower energy levels after being healed head-to-feet! Whereas there can be excellent results and perhaps cures of low energy illnesses, simply by healing feet-to-head! See point 3 below.

265

So therefore the healing energy cannot be so totally intelligent that it always knows exactly what to do.

2. If The Worst Problem Is Stress

Stress must be grounded, so the following exercise, as many healers know, will help most healees feel relaxed after a treatment.

> **Exercise 53 - Healing Stress – Head Down**
> **If the worst problem is stress, start at the head and finish at the feet to collect, ground and earth the stressed energy. This relaxes.**
> **Try this on yourself. How does it feel?**

3. If The Worst Problem Is Lack Of Energy

This is not taught on most healing courses, and may be one reason why many healers find healing low energy problems difficult. Healers are often surprised at how simple it is to help low energy.

> **Exercise 54 - Healing Low Energy – Feet Up**
> **If the main problem is lack of energy in daily life, start at the feet and finish at the head. This draws into the body the lower earth frequency of 7.83 cycles per second. This energises.**
> **Try for yourself and see how it feels.**

4. If Someone Has Stress And Lack Of Energy

Some sad people have both severe stress, and very low energy. In this case, discover the worst problem. And then heal accordingly.

If in doubt, it may be best to give a standard head to feet healing.

You should normally be able to check the best approach from the replies you get from the healee on the section 'Simple Record Keeping Form' in chapter 19.

WORKBOOK NOTES
On The Intelligent Nature of Reiki Energy

CHAPTER 15

HUI YIN AND KANJI

The Hui Yin

The hui yin is used to increase your flow of reiki. Remember that for all reiki practitioners, reiki should run through you and from your hands, not from your major escape points of energy. Thus by connecting energy meridians, you should be able to allow a greater, smoother flow.

1. Two Main Acupuncture Meridians

a. Central channel
The central channel runs from the mouth (under the back of the tongue) down the middle front of the body, to the perineum (which is between the anus and the genitals).

b. Governing channel
This runs from the perineum up the middle back of the body, over the top of the head, and finishes on the top lip.

2. The Mouth

It should be remembered that the above two meridians do not automatically connect by the mouth, and that, of course, there is a hole from the mouth going deep into the body. Therefore, when reiki is brought from above the head and through towards the hands, there is potential for the energy to escape into or out of the mouth on each in or out breath. In other words, much of the reiki energy may not reach your healing hands, and consequently the reiki healing will not be so intense.

To prevent reiki escaping in that area, simply connect the two disconnected meridians by touching the tip of the tongue gently against the gum above the teeth just inside the top of the mouth.

3. The Hui Yin

The hui yin is found by the perineum, between the anus and the genitals, the base chakra – or, as one of my students once said very politely, 'Between the number one and the number two'!

Do you realise that our bodies contain about 600 hundred muscles, yet we only use less than 75? If we were to develop all 600, we could become extremely fit and almost superhuman![110] The hui yin point is one muscle that is usually weak and underused.

However, like all muscles, the muscle at the hui yin point can be developed through exercise. This knowledge is used in various ways. For example, ladies about to give birth do pelvic floor exercises. And Kegel exercises also involve contracting the perineum.

In healing terms, if the hui yin is not contracted, some healers find that much of their reiki energy escapes from that point instead of from their hands.

Exercise 55 - Developing The Hui Yin
The exercise consists of contracting the area between the anus and the genitals. Imagine that point and then tense or contract it. Do this 30 times twice a day. Do not move the

---

[110] Private conversation with Dr Meir Schneider, with permission. He is an internationally recognised expert in the field of body movement, and has helped over 30 people out of their wheelchairs.

**'front or back bits', only the hui yin. You will
soon develop the muscle.**

4. Result Of Connecting Your Mouth And Hui Yin

If the two major escape points at the mouth and hui yin are connected at the same time, it will create better reiki healing energy flow.

This is because energy will not be able to escape from the two connected points and will instead simply flow within you and around the meridians. Therefore the energy is more likely to flow out of your designated area, e.g. your healing hands.

To connect the two meridians into a circular energy system, tense the hui yin whilst simultaneously touching the top front part of the inside of the mouth with the tip of your tongue.

5. When To Connect Your Mouth And Hui Yin

You will find that there will be times when it is not necessary to connect the meridians, because it will seem as if reiki energy is flowing in a relevant way, adequately and forcefully. Indeed, when I first heard of the hui yin, I blindly thought, 'What a waste of time'. I had always had brilliant results without connecting the two points.

However, there will be times when the connections are much needed. Indeed, my poor guides have had to work hard teaching me lessons. Shortly after I thought the hui yin was a waste of time, I was trying to heal someone when it suddenly felt as if nothing was happening. The energy was so weak, it was as if it had stopped flowing – or was escaping somewhere else instead of from my hands. I asked my higher consciousness what to do and was told, 'Contract the hui yin, now'. Immediately it felt as if the mouth and hui yin gaps had been plugged. As reiki came through me from above, immense heat built up within me. The subsequent healing was incredibly quick.

Exercise 56 - Reiki With Hui Yin
If you feel you are losing energy, try to hold the position with the tongue touching the roof of the mouth behind the teeth, and also the hui yin position, throughout the reiki treatment. If the hui yin muscle is underused, this will not be easy to begin with, but muscle-building practise will gain you much in results.
Bring down reiki.
Feel the difference between normal reiki and hui yin reiki.

Many good healers connect the hui yin and mouth points naturally, without thinking about it. Often they are surprised to discover why they made these unconscious connections. But it is simply a form of body language that is normal and natural.

Only use the connections when needed. And like any new method, practise until it can be done comfortably.

Reiki Flows

Where A Meridian Goes

Reiki Kanji (Or Mudra) Hand Positions

Kanji, or mudra, are hand body language that are historical and appear in most cultures around the world. In Hinduism and Buddhism there are many kinds of hand mudras, for example to help a being to be happy, to heal food, or to pacify Gods. Certain forms of karate have 10 kanji hand positions to help before a fight, and in South India, temple dancers use dancing mudras. The next time you watch television or a film, you may see scenes where directors ensure actors use kanji for unconscious effects on the viewer - business meetings often show a powerful board director in the kanji 1 hand position for extra power.

1. Unconscious Kanji

We all use kanji unconsciously. After reading the kanji 1, 2, and 3 positions, become aware of how people you talk with naturally go into those hand positions.

So for example, if someone goes into kanji 1 as you talk, they are unconsciously asking for extra power to be with you and whatever you are talking about. This is good.

And if someone goes into kanji 3 for extra understanding, perhaps they do not know what you are talking about! Maybe this is not good, and you will need to discover what they do not understand!

2. Kanji Meditation For Focussing The Mind

Meditate on a kanji to help focus your mind on the healing task. This in turn helps to centre and ground, and to receive help, guidance or answers from your higher self or spirit guides.

3. Seven Combinations Of Reiki Kanji / Mudra

Kanji can be used one at a time, or as a combination. So it is possible to use, for example, kanji 1 and 3 together, kanji 2 and 3 together, kanji 1 and 2 together, or all three together. See the photographs below.

There are seven different standard reiki kanji / mudra hand positions, including single and combination.

You may also recognise that if all fingers and thumbs are together in the prayer position, then all energy levels of kanji are being achieved at the same time.

Whilst on the surface this may seem like a simplified ideal, it is actually better to focus on the energy you need, and only use the relevant kanji to obtain the desired result.

Later in this section, non-standard positions are described.

4. When And How To Use Kanji

Be creative with kanji. Try to bring the energies of kanji into your life when talking with others, or thinking by yourself.

Exercise 57 - Using Kanji
Before each treatment, whilst at the head of the person if they are lying down, or from behind the person if they are sitting, take up one, or a combination, of the kanji positions to help each healing become more relevant.

Hold the hand position at your hara point, which is just below the navel.

This is the pivot point of your body's energy.

Contemplate why you chose this position, for about 30 seconds.

Also use for self-healing, before distant healing (after the Reiki 2 class), or other moments when the

273

energy purpose of one of the kanji positions could help you.
Experiment with different kanji as you heal or talk. See how they feel.

5.   Reiki Kanji 1 / Mudra 1 - For Extra Power

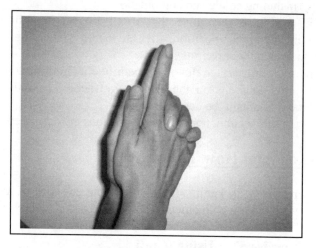

Figure 20:   Kanji 1

a.   Use
Kanji I brings in energy more powerfully. If you feel your healing needs extra power, or your communication, an energy frequency, or whatever needs extra power, please choose kanji 1.

b.   Position
Put the index fingers together with the fingertips touching, and interweave remaining fingers and thumbs on the outside of each hand.

c.   Warning
When healing, remember that many conditions need less power, not more.

274

Rather like homeopathy, the practitioner will give more or less energy to find the right dose for the right result.

This is explained in much depth in the Reiki 2 Manual. For now, if in doubt whether to use extra power or less power, please use either kanji 2 or kanji 3.

6. Reiki Kanji 2 / Mudra 2 - Extra Help From 'Above'

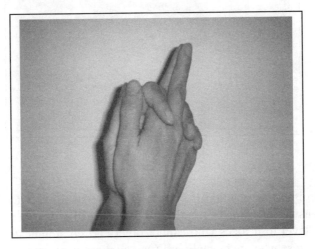

Figure 21: Kanji 2

a. Use

Asks for help from whatever you believe may help, like your higher consciousness, guides, masters, angels, your God.

It also helps spirits come much nearer. If you are a channeller, this could improve the quality of your connections to the masters, etc.

b. Position

Put your middle fingers together, and then interweave the remaining fingers and the thumbs on the outside of each hand.

7. Reiki Kanji 3 / Mudra 3 - For Extra Understanding

Figure 22:   Kanji 3

a.   Use

Go into this position if you do not understand what to do. This helps answer questions. Also use it if you need to speak on a silent mental level to healees who cannot otherwise communicate, such as babies, those who are mentally infirm, and those in a coma.

b.   Position

Your fingers should interweave, and face down towards your palms.

If you have asked a question silently, wait patiently for the answer.

Accept the first answer that comes, even if it is surprising. This is assuming you are not depressed because then you may receive a negative answer from your lower consciousness. And also assuming you do not have schizophrenia, when the answer could be incorrect due to inappropriate brain-chemical interaction.

8. Kanji Combinations

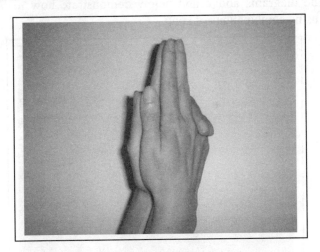

Figure 23:   Combination Of Kanji 1 & 2

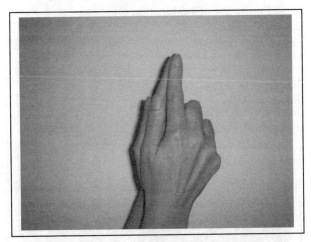

Figure 24:   Combination Of Kanji 1 & 3

a.   Common kanji combinations

The diagrams above and below demonstrate how to hold the hands using combinations of kanji.

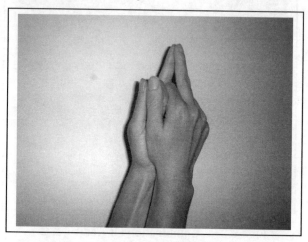

Figure 25:   Combination Of Kanji 2 & 3

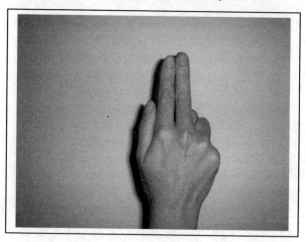

Figure 26:   Combination Of Kanji 1, 2 & 3

b.   Be guided

Do not use the same position automatically every session. Feel what is needed for each patient and each treatment.

9.   The Thumbs

Many students ask what to do with the thumbs. Twiddling is not the answer! Rather, the question is whether the thumbs should touch each other, or cross over each other. And if they cross over, should the right or the left thumb be on top?

a.   Touching thumbs

Thumbs should touch each other if you need greater connection to the oneness of all, and the universal God energy. Use this for greater awareness on all levels of being. As connection, oneness, and awareness are normally needed in reiki, the diagrams all show touching thumbs.

b.   Crossed thumbs

This is not easy to explain. The simple answer is to do what comes naturally and unconsciously.

The complicated answer is that, with crossed-over thumbs, the thumb on top should be on the hand from which the energy naturally flows in – but only if the kanji hand position is being used for a self-healing need.

Conversely, if the sessional need is for healing others, the thumb on top should be on the hand from which energy naturally flows out.

This complicated answer becomes more complicated when you realise that scientific studies as to which hand naturally has energy flowing in or out show different results.

Some studies suggest that the left hand flows energy in and the right hand flows energy out.

Other studies say the opposite.

This is complicated more with studies that conflict on whether energy flows in or out of the physically dominant hand (Benor v2).

So, unless you are certain which hand is your natural energy out flow, let the thumbs do what comes naturally and unconsciously.

10. The Ring Fingers (Next To Little Fingers)

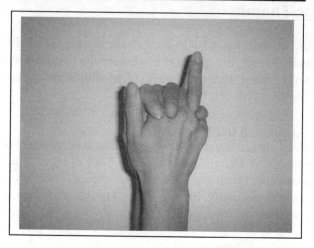

Figure 27: Ring Finger Kanji

a. Use

Plus energy flows on one side of the body, minus energy on the other.   Touching ring fingers connects these life forces.   Press together for 30 seconds. Breathe deeply. Feel energy flowing in your body.

11. The Little Fingers

a. Use

Connecting little fingers connects to knowledge. Use this position to access knowledge of anything, including from the Akashic Records (the universe's library of all that was, is, and will be).

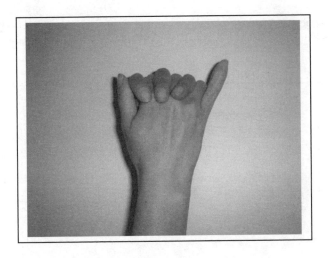

Figure 28: Little Finger Kanji

b.   Position
Place the little fingers together and interweave the remaining fingers and thumbs over the back of each hand.

12. Kanji For A Japanese Priest

a.   Use
On courses in the mid-1990s I unconsciously went into a certain combination kanji hand position, not realising why until one day a student explained. She said that many pictures of Japanese priests portray them in this particular kanji hand position to help them prayerfully have extra oneness, power, understanding, and knowledge.

b.   Position
Interlock middle and third fingers facing down towards the palms. Raise little and fore fingers up to touch the same finger on each hand. Touch the tips of the thumbs together.

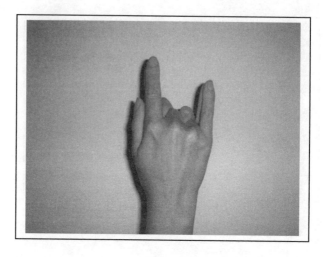

Figure 29: Kanji For Japanese Priests

13. Children's 'Reiki' Kanji

In many countries there is a rhyme learned during the school years, and seemingly passed through the ages.

'There's the church and there's the steeple. Open the doors and there's the people!'

This rhyme is chanted at the same time as children go into kanji 1 (the church), then kanji 2 the (steeple), and then, as they go into kanji 3, they wiggle their interlocked downward-facing fingers (the people).

Perhaps many centuries ago it was understood that this game would help children have the three main kanji energies, now used in reiki, of extra power, extra help from above, and extra understanding.

WORKBOOK NOTES
On Hui Yin And Kanji

CHAPTER 16

PROTECTION AND GROUNDING

Protection

1. Origins Of Protection – Spiritualist Healing

Modern-day theories about protection started in the spiritualist healing movement. Spiritualist healers open themselves up to spirit forces, and allow the energy body of the spirit guide to enter their physical body. This carries dangers such as opening up to other not-so-nice spirits, and the spirit that enters them not being willing to leave.

So spiritualist-healing groups developed various ways to protect against unwanted spirit intrusions or possessions. These included placing a cross on each major chakra, creating a circle of white or gold, or other coloured light around the healer, and saying various prayers before or after the healing.

2. Is Protection Necessary In Reiki?

Reiki does not allow spirit guides to enter in the same way as spiritualists. If guides are part of a reiki healing process, it is normally from outside the healer, almost never inside. Instead of guides working inside the healer, reiki practitioners use rei or ki energies. So protection is therefore almost never needed.

Rei is God, LOve, or spiritual energy. In Reiki 1, many healers believe that, if you bring healing energy direct from the highest source, protection is not necessary. Because if the source is highest universal energy, God's highest power, how can anything go wrong? It should not be necessary to protect against the LOve of God!

Ki is low frequency energy. And if Reiki 2 ki symbol energies are simply low frequencies in the same vein as a low frequency colour or a sound, why should it be needed to protect against a colour, sound or symbol?

3. Is Protection Needed From Others' Negative Energy?

One theory is that many people do not use total God-power or total spiritual energy, but their own energies. This has various 'kick-backs'. For example, if spiritual energy does not flow completely from above the healer's head, through the body, and then out of the hands to the healee, 'space' may be left for the healee's negative energies to flow back into the healer. So some healers would 'pick up' a healee's pain or emotion.

> ### Exercise 58 - Pre-Healing Fill-Up
> **Before your healee arrives, and certainly before starting your reiki session, ensure that you bring reiki energy from outside you, down through the crown, to pervade your body.**
> **Because weaknesses in your energy body are more likely to be filled up by using this technique, it will be more difficult for other unwanted energies to get in.**

4. A Simple Protection Method

Assuming healers only use rei or ki as stated above, protection in reiki is normally not needed. But many healers feel comfortable with some type of protection, so here is a simple rei protection method. The nearest colour to the highest spiritual rei energy is gold, so for compatibility with the spiritual rei healing, gold should be used as the protection method.

Exercise 59 - The Golden Cloak
Imagine a golden light, representational of God-LOve, completely filling your physical body.
Visualise your aura. Fill it with golden LOve.
Repeat before, during and after a treatment, or as often as necessary.

5. Potential Healing Conflict Of Gold Protection

Gold protection is probably ideal if using rei because rei and gold are similar energies. However, if this protection is used during a Reiki 2 low frequency healing, the high gold and low ki energies could contradict or fight each other, and a pure healing may not be possible. Similarly other protection colours like a 'violet flame' may conflict with a rei or different frequencies (a frequency is a colour) being channelled. Because on Reiki 2, healers have a choice of different energies, the Reiki 2 Manual gives a fuller explanation of clashing energies.

Grounding

1. Origins Of Grounding – Spiritual Healing

During rei or spiritual healing, healers' energies may be taken extremely high up in the frequency range. Whilst this is not a problem for most healers because the majority can automatically adjust quickly to high or low frequency energies, some healers stay too high for too long or cannot cope with the sudden rush of a God-LOve force. They may then feel light-headed, spaced-out, or reluctant to return. Or, when they do return, they feel sad, lonely, or depressed because they are away from God-LOve beauty.

This type of person needs a customised grounding process after a reiki healing session. For extreme cases, the customised grounding process can be used before the healing starts.

2. Is Grounding Necessary In Reiki?

a. Rei
See point 1 above for guidelines.

b. Ki
Grounding may sometimes be needed when using rei, but almost certainly not when using ki. Grounding is unlikely to be needed with Reiki 2 ki energies because they are already low frequency grounded energies, so should automatically ground the healer!

c. Biofeedback
Remember chapter 9 on '*Biofeedback*', that light-headedness and dizziness can occur in the healer or healee when an energy is received in a large 'dosage' that they have been low in for a long time. Remember that grounding is not needed here because it is not a grounding issue - simply allow half an hour of time for the large dose

287

of needed energy to be integrated into the energy system of the person and then a wonderful healing should occur.

Do not 'ground' this type of light-headedness, as grounding will take away and destroy the natural healing process.

3. Why You Should Customise Your Grounding

Few people's energy bodies are static, inflexible forces. So, if grounding is a need, spiritual healers probably need different grounding strengths on different days, depending on whether they are on a higher spiritual frequency, or a lower grounding frequency that day.

4. How To Customise Your Grounding

So, there must be a process to facilitate different grounding strengths on each healing occasion.

Using this technique, you may find certain grounding processes are sometimes totally inappropriate! For example, too much grounding, and you could feel so heavy, and your energies so low down into the earth, that, if you use grounding before a treatment, it becomes almost impossible for high frequency rei spiritual healing to flow through.

> ### Exercise 60 - Customised Grounding
> **Imagine your feet growing roots. The roots grow from beneath your feet to within the earth.**
>
> **Then ask the following three questions, and allow your energy body to project down into the earth. Through the differences, feel your need at that moment on that day.**
>
> **How deep?**

Feel how long the roots should be to effect a perfect grounding for you.
How thick?
Feel how thick the roots should be for perfect grounding for you at that moment.
What material?
Feel if the roots should be made of wood, metal, rope, or a material appropriate to your need.
Use a combination of deepness, thickness and material to project from beneath the feet, the exact grounding you need at that moment.

5.   Grounding During A Treatment

Unless needed, do not use the grounding method above during a treatment, as it may bring down the frequency of rei so much that it will not be rei energy any more, but some other lower frequency. However, do ensure that both feet touch the floor at all times.

Preferably, if you have a grounding problem, ensure that the healee also has both feet on the floor.

6.   Grounding Options After A Treatment

During self-healing, you will have been bringing the rei spiritual energy though your crown and into you – when healing others, the energy continues on its path to the healee. You will have been filled up with this wonderful healing force, and are therefore likely to receive a healing. Remembering that it takes at least half an hour for the majority of energy to integrate into your energetic systems, if you ground yourself immediately after the treatment, it could have the effect of 'pulling the plug out' and grounding – or draining – the healing energy before it has had time to work properly.

Only ground after a treatment if you feel it is needed. If it is, there are many options – find your own. The essential part of the process is to find something that will 'bring you down to earth' instead of being too high in the clouds of God-beauty.

Exercise 61 - Physical Post-Healing Grounding
As physical grounding is more needed by more healers, here are six options. Find the one most appropriate for you – or your own method.
a. Do grounding processes as in exercise 55
b. Take very deep breaths in and out
c. Think of your 5 senses, for a few minutes each
d. Have a very hot or very cold drink
e. Do a few press-ups or other exercises
f. Take a brisk walk

Exercise 62 - Emotional Post-Healing Grounding
Chat about mundane earthly emotional matters e.g. phone a friend and chat about relationships.

Exercise 63 - Mental Post-Healing Grounding
Watch TV (not a high frequency spiritual programme!)

Exercise 64 - Spiritual Post-Healing Grounding
For a few minutes each, imagine your energy field as first as gold, then as silver, then white, then slowly down through the rainbow colours of violet, indigo, blue, green, yellow, orange

and red. Only go down to the colour that helps you return to a 'normal' feeling. Any further down could again push you off-balance compared to your normal energy body needs.

Exercise 65 - All-Time Favourite Post-Healing Grounding
Eat Chocolate!

WORKBOOK NOTES
On Protection And Grounding

CHAPTER 17

PASSIVE AND ACTIVE REIKI 1 METHODS

Passive v Active Reiki I Methods

As in any profession, start from basics. A doctor in the first year at college would not be taught brain surgery! Instead, the medical curriculum would present basic knowledge from which the doctor could progress. Eventually the doctor would discover which branch of medicine he or she is good at or enjoys the most.

In reiki, as in any other profession, you must start from basics. Although reiki may take you down many potentially diverse healing, psychic or spiritual paths, it is the basics that will act as your springboard for future success.

For beginner reiki students, there are two basic methods of healing to choose from. The Passive Method, or the Active Method. Both should allow free flow of rei energy, which is the higher universal or God energy – the equivalent to spiritual healing.

Note that after Reiki 2, you will not only be able to channel the spiritual rei healing learned on Reiki 1, but also ki healing.

As with all matters in life, there are many sides of everything that may need to be considered. Before embarking on a definite healing method, please read the following and decide whether the passive or active method is for you.

Many healers find that the passive method is more appropriate to their personal needs and preference. Others discover that the active method is more appropriate for them because of aspects of how their being was made by their God. Most healers find the active method easier and more relevant in most ways.

About The Passive Method: Alpha Healing

When using the passive method of reiki, you will think of, or imagine, as little as possible. This allows the energy to flow in the most natural way.

1. Reiki As A Passive Method Of Learning Healing

Reiki is natural energy. If beginners need to learn the nature of this natural energy, they should be passive and allow reiki to flow naturally.

This is an excellent learning curve. In passive healing, you will discover the roots and heights of healing energy forces. And eventually you will begin to learn the fundamental principles of reiki flow, including your potential for magnetism. (See below *'Dangers Of Passive Healing For Beginners'.*)

2. Alpha Brain Waves

Alpha is the natural brain rhythm for passive healing. It is also the natural brain rhythm that you are in just before you go to sleep, or just after you have woken up.

This is why those two times of the day are best to do passive self-healing – you are naturally in the brain-wave pattern to allow The Passive Method of healing, and you should, after some practice, get easier or quicker results.

To allow alpha brain waves at other times of the day, relax or go into meditation for a few minutes before your reiki treatment.

Let no adverse thought enter your mind in this preparation time – peace is essential.

295

If you are stressed or ill, pre-treatment mental peace may be essential to allow the brain to be in alpha wave band and to allow the energy to be more likely to flow as needed.

See section '*Mental Peace Through Meditation*' in chapter 13 if necessary.

> **Exercise 66 - Alpha Techniques**
> **Relax with your favourite method – hot bath, sauna, cuddles, read a comforting book, yoga, walk in nature, meditate, pray, or whatever puts your mind into the type of state it is in before sleep.**
> **In studies in the 1960s, it was discovered that the most likely music to put someone's brain into alpha rhythm is Mozart or baroque; however, a teenager may prefer the latest music-style's hit record.**
> **Feel which technique is most likely to make you feel in that part-sleep, part-waking state.**

3. Eradicate Egotistical Attachments To Outcome

If you desire an outcome in passive healing, your brain wave pattern will probably not be in the alpha mode. This means that the intelligence of the energy may be impeded in its natural flow.

Nothing should matter. Whether you or the healee recovers or not should be irrelevant. In passive healing, the sole aim is that reiki energy flows freely through you to where you or the healee needs it.

4. For Beginners: Trust Energy Goes Where Needed

As stated in chapter 14, '*The Intelligent Nature Of Reiki Energy*', the healing energy is not always so intelligent that it knows exactly where to go under all circumstances. (See exercises in that section to prove to your self this point.)

However, it is important that beginners begin to feel energy (if they can) and hence begin to understand energy. After some time you will notice that the energy sometimes has an innate intelligence. It can sometimes find its way to an area in need, for example an old injury site that your self-healing did not go near.

On other courses you will learn different aspects to this, for example that energy may flow in a way that the healee does not need in order to obtain a good result, and that you should therefore take action for the highest good of all concerned. Passive healing practice will help your eventful and eventual understanding.

Remember that a doctor must start somewhere with his training. So must you. Trust in your passive healing method.

5. Dangers Of Passive Healing For Beginners

a. Magnetic healers

To give beginners time to understand their magnetic nature, this is covered in depth in the chapter, '*Electrical And Magnetic Beings,*' in the Reiki 2 Manual. If the energy body of the beginner healer is less electric and much more on the magnetic scale, there is a chance that the healer will unknowingly magnetically attract 'bad' energy from the healee.

A beginner magnetic healer may be unaware that good energy is not flowing from the hands, but that bad energy is flowing in. It is the beginner's lack of experience and lack of ability to discern energy flow that is the danger.

Left unchecked, the beginner healer could take on much negative energy and eventually become ill.

For this reason, I prefer beginner healers to use the active method.

The following technique is excellent for helping you understand your energy body – an essential part of reiki if you are to stay healthy.

Exercise 67 - Preparing For Magnetic Attraction

Just before you meet a friend or family member, become aware of your body. How do you feel? Where are the hot, cold, electrical tingling areas?

This allows you to understand when someone else's energy comes into you.

Exercise 68 - Feeling Emotional Magnetic Attraction

Can you feel an emotion within you? If so, what does the emotion feel like? Ask if your friend has that emotion in the area where you feel it.

Exercise 69 - Feeling Physical Magnetic Attraction

Whilst with someone with a physical pain, feel your body. Can you feel a pain in the same area in you as their problem? If so, ask if your friend has a pain in the exact spot as you feel it.

If friends regularly confirm that you are magnetically picking up their pains and emotions, please only do the active method. However, if you progress to Reiki 2, there will

be coping strategies in the chapter, *'Electrical And Magnetic Beings'.*

b.   Professional responsibility for actions and results

Another danger in the passive method is that some healers may believe so passionately that the energy does not come from them, they take no responsibility for their actions or for the results. If reiki healing is to become accepted by the governments and medical establishments, healers must accept that they are either allowing (passive method) or creating (active method) the healing energy flow, and then take professional responsibility for their actions and results.

About The Active Method: Fast Beta Healing

    I prefer this method of healing for the average beginner because of the dangers as noted above.

    When using the active method of reiki, you will think of, or imagine a visualisation to allow the brainwave pattern to be in fast beta.

1. If You Are Unwell, Need A Kick Start, Or If Your Mind Wanders Too Much

    The active method is usually needed for a beginner who needs a 'kick-start', or a healer who cannot achieve alpha brain wave passive healing due to being too stressed or ill.

    Also some students who are unfocused, or who find it hard to use the passive method, may find the visualised active healing process easier.

2. Fast Beta Brain Waves

    In the active healing method, the brain wave pattern of the healer is likely to be in fast beta.

    Once Reiki 1 basics have been practised and understood, on higher-level classes various techniques are taught based on fast beta active healing to essentially create a flow of energy by the creative use of mind.

    The method is used outside reiki by other healing organisations, for example the healing method used by USA nurses, Therapeutic Touch. But reiki attunements usually make reiki even better!

3. Are You A Magnetic Healer?

If you are with a person who is sad, do you feel sadness as well? Or other emotions or pains of people? If so, it is essential that you use this active method reiki to prevent you magnetically attracting and allowing the bad energy to flow in the hands and up the arms.

Therefore it is a priority for magnetic healers to master an active method of healing that will only allow a one-way flow of good energy to leave the hands.

4. Dangers Of Active Healing For Beginners

The main danger is ego. If the beginner healer starts to think that he or she is the creator of the energy flow, huge egos can result. Ego then becomes a danger to the personal growth of that person - and also a danger to how they interact with friends, family and healees.

To overcome this potential problem, simply accept that this is a reiki method that needs to be learned and mastered. As with most things, accept that there will be a long learning curve.

Using The Passive Or Active Method

Before choosing one of the following two options for your self-healing, please read thoroughly the previous two sections about passive and active healing. If you are a beginner healer, it is probably better to choose the active method.

1. The Passive Method

This philosophy suggests that, after you have had the attunements in the reiki class, most people are more able to passively and unconsciously allow a reiki flow. Part of the attunement process adjusts your crown chakra, central channels and palm chakras. This allows highest universal energy to flow through you.

> **Exercise 70 - The Passive Healing Method**
> **In the passive method of healing, you simply release your thoughts, and go through the reiki hand positions. Reiki healing is supposed to flow naturally through your crown, through the head, down the shoulders, down the arms, out of the hands and into the person you are healing.**

2. The Active Method

There are many ways to pour down the white light through the crown – seek the way that works for you, even if you see nothing, and simply have to have the intention of flowing white light.

Be creative if necessary!

Once you find a method that suits you, reiki healing should flow actively through the crown, through the head, down the shoulders, out of the hands and into the hand position.

Exercise 71 - The Active Healing Method

Imagine that above your head there is a beautiful, bright white light. Maybe you can see the white light exactly, as if in a painting or a video. Maybe you see white light as if through a mist or a haze. Or maybe you cannot see the white light at all - you just have an intention, or an inner understanding, or *know* that it is above the head.

Then simply find a way to allow that white light to come down from above. For example, some students see a large tube or straw attached to the head going up to bright white light, and then see white energy poured down the tube by a jug or a hand or an angel. Others see it as a white cloud descending to the crown and entering the head. Find your creative beta-brained way to allow white light to flow readily.

What Should Healers Say? 'It's Not Me' OR 'I Am Only The Channel' OR 'It's Me'

These three phrases are often heard in the healing movement. But how did they originate? What is their literal meaning? And how do they apply to reiki?

1. 'It's Not Me' – Spiritualist Healing

a. Origin – spiritualist healing with guides

This phrase started in the English spiritualist healing movement. In spiritualism, the etheric body of the spirit guide or spirit doctor enters the physical body of the healer. Once inside the healer, the ectoplasmic force of the spirit guide begins to work. (Ectoplasm is the material the spirit consists of.) It works its way through to and out of the hands of the healer, into the body of the healee.

Thus, because the spirit beings do the work, spiritualist healers say 'It's not me.'

b. Does this apply to reiki?

The simple answer is 'No.'

In reiki, we may have our reiki guides helping our healing sessions. However, these guides normally stand back and help in various ways from a distance. The closest reiki spirit guides may come to the healee is when, separate from the healer, they put their hands on an area that they know needs reiki. Often, the healee will then say afterwards that they felt as if another pair of hands was there. But the reiki practitioner was still doing his or her own healing work.

This is very, very different to spiritualist healing where the ectoplasm of the spirit guide enters the healer's physical body.

Therefore although spiritualist healers can truly say 'It's not me,' this aspect of guides does not apply to reiki.

N.B. It should be noted that there might be the occasional reiki practitioner who suddenly has spirit guides entering in the way described above.

If this is the case – and do not confuse this with the natural reiki energy flow – then the practitioner should find an organisation to help their understanding and practice of spiritualist healing.

Then of course they will be able to say 'It's not me', because the spirit guide will be doing all the work.

2. 'I Am Only The Channel' – Rei And Spiritual Healing

a.   Origin – spiritual healing with LOve

The phrase 'I am only a channel' started in the spiritual healing movement. The objective is for spiritual healers to release their own normal consciousness and raise themselves higher towards the highest spiritual or God-type LOve energy.   In effect they then become 'only a channel' for the high LOve force.

b.   Does this apply to reiki?

Yes.   Although strictly speaking, it does not apply to reiki, it applies only to rei.   On Reiki 1, practitioners learn to bring through rei, the highest spiritual energy of LOve.   When using rei energy, reiki healers can say 'I am only a channel.'

However, on Reiki 2, the conscious choice and flow of a particular ki energy creates the low frequency healing.   The reiki healer must control this to ensure the correct ki energy flows out. Therefore the Reiki 2 practitioner using ki is much more than 'only a channel.'

3. 'It's Me' – Ki And Technique Healing

To elaborate, with Reiki 2 healing, practitioners have a choice of different energies and techniques to use on each healing occasion. Attunements can help healers channel energy, but it is the conscious choice that makes it possible for reiki healers to say 'It's me.' Unless the right energy or technique is deliberately chosen and used, there may be less chance of a successful healing.

a.   Different reiki energies

Practitioners have extra energies to choose from on the Reiki 2 level, so many pages are devoted to this topic in the Reiki 2 Manual.

For example, it can be proved scientifically, energetically, and clairvoyantly, that the healer must focus on the energy symbol for physical healing, or the one for mental or emotional healing, or whatever other reiki symbol.

If not, there will almost certainly be a different energy flow, and it may not be the best for healing. Because this is more a topic for Reiki 2, exercises are given in the Reiki 2 Manual to prove this.

So healers must first choose an energy, then focus to use it. The reiki healer will ultimately be able to say 'It's me' doing the work.

b.   Different reiki techniques

Dr Usui taught many techniques to try to effect quicker healings. It is the conscious choice and skill in application that makes the reiki practitioner able to say 'It's me' getting the results.

c.   Responsibility

Because of a. and b. above, Reiki 2 and above healers eventually need to own up to their responsibilities for outcomes.

On the Reiki 1 level, you will be saying 'I am only a channel', at the same time as trying to release yourself to highest LOve energy.

4.   Eventual Healing Mastership

The ultimate goal for healers is that all three above options are automatic, without conscious thought or effort, for any need.

However, this can only be achieved after much practice. It is only practice, practice, practice that will programme the mind to understand unconsciously the energy need at any moment.

WORKBOOK NOTES
On Passive And Active Methods
Reiki 1 Methods

CHAPTER 18

HEALER HAND AND
HEALEE BODY POSITIONS

Ways To Hold The Hands for Healing

Hand positions are important – so is how to hold the hands. All can be touch or non-touch methods.

1. The 'Normal' Way

Hold hands flat and palm downwards, adjacent to each other, as you move through the hand positions. Keep fingers together to focus the energy into where you need it.

2. Thumbs

Thumbs are worthy of special attention because, during healing, beginners – and even some 'experts' – have a great habit of sticking their thumbs out at a different angle to the fingers.

Reiki energy may come from palm, thumb/fingertips, or between the fingers/thumbs. If energy comes from thumb/fingertips, reiki becomes concentrated where the fingertips of the healer touches the body.

If the thumbs stick out, the energy from the thumbs will almost certainly shoot off in a different direction to the rest of the fingers. Whilst this is not a drastic problem if the issue to be healed is an all-over disease, if the problem is localised, reiki energy will be more strongly concentrated into the needed area if the thumbs are kept adjacent to the forefingers.

3. The Reiki Hand Stack

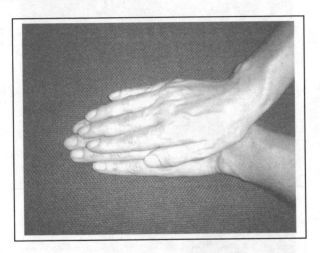

Figure 30: Reiki Hand Stack

Hand–sized healing areas on the healee need hand-sized reiki entering them!

For example, if your hands were placed side by side on a fractured or broken bone or an arthritic joint, the energy from your hands may be too widely spread to be able to concentrate the energy to the problem area. Therefore the energy becomes unfocused, and diluted into areas that do not need reiki. This means that it can take longer to heal the needed area.

To provide a more appropriate and greater concentration of reiki in an area of need about the size of one of your hands, simply place one hand on top of the other in a Reiki Hand Stack. Pour reiki through.

Don't waste reiki. Concentrate it to where it is needed.

4. Reiki Laser Coning

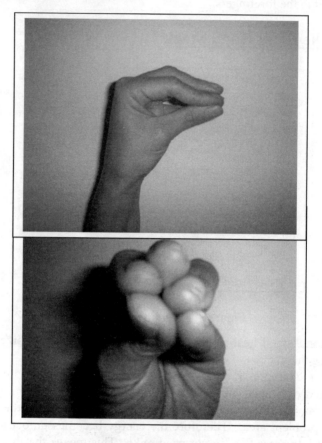

Figure 31: Laser Coning Hand Position, Side And Front Views

Reiki Laser Coning is used when the healing area is very small, such as a pinpointed pain.

Hold the thumb and fingertips of one hand together, so that all tips touch each other. This will allow reiki to be channelled from the palm chakras, and from between the fingers, and from the fingertips, as a laser beam into the pinpointed need.

5. The Reiki Spread

Figure 32: Reiki Spread

If in a rush, without enough time for a full reiki treatment, use The Reiki Spread for 30 seconds to one minute in each hand position.

In each position, spread fingers and thumbs as wide as possible. This spreads reiki from each finger and thumb into a very wide area.

The healing will almost certainly not be as intense as one of the above methods, but at least it is better than nothing!

Exercise 72 - Handy Experiments
When self-healing, try holding the hands in different ways. Assuming as a beginner you can feel energy, feel the differences.

The Basic Twelve Hand Positions For Self-Healing And For Healing Others

1. The Traditional Twelve Hand Positions

The following are the standard traditional hand positions as taught in Japan by the Iyashi No Gendai Reiki-ho, the modern Japanese reiki method for healing. Each position has a letter and a number so that biofeedback in each position can be recorded after the treatment.

They are reputed to be original Dr Usui hand positions, and allow for a reiki treatment to be a 'can't miss' system – all major glands, body parts and organs will automatically receive healing.

However, most students find that their greatest healing needs are in the head and/or the body, so they concentrate effort and time mainly in those two areas. The head often needs more healing due to such balancing needs as the hearing, third eye, unconscious mind, eyesight, neural pathways, and interactive brain chemicals. The body often needs more reiki due to the healing needs of major internal organs such as the heart, lungs, liver, kidneys, stomach, bladder, and intestines. Arms and legs usually need least energy, and unless there is a problem are not normally healed on every session. Heal the arms and legs regularly if you have time, or when needed.

If it is difficult for you to reach your back, use intention to send the energy from the front to the needed area in the spine or back. Reiki will enter the chakra system at the front and travel to the back. Many clairsentients can feel this.

The Head

H1. Full on face
H2. Sides of head
H3. Back of head
H4. Front of neck

Front Of Body

F1. Above the chest
F2. Below chest
F3. Either side of navel
F4. Below navel

Back

B1. Shoulders
B2. High up on rib cage
B3. Lower back
B4. Base of spine

Arms

A1. Shoulders
A2. Elbows
A3. Wrists
A4. Hands

Legs

L1. Hips
L2. Knees
L3. Ankles
L4. Feet

2. If You Cannot Reach A Particular Hand Position

Some people have constricted movement in their arms. For example, someone with bad arthritis in the arms and shoulders may not be able to move their hands far enough to heal the head or the back or the feet.

In this case, energy can be sent through from one side of the body to the other. Or it can be sent up to the head, or down to the legs or feet. As most reiki classes teach this as a Reiki 2 technique, please see the chapter on '*Beaming*' in the Reiki 2 Manual.

3. If Some Positions Strain Your Arms

Assuming you are physically healthy, you may not be able to stay in some positions for long if you have not done your press-ups for a long time! Your arms may ache…

Some students, even if they have done regular keep-fit exercises, find that healing causes arm ache because it uses different muscles. Go through the slight pain barrier - it does not take long to tone the muscles.

Exercise 73 - Hand Position Practice
Before starting self-healing, go through the various hand positions until you can remember them by heart. Then, when you are in the healing mode, you will not need to think about what position comes next, and be in danger of changing your brainwave pattern away from the needed alpha or fast beta.

Healee Body Positions
On A Chair Or A Healing Couch

Whereas self-healing is normally done lying down, healers have individual preference as to whether they feel it best to heal other people on a chair or on a healing couch. Personally, I have always preferred chairs, because there are fewer dangers and more benefits. If you learn how to heal on a chair, you can heal almost anywhere in the world. However, some healees prefer a chair, and others prefer a couch. Choose the option that is mutually comfortable for you and your healee.

1. Healing On A Chair

The sitting position needed for healing is often called 'The Egyptian Position', because ancient scrolls, parchments and drawings portray a Pharaoh sitting peacefully upright as in the following.

a. The healee's position

i. The legs and arms of the healee should be uncrossed. This is because down one side of the body there is plus energy, and down the other side there is minus energy. If the arms or legs were crossed, this would result in crossed energies and there would not be such a good flow of healing energy. It is far better to ensure that the rei energy has a chance to flow unimpeded to heal the plus and minus sides of the body.

ii. The feet of the healee should be flat on the floor. The high frequency rei energy is then less likely to create light-headedness, because there would more likely be an automatic positive grounding effect. Please see section on *'Grounding'* in chapter 16.

iii. If the legs of the healee are too short for the feet to reach the floor, place a cushion either under their feet or behind their lower back.

iv. Hands should be placed one on each leg. (On their own leg! A beginner student on a course once misunderstood...) This allows the flow as in 1.a.i. above.

v. Hands should not be near the knees as this stretches the arms out too far and puts tension into the upper parts of the arms, shoulders and body. Stressed persons often place their hands near the knees and create even more stress and tension.

vi. Instead, the hands on the legs should be closer towards the body. This relaxes much more.

Practise placing your hands near your knees and then closer to your body and feel the difference.

vii. Base of spine should be against the back of the chair. This puts the back upright and the head and neck are likely to be in line with the spine.

This creates a more positive flow of healing energy.

Zen Buddhism teaches that this type of straight back will allow energy to be channelled through the being to create enlightenment.

viii. Eyes of the healee should be closed so as to passively perceive biofeedback responses instead of looking around the room actively and creating a different, perhaps blocking, energy through thought.

ix. However, if the healee has a phobia about having the eyes closed, do let them have their eyes open, as experience of the phobia would be an even worse blocking energy.

b. Advantages

Once practised, you can heal almost anywhere in the world. Hotels, bars, shops and restaurants etc. all have chairs you could use when someone is in need. (And if you heal there, you may well get free food and drinks!) Other advantages are:

i.   If you are short and your healee is tall, chairs enable almost everyone to simultaneously reach and heal the head with one hand and the feet with the other.

ii.   Chairs are, on average, more comfortable for more people, e.g. those with back problems, burns or injuries.

iii. It is easier to heal in private homes on the healee's chair.

iv.   Private transport is not needed to carry a couch around.

v.   Can more easily heal the back and front of the person at the same time.

vi   If needed it is easier to hold both your hands around the healee's arm or leg.

c.   Disadvantage

i.   During healing, the healer often has to bend low down, or kneel or sit on the floor. This is uncomfortable or even impossible for some healers.

d.   Danger

i.   If the healee relaxes too much he or she may fall asleep and fall off the chair.

      If you notice your healee swaying to one side, whisper gently in the ear 'Are you alright?' Often, the healee will respond 'Yes,' because the swaying is simply an energy rebalancing.

      If they say 'No,' ask if they would prefer to lie on a couch or the floor.

2. Healing On A Healing Couch

Some people consider healing with a couch to be the classic way to heal others, the professional method for every therapy and therapist.

a. The healee's position

i.   Because every healee's head would be on the same pillow, ensure that tissue is placed on the pillow beforehand to provide cleanliness.

ii. Similarly, many healers buy a roll of special 'couch paper' and tear off a couch-length piece for each new treatment for the healee to lie on.

iii. Give gentle assistance as the healee gets on and off the couch – there have been cases of healees falling, especially as they try to get off the bed not realising they are still in a light-headed state of being.

iv. Just before the healee lies down, ask if he or she would prefer to have support from a cushion or pillow or rolled-up towel under the head. Some head or neck or shoulder injuries would be too painful without support.

v.   Or is similar support needed under the small of the back? (To help support arches, deformities, scoliosis, injuries etc. that may be too painful without support.)

vi. Or is support needed under the knees? If the legs were stretched out taught and tight, it could create pain for many conditions, especially the lower back.

vii. Limbs should be uncrossed as in the previous 1.a.i.

viii. Eyes as in 1.a.viii.

ix. Although some atmospheres are adequately warm, or some healees may not want a blanket, it is better in most circumstances to place a clean healing-coloured blanket over the healee, because if he or she falls asleep, the body could become cold.

b.   Advantages

i.   Easier for some healers to heal whilst standing.

ii.   Standing is a more comfortable position for some healees.

iii.   Looks professional.

c.   Disadvantages

i.   If you are short and your healee is long, you probably could not reach to heal the head and feet at the same time. Although not normally needed, this could be a disadvantage in cases where energy meridians have been damaged through injury, and a line from the head to the feet needs to be healed.

ii.   A couch is expensive, and difficult to carry to other people's homes.

iii.   Healees are more likely to fall asleep, and not experience the healing process.

iv.   Many illnesses make it impossible for healees to lie down or turn over comfortably.

d.   Dangers

i.   There is a potential for a Court case against a healer if the healee accidentally falls off the healing bed, especially whilst trying to get on or off the bed, and sustains an injury. Some healees have left in a worse condition than when they arrived.

ii.   It is possible for the bed to collapse, especially whilst getting on or off.

iii. When healing, it is not always easy to be aware of where your healee may have moved the arms or hands, especially if they are hidden under a blanket. Be aware and wary not to push your body unwittingly against the healee's hand (that often hangs just over the side of the couch).

iv. Because the healee does not have both feet on the ground, when using rei spiritual healing energy there is more likely to be an ungrounded light-headed or dizzy feeling after the treatment.

v. I have heard some people say that grounding comes from the table legs. If this is true, it means that the healee's energies are being grounded at both the feet and the head! This may lead to imbalanced low frequency energy throughout the body. (Most people need higher frequency at the head for higher frequency channelling, healing, psychic, and spiritual purposes.)

vi. If a healee is lying face up, there is a possible problem when trying to heal the back of the head. If the healer tries to lift the healee's head to get their hands at the back, it is very easy to cause further damage to many conditions such as whiplash, osteoporosis, fractures or unperceived innate weaknesses. Although there is a supposedly 'safe' method for turning the healee's head to get your healing hands underneath, severe neck weaknesses may still occasionally cause movement problems. Thus the head should not be lifted – the back of the head should be healed when the person is laying face down.

vii. Turning a healee over to heal the front first and then the back is also potentially dangerous for some healees with certain injuries and weaknesses.

Head Hand Position H1 – The Face

This hand position may help issues such as of the retina, cornea, conjuctiva, pupil, optic nerve, iris, and lens, sinus and nasal areas, jaw, facial tension, mucous membrane, pharynx, third eye development, taste buds, and areas of the brain such as those used for complicated thinking, speech, and body movement.

The brow, eyes, cheeks, and mouth hold tension. Keep fingers together, and de-stress as much of the face as possible.

Caveat. Especially when healing others, beware of possible claustrophobia if the face is covered. When healing others, place the heel of the hand gently against the person's eyebrows and let the fingers cover the face. Do not touch eyes or mouths as they are delicate areas.

Workbook notes on hand position H1:

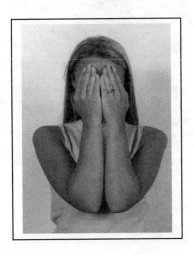

Figure 33: H1 – The Face

321

Head Hand Position H2 – Sides Of Head

May help issues such as of the cochlea, ear drum, hearing, balance, adenoids, eustachian tubes connecting ears to throat, hormonal problems via the pituitary gland at base of brain, thalamus, hypothalamus, and areas of the brain relating to smell, taste, and touch.

Caveat. If you or the healee wears a hearing aid, beware of healing over the ears. Often, reiki will make the aid emit a high-pitched whistling.

Workbook notes on hand position H2:

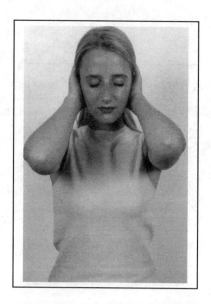

Figure 34: H2 – Sides Of Head

Head Hand Position H3 – Back Of Head

This hand position may help issues such as of the cerebrum, cerebellum, unconscious thoughts, attitudes, and memories, and the area of the brain relating to vision.

You may place your hands anywhere on the back of the head, but not on the back of the neck, as this would not heal the desired areas.

Workbook notes on hand position H3:

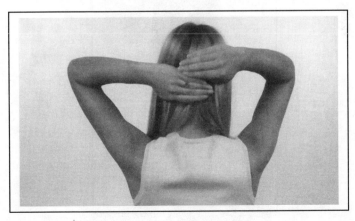

Figure 35:   H3 – Back Of Head

323

<u>Head Hand Position H4 – Throat</u>

This may help issues such as of the glottis, epiglottis, larynx, vagus nerve, thyroid gland, start of spinal cord and spinal vertebrae, oesophagus, trachea, vocal cords, jugular vein, tonsils, adenoids, and the upper part of the thymus gland.

Caveat: Do not touch the 'Adam's apple' area of the throat as it is very sensitive, and often leads to a feeling of being strangled, or even a past life death memory.

Workbook notes on hand position H4:

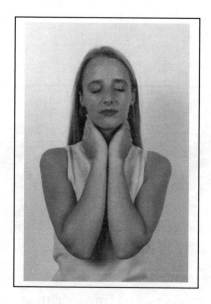

Figure 36: H4 – Throat

Front Of Body Hand Position F1 – Top Of Chest

This position may help issues such as of the pleural sac and membrane, pericardium, pulmonary arteries and veins, carotid arteries, the lower part of thymus gland, atrium, ventricles, sternum, blood vessels to and from the lungs, bronchus, bronchiole, and the upper areas affecting heart including most of the cardio-vascular system.

Caveat: When healing a lady, even if you are female, keep your eyes open and do not touch her front. Someone who has been raped could be traumatised even if you touch just over the shoulders. There is potential for a court case against a healer even if sexual abuse was not intended.

Workbook notes on hand position F1:

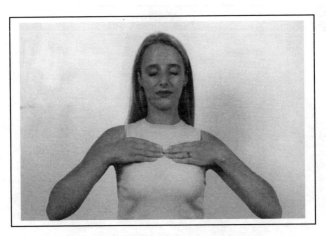

Figure 37: F1 – Top Of Chest

Front Of Body Hand Position F2 – Below Chest

May help issues such as of the diaphragm, liver, renal artery, kidney, adrenal glands, lower areas affecting heart, spleen, pancreas, stomach, gall bladder, duodenum, rib cage, abdominal aorta,

Caveat: see previous page.

Workbook notes on hand position F2:

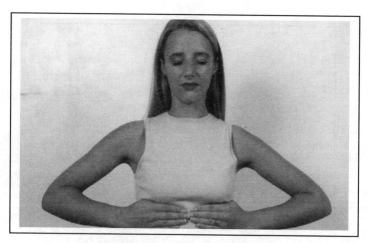

Figure 38: F2 – Below Chest

Front Of Body Hand Position F3 – Around Navel

This position may help issues such as of the colon, small intestine, lower aorta, digestive issues, upper bowels, ureter, and sacrum. It is considered by many that the hara, the energy fulcrum of our being, is situated about 5 centimetres below the navel.

Be guided. Place your hands a little above or below the navel, as you feel necessary.

Caveat: see F1.

Workbook notes on hand position F3:

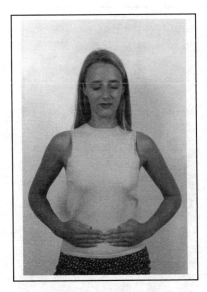

Figure 39: F3 – Around Navel

Front Of Body Hand Position F4 – Below Navel

This may help issues such as of the rectum, ovaries, testes, uterus, bladder, urethra, prostate gland, penile and vaginal issues, anal canal, fallopian tubes, lower bowels, and cervix.

Move hands slightly above or below this position, as you feel necessary.

Caveat: When healing others, do not touch a sexual area. Keep your hands a few inches from the body and with your eyes open. With closed eyes, you may inadvertently move and touch a 'private' area.

Workbook notes on hand position F4:

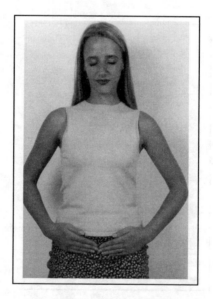

Figure 40: F4 – Below Navel

Back Of Body Hand Position B1 – Shoulders

See F1 for potential help from this hand position. This may also help stress, tension, upper back and shoulder issues.

Be careful – do not overstretch in this position if your arms do not reach.

Remember that energy can travel through what we perceive to be solid objects. If you place your hands on your front and send energy through, you can give reiki to any back position.

Workbook notes on hand position B1:

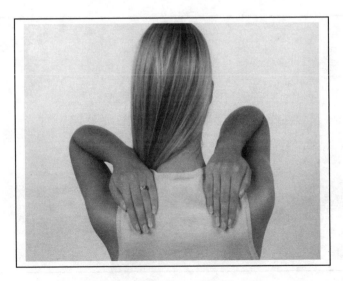

Figure 41: B1 – Shoulders

Back Of Body Hand Position B2 – Rib Cage

See F2 and B1 for potential help from this hand position.

If you can move your arms freely, this position may help many problems in nearby organs.

Workbook notes on hand position B2:

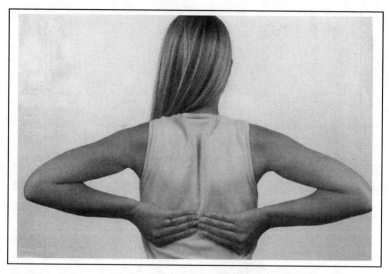

Figure 42: B2 – Rib Cage

<u>Back Of Body Hand Position B3 – Lower Back</u>

See F3 and B2 for how this position may help.
Workbook notes on hand position B3:

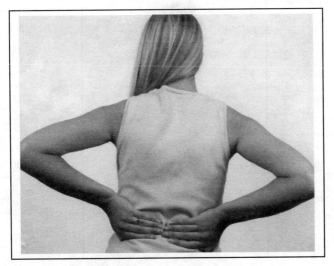

Figure 43: B3 – Lower Back

<u>Back Of Body B4 – Base Of Spine</u>

See F4 and B2 for how this position may help.
Workbook notes on hand position B4:

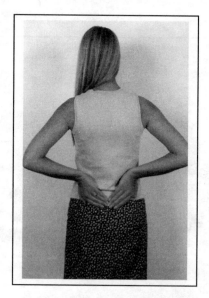

Figure 44: B4 – Base Of Spine

Joints Of Arms A1 – Shoulders

The joints of the body hold much negative energy due to friction and energy interchange issues. Therefore healing the joints may help release problems before they manifest.

Workbook notes on hand position A1:

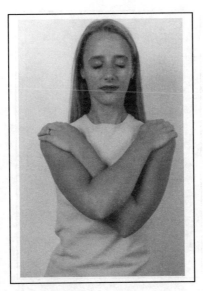

Figure 45: A1 – Shoulders

<u>Joints Of Arms A2 – Elbows</u>

See A1 above.

Workbook notes on hand position A2:

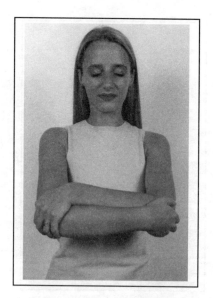

Figure 46: A2 – Elbows

Joints Of Arms A3 – Wrists

See A1 above.
Workbook notes on hand position A3:

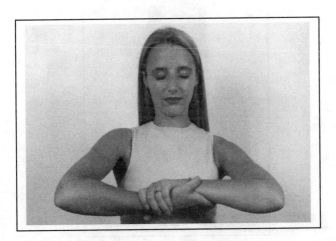

Figure 47: A3 – Wrists

__Joints Of Arms A4 – Hands__

See A1 above.

Workbook notes on hand position A4:

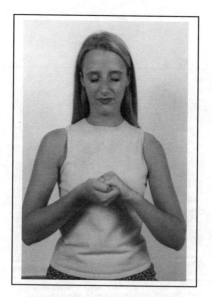

Figure 48: A4 – Hands

<u>Joints Of Legs L1 – Hips</u>

See A1 above.
Workbook notes on hand position L1:

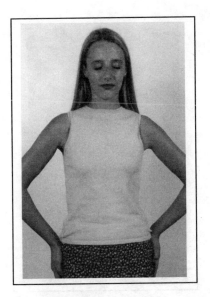

Figure 49: L1 – Hips

<u>Joints Of Legs L2 – Knees</u>

See A1 above.

Workbook notes on hand position L2:

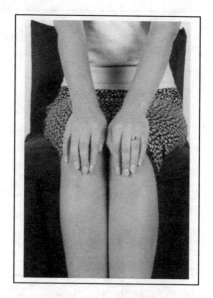

Figure 50: L2 – Knees

Joints Of Legs L3 – Ankles

See A1 above.
Workbook notes on hand position L3:

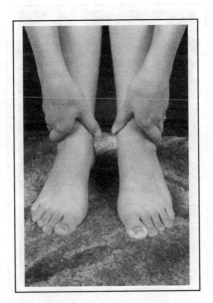

Figure 51: L3 – Ankles

Joints Of Legs L4 – Feet

See A1 above.
Workbook notes on hand position L4:

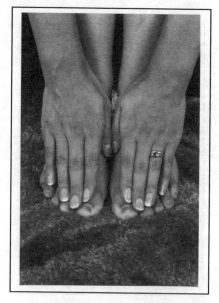

Figure 52: L4 – Feet

WORKBOOK NOTES
On Healer Hand And Healee Body Positions

CHAPTER 19

THE COMPLETE REIKI 1 METHOD

If You Clean Your Teeth You Should Also Cleanse Your Energy Daily

I usually ask students on a Reiki 1 course:
'How would you feel if you didn't brush your teeth for a month?'
Screwed up faces tell the answer! I continue,
'That's how reiki people feel if they haven't done self-healing for a month! They feel the difference!'
Self-healing is like cleansing the teeth, but on an inner level!

Exercise 74 - Testing Your Self-Healing
Try reikiing yourself for a year. It will become a good habit, like brushing the teeth. But like brushing the teeth, it is often not appreciated until you stop. So after enough time has elapsed for you to become healed, say one year of self-healing, stop for one month. Most people feel the difference, and start cleansing again within the week!

How To Give Yourself A Reiki Treatment

Practise, practise, practise!

Only practice will give you the healing you need. Only practice will give you wholesome balancing. And only practice will give you the understanding of all aspects of a reiki treatment.

1.   How Often Should You Practise Self-Healing

Do reiki self-healing twice a day. The best times are in bed, just before rising in the morning and just before sleep at night when the brain is usually naturally relaxed and is more likely to enhance healing energy. But, if your life-style doesn't allow this, e.g. kids or pets or a spouse that jumps on you to wake you up, find an alternative time.

2.   What If You Miss A Treatment

Busy lives mean that treatments will be missed. This is acceptable. However, it is easy to lapse into bad habits.

Few people want to keep their problems. Continue self-healing as soon as possible.

3.   Falling Asleep During Self-Healing

If you often fall asleep at night, with your hands in the same position, good! This position is probably where you need the energy the most. It is likely that your higher consciousness or guides take you out of the healing equation so that you cannot interfere with the healing process. You may regularly fall asleep in that position until the healing has been achieved.

Some beginner healers have told me that if they fall asleep, they wake themselves up again and carry on. I always wonder, 'How do they do that?' It is better to let 'sleep healing' continue to heal the need.

But it would not help all-over health if you always fell asleep during the first hand-position! So if you feel that other hand-positions are 'missing out', occasionally start elsewhere.

4. The Self-Healing Dosage

Twice a day is the normal requirement for the average self-healer.

If you are ill, increase self-treatment to three or more sessions daily.

It is no different to taking painkiller tablets; the worse the pain, the more you take, up to a certain dosage. The majority of reiki energy is absorbed within half an hour, so in theory you could reiki yourself at least every hour!

Ideally spend 3-5 minutes on each position.

5. If You Have Little Spare Time

If time is limited, a little reiki is better than none. Reiki especially the head and front body as they are usually more in need than the back or limbs.

Reiki yourself when possible, such as when listening to the radio, when soaking in the bath, whilst eating a meal, or waiting in a traffic jam. Any safe place is good where onlookers will not consider you a candidate for a mental hospital.

Be creative with your time, and you will soon feel good.

In any case, there are always opportunities to practise exercise 41, 'Healing With Two Consciousnesses.'

6. Should Reiki Be Turned Off

The simple answer is 'Why should you turn off something that may heal you?'

If nothing adverse occurs from keeping rei switched on, such as being permanently too light-headed due to being too high in your energy body frequency, keep rei on and enjoy it.

An ultimate goal is that you become so healed from the permanent flow of energy through you that you become like Jesus – there will be such a beautiful excess of healing energy around you that people nearby or touching your clothes may be spontaneously healed!

Self-heal
And feel
The difference

The Complete Reiki I Method

Remember that this is your foundation treatment, the 14-step baseline method from which many other techniques can be empowered. In the future, if all else fails with a certain illness, you have this foundation treatment to fall back on. But this method must be learned and understood first.

This method is used both for your self-healing, and for providing spiritual (rei) healing to others.

1. To Touch Or Not To Touch

Reiki has developed as essentially a touch method of healing. Some other systems of healing such as spiritual healing have developed as essentially non-touch systems. However, it is not your choice whether to touch or not – you should ask healees whether or not they prefer to be touched.

With the non-touch method, the hand is so close to the body that reiki energy radiating from the hand will have virtually the same effect as if the hand was touching.

a. Touch

'Touch' means hand-contact - physically touching the hands on your or the healee's body. It is the traditional reiki way.

Use this method for those healees who may think that, if you did not touch, you are not doing anything. Healees would especially think this if they did not experience any biofeedback from the energy. Touch healing would prevent them from feeling 'cheated.'

b. Non-touch

'Non-touch' means close-hand contact - holding the hands in the aura, close to the body, a few inches / centimetres away. It is the traditional spiritual healing way.

Use this method for those healees that may have a phobia about being touched, for example someone who had recently been raped.

Use this method for healees who have an illness or condition, such as, for example severe burns, that mean they cannot be touched adequately.

2. Healing From The Head Down Or The Feet Up

Decide which is the worst problem the healee has at that moment, stress, in which case heal starting at the head and work downwards, or low energy, when you should start at the base and work upwards.

Get into a comfortable position ready for starting the treatment.

Remember that you do not have to heal the feet or legs – the head and body normally have the major healing needs.

3. For The Highest Good Of All Concerned

In reiki, there are various protection methods that try to ensure reiki is only ever used when the receiver needs it. Before any reiki healing treatment, or after if the treatment was an emergency when there was no time to say this prior to treatment, contemplate for about 30 seconds that 'this reiki treatment will be for the highest good of all concerned.' And understand deeply within you what the words mean.

4. Help From Above

Consider your belief systems. Do you believe in guides, masters, angels, etc? If so, for 30 seconds, ask one, some, or all of the highest guides, reiki guides, healing angels, Dr Usui, Dr Hayashi, Mrs Takata, or your ascended masters to help the reiki healing process. If you are a Marxist, or do not have any of these beliefs, ask for help from your higher consciousness. Or inwardly ask for help from your reiki master. Or whatever or whoever else you believe may help.

5. Kanji

Consider which kanji hand position (1, 2, or 3, or a combination of the kanji) is needed for that particular healing. You may need a different kanji hand position for each session.

Contemplate why you chose that position for about 30 seconds.

6. Place Hands On Or Near First Position

See chapter 18, 'Healer Hand and Healee Body Positions'.

7. Eyes Open Or Closed

This is relevant only to healing others.

a. Eyes open – logical biofeedback

Understand that, if you keep your eyes open when healing others, you will be more logically aware of their biofeedback and signs of release. This may help you decide how to progress the healing.

Although there may be great value in keeping eyes open when healing others, if you keep your eyes open when self-healing, you may be distracted by surroundings, and not have such a good result.

This distraction does not usually occur so much when healing others because you are concentrating on watching the person in front of you.

b. Eyes closed – psychic biofeedback

If you keep your eyes closed when healing others – or yourself – you will have more potential for your own inner psychic biofeedback such as visions or hearing sounds or messages etc. This is only if you are built in that particular way. See section *'Biofeedback Through Your Seven Senses'* in chapter 9.

For most beginners, it is best to experiment with and develop both abilities of open and closed eyes. This will create understanding of how you are built as a healer, and how you may develop.

Remember that all biofeedback you see or experience should be used for your own reference to ascertain how to progress the healing, and should not be imparted to a healee.

8. Decide Passive Or Active Method

Choose the active or passive method as described previously.

9. 'Rei On'

Say, within your mind, 'rei on.'

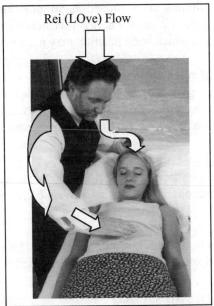

Rei (LOve) Flow

Figure 53: Representation Of Rei (LOve) Flow During A Healing. The rei is brought in through the top of the head, down the arms, and out of the palms of the hands into the healee.

10. Spend 3 - 5 Minutes In Each Position

Allow rei, or the chosen reiki energy if you are a Reiki 2 practitioner or above, to flow through passively, or make it flow through actively, for 3-5 minutes in each hand position.

Beginners may use relaxing music that also has a bell or sound every 5 minutes to determine when the hands should move on.

However, this is only to help beginners programme themselves into an understanding of how long 3-5 minutes is. Soon it will be learned that more, or less, time may be needed in each position for more appropriate and effective healings.

11. Return To Where Most Energy Was Needed

After completing all standard hand positions return to the position where you felt most energy was needed. There are three ways to understand which hand position may need extra healing.

a. Sign of release

If the healee gave biofeedback signs of release in one particular hand position, e.g., gulp, yawn, sigh, cough etc, give that position extra healing. You may find that the same biofeedback reoccurs.

b. Extra biofeedback

If in one position you felt more heat, electric or other biofeedback sensation, return there to provide extra energy.

c. Hands 'stuck'

If your hands felt stuck in one position and could not move on easily, return and stay there for as long as is needed.

12. Come Around Gently

After the self-healing treatment, only open your eyes when you feel that the energy has integrated or subsided.

When healing others, allow them space to come around in their own time. Stand in front of the healee, perhaps in the prayer position, with a smile on your face.

13. Evaluate The Session

Whether the treatment was for you or someone else, complete the forms towards the back of this manual. Programme yourself to get into this good habit. It will help you keep adequate records, know how to progress the healee, and formulate your personal research programme.

It should be noted that more comprehensive forms, for those who wish to become reiki practitioners, are included in the Reiki 2 Manual.

14. Make Next Appointment

Ensure you make a further appointment with your healee – or with yourself. As you progress on your healing learning curve, you will realise that some illnesses require appointments on consecutive days (e.g. broken bones), whilst other conditions may require weekly or other time spaced appointments to help keep the health issue under control.

Exercise 75 - Remembering The Complete Reiki I Method
Because you need to concentrate on energy flow to get the best results, it is best to learn the above 14 steps before practising self-healing. Write them out or study and learn the steps thoroughly before your first reiki treatment.

Exercise 76 - Annotation Of First Self-Healings

Using the workbook notes page, record the
various biofeedback experiences in each of the
hand positions for your first evening and first
morning self-healing. Record especially the
differences felt in each position H1, H2, etc.

Simple Record Keeping Form

Superior practitioner forms are in the Reiki 2 Manual for those taking reiki more professionally. This form will help beginners by scoring symptoms of friends or family practised on. Results are seen objectively. If scores are not kept, friends may think subjectively it hasn't worked and be against your reiki or even you. Keep symptom scores, even of your mum or best friend. It looks professional, and you and your reiki are more likely to gain respect.

Records will give you feedback of how different illnesses respond to reiki in different ways – a necessary part of your learning on the reiki path.

As discussed in chapter 2, placebo possibly works within an across-the-board-of-conditions average in about 30% to 35% of cases automatically – even if you did nothing except place hands on a person, about 30% to 35% may feel better. Your job as a healer is to increase the success rate as far as possible above the average 30% to 35%. Indeed, improvement of 35% is considered the low end for drugs to get on the market, so it is a good idea to use that figure as your low end for your across-the-board-of-conditions success rate as a Reiki 1 healer.

Please remember that some conditions are more difficult for rei energy to heal than others; so do not expect the scores of all illnesses to reduce by 35%. Over a period of time you will understand that some symptom scores will quickly reduce by far more than 35%, whilst other symptoms will take far longer to reach even a 10% score reduction. It is therefore your average score reduction of 35% that is your target.

Watch the symptom scores before and after reiki. If – on average of all illnesses you treat – they do not come down by at least 35% within say seven sessions, re-evaluate what you are doing by going back to basics, and ensure reiki is channelling through you correctly.

If there is still a problem in reducing symptom scores, use a relaxation process for about 10 minutes before you start a reiki treatment. Please see section 'Releasing Stress Before Reiki' in chapter 13.

If the scores still do not reduce, see your reiki master and ask for help. As a last resort, ask for a re-attunement to give you a kick-start.

The law states records should be kept, and are confidential, and should therefore be kept locked up or somewhere safe from prying eyes.

Exercise 77 - Recording
Use the form on yourself. List your symptoms. See if the scores come down over seven sessions. Then practise with the form on a trusted friend. See the objective value of records.

Reiki 1 Record Keeping Form

You may use, or add to, this form, providing you include the following (please then use freely):

(10 = worst and 1 = nothing)

"© Universal Copyright 2001, Dr Allan Sweeney
Reiki 1 Record Form by Dr Allan Sweeney www.reiki-healing.com

Healer's name..

Patient's name ....

Doctor's diagnosis...

Address ....

Phone number ....

Date of birth ....

How long has the condition been present?.......................

Symptom A ....

Score before healing out of 10 ....

Score after healing out of 10.......................................

Symptom B ....

Score before healing out of 10 ....

Score after healing out of 10.......................................

Symptom C ....

Score before healing out of 10 ....

Score after healing out of 10.......................................

Comments of healee after reiki ....

....

....

Comments of healer after reiki ....

....

....

....

Signed..

Date ...."

Students' Comments On First Self-Healings

As overnight homework on a Reiki 1 class, I ask students to give themselves self-healing before bedtime just before sleep, and in the morning, before getting out of bed. I also ask them to record what happened so as to keep a record of their first ever self-healings.

The following are records of these events, and have been chosen to show the wide variety of self-healing experiences.

These records are also included because so many people ask what they could expect to experience from self-healing. Remember that the experiences are unique for the individual, depending on what is needed, and which sense the person uses the most powerfully for reiki biofeedback. Whatever you experience in which hand position is right for you at that moment.

'Evening, positions H1, H2, H3, H4, felt sensations over sternum lengthening and opening up. Position F1 felt a lot of heat/energy in my hands. Position F2 felt curl-shaped pool of heat/energy. Position F3 felt a glow. Position F4 felt lots of energy in my feet especially the right one.

'Morning position H1 & H2 had a sense of calmness. Position H3 opening up of sensation area over sternum. Position H4 felt a sense of calmness. Position F1 felt a slight sensation at top of sternum. Positions F2, F3, & F4 felt a sense of calmness.' DN

'The positions seemed easy to do – although it wasn't easy to hold the positions longer than a few minutes. My headache was gone in the morning and I seemed more positive and less afraid.' OK

'I used the self-healing reiki in bed. Initially I found myself checking the clock when I changed to the next position and was taking around three minutes per position. In the first head positions, I wasn't aware of any sensations. In the second position I initially had pain in my temples. In the third position I saw a string of white,

bright lights in a random pattern. I then had a pain in my left elbow
and had to change position. In the fourth position I wasn't really
aware of any sensation. In the first body position, initially I was
aware of heat in my chest and then vivid purple light which had
tinges of vivid orange mixed into it later. In the position two I was
aware of heat and then had images of a big brown bear's face. (I
believe the bear to be one of my power animals.) I felt very happy to
see my bear again. In position three I felt cold and as if there was a
layer between my hands and body. I caught fleeting images of a
black dog and then a tingling travelling up my spine until I changed
position. In the last position I was aware of cold and could still feel a
sensation in my spine.

'In the morning I woke up feeling as though I had had a deep
dreamless sleep – (despite the neighbour's cat crying at my window
at 4am and getting up to let him in!)

'During this morning's self-healing I was aware of feeling warm
throughout. I averaged 4 minutes + per position. In position one of
the head I was aware of sensation in my stomach area as if my
stomach was going to be upset in some way but not quite. This
carried on through the position 2. In position three I had tingling
around my left palm and pain in the wrist. I was also aware of my
stomach. In the fourth position I was only aware of the sensation in
my stomach and tried to decide what the sensation was exactly but
couldn't. In position 1 of the body I was aware of cold along my
back although my front continued to be warm. In position two I felt
as if I was leaning my head and torso towards the left. In position 3 I
felt tingling in my thighs and then felt heavy. In the final position I
was aware of bright yellow light in bands, one or two at a time,
curving with some white ones coming in.' GH

'Night, cobalt blue then fell asleep.
'Morning, little heat but much calm.' MS

'Evening, little happened initially – some heat in hands whilst
hands on neck. Fell asleep shortly after placing hands on upper chest.

'Morning, a little throbbing at crown chakra, again heat and light tingling in hands. No visualisations.' KN

'Night, first four positions on head were most powerful, with flashes of blue (orange to a lesser extent) on positions H1 & H2. (again at the end when returning to position H1.) Other positions gave a very relaxing feeling – a soft warm breeze was felt.

'Morning, a very peaceful experience (almost yoga-like) during the movements. Again purple colour. A symbol like Japanese writing was seen in lower right vision. Noticeable increase in heat/energy around hips.' SP

'Evening, headache lifted 10 minutes after finish of reiki. Felt very warm and relaxed.

'Morning, felt very light as though I was floating above the bed. Felt very energised yet relaxed and calm.' TC

'Evening, have never seen such wonderful colours. Red, orange, yellow, green, blue, violet. A pattern in black (very fine) like crazy paving. One or two faces. Heat in hands and also felt very relaxed.

'Morning, nothing to report.' EY

'Evening I didn't feel anything, just very tired and I fell asleep. Morning when I did it all I saw was dark red. After healing (last night) I got a good night's sleep and my back problem was nearly gone. Thank you!' SI

'Found it very relaxing. Pains in head and neck developed suddenly which is where I have major problems. Hands wanted to stay in solar plexus area. Today I feel better in health generally.' IP

'Felt very calm and grounded' and had a very peaceful sleep. It was not interrupted. In the morning I felt very calm and in rhythm with my being. I look forward to more healing with myself.' WC

'Bedtime, H1 eye tiredness drawn out by warmth and pulsation then I fell asleep. Morning, H1, H2, H3, no noticeable response. H4 strong pulsation. F1 seemed to notice lumber and pelvis to relax, F2, no reaction. F3 and 4 strong pulsation. B1 Reaction down back. B2 & 3 little reaction. B4 Strong pulsation.' GD

'Last night I felt very relaxed, usually I can't sleep because I'm always worrying about not getting everything done by a certain time or I'd be thinking about the past. I had a very deep peaceful sleep and the funny thing is I can't even remember falling asleep! That has got to be a first. Cold energy swirling around. I felt like a big floppy pillow.

'This morning I woke up feeling really relaxed no worries it was quite amazing a calm mind. I felt so relaxed doing the self-healing I thought I would fall asleep again but after I got up to prepare my work to hand in. I have to say Allan, I feel great!' ND

'Night, I felt very comfortable and relaxed. My hands were very hot and my feeling was of a deep sense of peace with an awareness of stress drifting away. I saw the colour pink and felt as though I was enveloped in love.

'Morning, my hands were extremely hot and a very bright white light appeared which changed to pale green and yellow. I placed my hands on my lower back as I had back pain. My hands became even hotter and the pain gradually drifted away. My feeling was of total peace.' BI

'I slept very well last night. I usually have some vivid dreams that linger on in my mind the next morning. But today, I woke up to quite a calm, peaceful self.

'I usually need quite some time to kick start myself in the morning, but with 15 minutes of self-healing practice, I was ready to go! I had a heavy head last night, which has also disappeared.' ET

Millions of people worldwide have helped or healed themselves with reiki. With you reading this book, is it your turn next?

WORKBOOK NOTES
On The Complete Reiki 1 Method

WORKBOOK NOTES
On Your First Self-Healing

CHAPTER 20

AURAS AND CHAKRAS

Auras

An aura is a subtle energy field outside the physical body that consists of a combination of parts, colour frequencies, layers, and densities.

It is a unique force working for the individual within it, and trying to balance and nurture and encompass and release the various internal and external energetic influences.

Each aspect of each aura has a different purpose and has the potential for constant change, making the aura difficult for scientists or clairvoyants to agree on and understand. If you search the net, for example, there are many disagreements of measurements of the aura.

The complex, chaotic nature of auras are specialist subjects, and are described more fully in higher-level manuals when practitioners are more likely to be, through practise, more understanding of the complex issues involved.

Until then, the following may help initial understanding.

1. The Unique Charge Of An Aura

The aura is a type of electro-magnetic force with plus and minus aspects, positive and negative ionic charges. The charges are different for everybody so an aura is a unique force that is yours and yours alone.

Your physical body has its own uniquely positive charge and the aura has its unique negative charge. As positive attracts negative, your aura cannot leave you. If you stand by the side of the road and a bus full of people passes next to you, your aura does not leave with the bus!

2. Feel Your Own Aura

This is a classic exercise that has probably been taught since people first understood they had energetic bodies.

Exercise 78 - Feeling Your Own Aura
Hold your arms at least one metre apart, slightly in front of your body, with your palms facing each other.

Put your thoughts into the skin of your hands. Only think of the skin of the hands, nothing else, and feel any sensation there. Feel any heat or cold, pushing or pulling, breeze or fluttering, vibration or whatever is there.

Do not be concerned how much or how little you feel. Do not analyse. Do not think things like, 'I always feel sensations like that.' Release your logic. Trust in the process.

Slowly bring the hands together – very slowly – with your palms still facing each other. Be

aware only of the palm sensations. When the
hands touch, go out and repeat the process.

As you come in again slowly, think of any
sudden changes that are happening, maybe in
one area of a hand there will be sudden heat,
another area sudden cold, another area maybe
a pressure as if there is something hard to
push against. It might be as if you find
different layers at different positions. Very
occasionally you may find it almost impossible
to push your hands further together. On
other occasions you might get to a point where
you feel that the hands are suddenly being
drawn together.

Do that a few times and see if these layers,
these pressures, these feelings occur at about
the same distance away as on previous
occasions. If so, you have discovered your
own auric field and its layers or energy spots!

Please read chapter 9, '*Biofeedback*', for
sensation explanations, and chapter 21,
'*Scanning*', for what to do next!

3. Filling Your Aura With LOve

Auras are a sort of filter. For example, they filter unwanted
energies from entering you. This means that they can become filled
with 'debris' and can benefit from occasional cleansing with a shower
of rei LOve.

Exercise 79 - Rei Shower
Sit, stand, or lie in a comfortable position.
Tune into rei energy by putting your thoughts

up to your version of God or the highest power you believe in. When your thoughts are up high, take your thoughts higher still. Then higher again. When you have gone as high as you can go, as you breathe out, imagine a rei shower of golden rays of light raining down towards your being, about four metres all around you. Let the golden rei energy wash out your aura in a gentle LOving shower. Do this for about three minutes on each out breath. Take notes on how you feel.

4. If You Cannot Feel Anything

It is important to repeat here that if you feel nothing you should not be concerned. Dr Usui understood that these techniques need more practice for some than others. So if you feel nothing, just accept that is how it is! And concentrate on healing with reiki energies in different ways.

Please see chapter 10, 'Developing Strengths'.

Chakras

Chakras are energy wheels that let good energy in and bad energy out of a body and help the body stay in harmony. Sometimes, like any other part of the body, they can malfunction - and there are many ways malfunctions can be returned to normal by various types of healers.

Like auras, chakras are extremely complex. Since they manifest as unique forces for each individual depending on how the person interacts with the world inside and outside, they are discussed more fully in a higher level manual by which time practitioners are more likely to understand the issues due to practise of self-healing. For now, on Reiki 1, please accept that everything is a progression of learning; not everything can be taught at once; and delicate energetic chakras can be damaged by a healer using forceful energies inappropriately, in a not dissimilar way to how a blood vessel can be damaged by a sledgehammer.

Thus it is of paramount importance for Reiki 1 practitioners not to deliberately try to heal a particular and complex chakra. Instead, the beginner healer should allow energy to gently flow into each chakra as is needed, and to feel and to move on when it seems that the flow of energy has ceased.

Exercise 80 - Unconscious Chakra Balancing

Simply and unconsciously allow reiki's nature to flow less or more energy automatically into each hand position without any 'control' by you. This will create wonderfully gentle healing effects, without the potential for damage.

Feel in your hands where more – or less – flows and record the flow.

WORKBOOK NOTES
On Auras And Chakras

CHAPTER 21

SCANNING

<u>Scanning With Hands And Eyes:</u>
<u>Byosen and Hibiki</u>

<u>Scanning</u>: is the Western name for the technique of feeling around the layers of the aura and finding spots in need of healing. Scanning is therefore the method of feeling the aura's 'negative energy spots' (NES's), or feeling the byosen (source of the illness) by using hibiki (sensation in the hand). I, and many others, have always taught this on beginner reiki courses, so it was comforting to discover that Dr Usui did the same. It surprises some reiki practitioners when they hear that Dr Usui taught how to scan and heal the aura. He felt that scanning with the hands was simple enough, but also important enough, to be taught at the first level of the first level of the first level.

On the second level of the first level of the first level, Dr Usui taught how to scan with the eyes.

This part of the Reiki I Manual will therefore provide in-depth coverage of both scanning with the hands and the eyes.

In Japan, there are two words to describe the process of damage and healing in the aura.

<u>*Byosen:*</u> *is the word used in Japanese reiki to describe an auric energy that comes from the source of a physical illness.*

<u>*Hibiki:*</u> *is the Japanese reiki word to describe sensations that can be felt in the hand of the reiki practitioner who feels the byosen.*

<u>*Auric weakness:*</u> *is another way to think of this. Good clairvoyants can see weak spots in auras. When a healer's hand scans over that spot, he or she can see the aura opening to let reiki energy in to heal.*

Some suggestions are made that the feeling in the hand when scanning is due to feeling the negative energy of the dis-ease. However, the evidence of clairvoyants shows that the tingling or other sensation a healer feels in a NES is due to the reiki energy flowing more strongly from the hand to heal the weakness.

1. Hibiki Sensations

a. What you may feel

i. As you scan, you may feel tingly spots. Or hot, cold, electric, breeze, pushing, pulling, shaking, fluttering, or vibration spots. Or you may feel many other sensations.

ii. Go with your strongest sensation. For Matthew Manning, a famous English healer, it is the tingly spots that matter. For Ray Brown, another English healer who has been on TV, it is the cold spots. For me it is feeling electric spots that portray byosen.

Any sudden change in sensation you feel as you scan the aura could mean a healing need.

b. What if you do not feel

i. Although almost everyone can scan and feel, there is, very occasionally, a person who cannot feel any hibiki in the hand whatsoever.

If you are one of those very few, please do not be concerned. Understand that this is how your God has made you.

Concentrate on the things in reiki that you are good at.

Concentrate on your reiki strength, not your weakness as explained in chapter 10, 'Developing Strengths'.

ii. Most of the few who feel no hibiki at the beginning will eventually feel hibiki perfectly well. One lady student could feel nothing for about nine months. Suddenly she could scan and feel everything. And she still can.

iii. So persevere. Trust. Some healers will feel a lot, some will feel very little.

The important thing when scanning an aura is to eventually feel some change somewhere.

2. Scanning As A Tool For Diagnosis

a. Healers should never diagnose

Diagnosis is a doctor's responsibility. We should work with doctors, and never diagnose against their medical decisions.

In any case, unless a healer had a qualification allowing diagnosis, and relevant insurance, normal reiki insurance would not cover healers if they had a claim against them for wrong diagnosis.

b. Scanning provides a simple way to 'diagnose' where there is an energy problem

i. Having said that healers should never diagnose, practitioners can still scan as described below.

ii. Without knowing that the healee has an illness, the healer will normally feel extra energy flow from the hands over a point of need.

c. Scanned information is only for the use of the healer

i. Information gained from scanning should not be imparted to the healee. This is because the information may conflict with a doctor's diagnosis and cause the healee confusion.

For example, if the doctor has given a diagnosis of a stomach problem, and you then tell the healee that you felt some type of byosen in the top of the forehead (a standard place for a meridian spot relevant to the stomach) some healees may become confused and think they have a disease in the head!

ii. Use the scanned information only to tell you where to heal.

3.   Preparation

See previous sections.

4.   Thoughts

You need to let go of current thoughts otherwise you are more likely to be analytically left-brained, and less likely to feel the energy. Although some people may think this exercise is simple, for some more analytical people it is essential.

> ### Exercise 81 - Letting Go Of Thoughts
> **Think of your thoughts for 30 seconds.**
> **Let go with your mind for 30 seconds.**
> **Put all your thoughts into the palm of your hand for 30 seconds.**
> **Let the thoughts leave your hand and go up to your version of God.**
> **You are now ready to scan.**

5.   Which Hand To Scan With

For beginners, scanning should only be done with one hand. This is because there will be different sensations in each hand due to plus energy being on one side of the body, and minus energy on the other. This will confuse the feelings of beginners.

The hand you should use should be the hand your energy flows out of so that the aura weaknesses can be healed with natural reiki flow from your hand. Some say that this should be the dominant hand, or the hand you write with. However, my experience with clients and students over the years show that most healers' energies flow in the right and out the left hand, and have nothing to do with whether you are left or right-handed, although I have seen a study stating the opposite flow (Benor v1)). If in doubt, you should use your left hand.

Ultimately, good healers should become ambidextrous, with reiki able to flow in or out of either hand, but that will take practise.

Exercise 82 - Which Is Your Dominant Energy Hand?

Although this method is not fool-proof, it is the closest technique available for this purpose. Scan around your head and body with one hand only, and remember where the biggest sensations were felt. Then scan the entire head and body again with the other hand only, and see if there were more or less sensations this time.

Repeat. The hand in which you felt most energy from the Negative Energy Spots is almost certainly the hand that your energy naturally flows from.

Meaning that the other hand is where your energy will naturally flow in.

6.   Scanning Method

There are many component parts to understanding whether or not you are feeling byosen. Each has an exercise to practise. Enough practice of each of these parts will prove invaluable later on your healing path.

Exercise 83 - Feeling The Closest Layer Of A Person's Aura

Hold the palm of your hand you believe your energy flows out of, or your left hand if you

are unsure, towards the healee from a distance of about 1 metre from the back of his or her head.

Slowly bring your hand towards the head.

Feel for changes, especially in pressure. This is the change in density between the auric layers, e.g. between the emotional and physical layers.

Feel for the closest pressure - usually this is between 5cms and 20cms from the body.

Exercise 84 - Test For Breathing Hibiki

Be wary and aware of your breath. This is because most healers feel extra sensations in the hands whilst breathing in or out. This could be confused with hibiki.

To prevent this confusion, only scan whilst holding your breath.

If you do breathe, and feel hibiki whilst you breathe, treble check that it really is a byosen you are feeling by scanning a total of three times on the same spot.

Or, deliberately breathe out as you scan, and feel the extra sensations in your hand. Then check to see if the sensation can be scanned again whilst holding your breath. The sensation will probably not be there, as it was 'breathing hibiki', not byosen.

Exercise 85 - Scanning For Byosen

Very slowly scan with your hand in the aura around the head.

Keep the hand about the same distance from the physical body.

Occasionally test if the physical aura is further in or out. E.g. one side of the body may have the aura closer than the other.

Adjust the hand position if needed. Be guided. Continue by scanning the head, shoulders, down each arm, back, front, thighs, and lastly down each leg.

Feel any changes.

Remember any tingly or other relevant NES or hibiki, as these will show where the byosen needs to be healed.

Exercise 86 - Treatment Of Byosen

Return to the biggest NES, the strongest sensation of hibiki, first.

Give reiki to this spot for a few minutes.

This may be through the auric spot outside the physical body where you felt negative energy.

Or, because you are probably scanning close enough in to feel the physical energy emanating from the body, you can place your hands on the healee's body directly on the spot in the aura where you felt the byosen. (Assuming it is a polite area.)

Let reiki flow through you into the area using the passive or active methods.

Stop when it feels as if the energy has stopped flowing through your hands.

Check the aura again to see if the tingling has gone.

If necessary, give further reiki treatments until no tingling is left.

Move to the next biggest NES, the next strongest sensation of hibiki, and repeat the treatment.

Continue until the entire aura feels smooth and clear and balanced.

Exercise 87 - Scanning Memory Jogger

Trust in what happens.

Pass your hand around the aura.

Think only of the hand sensations.

You may feel heat, cold, electric, or any other sensation.

Concentrate on the changes in sensation.

Do not be concerned with how much or how little change you feel.

Remember where the biggest changes are, regardless of how big or small the changes may be.

Trust in what you experience.

If unsure whether you felt a change, scan the spot again and see whether the byosen you thought was there the first time, is still there the second time.

7. Young Children And Animals

Although some children and animals such as cats and dogs love reiki, most will not stay still for long enough for hands-on healing.

Try healing twin Siamese cats!

Although animal healing has its own methods, over the years the following is the only method I have ever needed. Indeed, many severely ill animals have had remarkable results.

If you have difficulty with a child or animal not staying still long enough for healing, try the following.

Please also see the sections 'Giving Healing To Children Under Age Of 18' and 'Codes And Laws' in chapter 25.

a.   Wait until the child or animal is asleep.

Most parents or animal owners know approximately when it is the child's or animal's bedtime.

Make your healing appointment for that time.

b.   Scan the aura

Scan and treat as above to heal through the NES into the byosen.

c.   Often the child or animal will turn over in sleep

Children and animals often seem to unconsciously know where the healing energy is needed. Even in sleep they may turn over into a better position to allow you get to the exact area to be healed!

d.   Continue as point 7 above.

Continue scanning the aura, and healing through the NES until the aura feels smooth all over.

8.   Self-Healing With Scanning

You can scan and treat yourself, friends, and family members.

a.   Yourself

Daily scan your head, arms, legs, front of body, and every part of your back you can reach. You will:

i.   Detect existing problems and potentially heal them through the negative byosen, and,

ii.   You will also be able to heal auric knots before they have entered the body and created a physical problem.

You could become healthier, and then stay healthier!

Exercise 88 - Practise Daily Self-Scanning
Each day, scan your aura, feel the byosen and heal yourself.   Eventually, you may feel wholeness returning.

b.   Family, friends, other people
Practice makes perfect. Practise first on yourself. Then practise on your closest family and friends before you progress on to scanning and healing other people. Choose close family and friends who will give you constructive, not destructive, feedback.

9.   Scanning With The Eyes

As mentioned, the first healing technique Dr Usui taught as level one of level one of level one, was healing by scanning with the hand.

And the second technique Usui Sensei taught as level two of level one of level one was scanning with the eyes.

The latter is a technique I have taught for many years, although previously only on more advanced courses, as I believed it too difficult for most beginners to achieve adequately.

However, because Dr Usui taught these methods, and because many people are now trying to integrate both Japanese and Western healing systems into the teachings of reiki, it now feels right to teach scanning with the eyes on Reiki 1 courses.

Exercise 89 - Unfocussing
With your thoughts and your eyes, focus on the area to be scanned using the method above.   Concentrate.   Feel an energy

connection from your eyes to the scan area. Try not to blink.

Then 'unfocus' by imagining that you can bring the 'focus' of your eyes a few inches or centimetres towards you.

This may take practice – eyes may ache if eye muscles have not been used in this way. However, like any muscle, regular exercise soon tones them up.

Exercise 90 - Scanning With The Eyes

Keeping the energy connection from your eyes to the scan area, very slowly scan just outside the body or object with your eyes.

Keep the focus of the eyes about the same distance from the object being scanned.

Feel any changes in sensation in the eyes.

Remember any tingly or other relevant biofeedback or relevant NES/hibiki.

If you think you have found byosen, scan with the eyes three times to ensure you are correct.

10. Healing Through The Eyes

a.   The difficulty

The eyes are the windows of the soul.

This seems true, especially when you think of some of the common phrases about the eyes, such as hate-filled eyes, a look of daggers, a glint in the eyes, sad eyed, bright-eyed, tired eyes, a glare of anger, a loving look, pie-eyed, shifty eyes and so on.

It is one thing to be able to scan with the eyes, and quite another to heal through them. Because, to project energy from the eyes, you must be sure you are projecting positive reiki, not one of your natural negative energies as above!

I remember a newly qualified reiki master whom I met in Australia. She had struggled to heal her life-long inner hatred, and asked me, 'Allan, why is it that when I try to send love to people through my eyes, they glare at me, or even make a negative remark?'

She was the type of person who would not have taken the answer lightly. In fact, her character and personality were so fragile the answer would have set her development back at least many months.

Therefore I could not tell her the truth.

The truth was that she needed much more self-healing for her inner hatred, because she was not projecting love from her eyes. She was projecting inner hatred that still needed to be healed. So be careful.

Remember that it may be relatively easy to scan with the eyes to feel where the byosen is located, but that it is relatively difficult to heal through the eyes because, unless you have done your self-healing adequately, you are likely to transmit whatever is deep within the windows of your soul.

<u>Exercise 91 - Healing Through The Eyes</u>
Look at the byosen. Concentrate your eyes on the area to be healed.

Allow rei to flow from above your head, through your crown, and out of your eyes.

Let rei be like a river of energy flowing from your eyes, into the problem and healing it.

Ensure that it really is rei flowing through and out, and not some other energy connected with your non-concentrated thoughts or soul-window.

Remember that if you lose concentration, another energy, maybe your own negative energy, may flow to the byosen instead.

Continue until you can feel no more sensations
in the eyes from the negative byosen.
Scan the area with your eyes to ensure a healing
has been achieved.

Scanning For Old Scars

Is Like

Panning For Gold Bars

Eureka!

A Golden

Healing Opportunity

<u>Scanning The Aura – 1</u>

Start at the head, and scan all around the healee. Wherever you find the biggest 'negative energy spot' (NES) or hibiki, let reiki flow through until the area feels smooth.

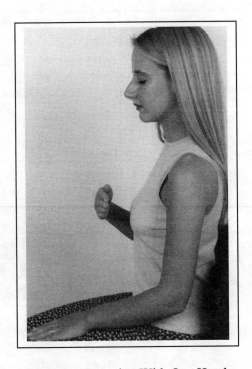

Figure 54: Scanning With One Hand

Scanning The Aura – 2

If you find two 'negative energy spots,' let reiki flow into both at the same time, even if one spot is further outside the body than the other.

Scanning The Aura – 3

A positive self-healing method to create health and balance is to scan your own aura and heal through wherever you feel any hibiki, or 'negative energy spot.'

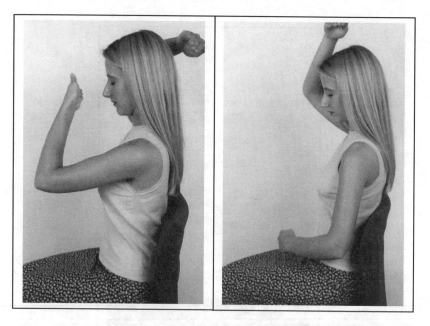

Figure 55: Scanning 2 Negative Energy Spots At The Same Time

WORKBOOK NOTES
On Scanning

WORKBOOK NOTES
Biofeedback Of First Scanning

CHAPTER 22

JAKIKIRI JOKA-HO

Jakikiri Joka-ho: Chopping And Releasing Stubborn Byosen

Jakikiri Joka-ho is the phrase used by Japanese reiki masters to describe a purification of negative energy by making a chopping movement of the healer's hand. This is used when there is a strong sensation of hibiki in the hand from a byosen, and all normal attempts to shift the byosen do not work.

1. When To Use Jakikiri Joka-ho

a. Byosen is too large or strong

If the negative energy from the source of the illness is too big, simply putting in good reiki energy into that area may not be enough to disperse the bad. You will know that this is a possible problem if:

i. You normally disperse byosen within a short period and it does not budge even a fraction.

ii. There is a very large area (at least the size of a football) where you feel hibiki in the hand.

b. Byosen cord connection to physical is too strong

Sometimes the negative energy of the byosen in the aura has a 'cord' attached to it, connecting it to the physical body. Even if you disperse the aura's bad energy byosen, the attached cord will pull it back into the original position. You will know that this may be a problem if:

i. You think that you have healed the byosen but it returns soon after.

ii. The byosen 'jumps around,' but always returns to the original spot.

c. The healee has too big an emotional, or mental, or spiritual attachment to their byosen

Some healees are unconsciously too attached to the source of their illness. The byosen has become like an old friend that is not liked, but that has become such a comfortable bad old friend that the person is in a rut that is too difficult to break away from. You will know this is a possible issue if:

i. The byosen is difficult to budge or soon returns to the original spot, *and*

ii.   The person has a fear of what they may be like if they were cured.

For example, the illness provides attention or love from others, and without the illness, how would that love come?

Or maybe the person's illness has simply allowed a comfortable rut of life, and if there was a cure, there is a fear of what the unknown life would be like. Many people are comfortable with what they know, and uncomfortable with change.

iii. Please note: if you consider that if this point above (c.ii.) could be the problem, *and* if you have been trained in counselling or psychotherapy, it may be wise to discuss the issues with your healee.

Or, refer to a qualified, professional counsellor. Once the issues are brought to the conscious mind, the healee can usually make a rational decision to release the byosen, and you can continue with Jakikiri Joka-ho.

iv.   Please do not introduce or discuss the problem if you have not been professionally trained - you could make matters worse.

2.   When Not To Use Jakikiri Joka-ho

a.   Healee's decision

Occasionally, after receiving counselling about the attachment to the illness as in c.ii. and c.iii. above, a person may decide not to be healed. This is perfectly acceptable as part of the healing process.

b.   Healer's respect for the healee's decision

Reiki 1 practitioners should respect the wishes of that healee, even if intuitively we believe that the person should continue with their course of reiki treatments. Remember that no clairvoyant or healer is always right, so accept the decision gracefully.

c. A possible start of healing

Understand that, even if the person refuses further reiki treatments from you, there has probably been created at least the start of a healing process simply by helping the person understand that they have an emotional, or mental, or spiritual attachment to their illness.

On some occasions, it is the very act of the person recognising that they have an attachment for a particular reason that becomes the actual healing cure.

For example, people who suddenly discover that they do not want to release their problem because it allows them to receive love will often be shocked initially. But they are usually able to come to terms with the issue themselves, and progress on without further healing.

However, if professional counselling or psychotherapy has brought the issue of attachment to the surface of the conscious mind, the healee may be helped by further counselling, or by referral to a third party specialist.

3. How To Use Jakikiri Joka-ho

If you can scan and feel byosen in an aura relevant to an illness, this means that the negative energy is emanating from the physical bodily illness into the aura. Therefore there is a connection cord between the byosen and the body. If the connection can be broken, the byosen can then be more easily healed or released.

Exercise 92 - Jakikiri Joka-ho
Make a chopping motion with one hand, holding the hand at right angles to the body part, between the place in the aura where you feel hibiki, and the nearest part of the physical being. In normal scanning of the close energy

field, this chopping motion will be about two inches from the physical.

Take care not to touch the person.

Repeat two more times.

Then give reiki to the byosen to see if it can be healed, dispersed, cleansed or released more easily.

If the byosen is still stubborn, give a few more chopping movements from different angles between the auric NES and the body, and continue to pour reiki in until there is no more hibiki.

WORKBOOK NOTES
On Jakikiri Joka-ho

CHAPTER 23

THE 21-DAY CLEANSING OR HEALING PROCESS

Receiving an attunement may, for some students, be similar to receiving healing. Many reactions can occur. In Western reiki, the process students may go through after the attunements is called 'The 21-day cleansing process' because of Mrs Takata's story that Dr Usui spent 21 days on Mount Kurama - and it was only on the last day that he discovered the true value of the reiki system in a flash of inspiration.

However, there appears to be no record of any cleansing process in either Dr Usui's or Dr Hayashi's writings or records. The '21-day cleansing process' started from the USA, and is probably one of Mrs Takata's ideas. I prefer to call the period after an attunement a healing process – a healing process that could last for any length of time, not only 21 days.

Although many students do not have a healing process, if you do have one it could be due to one or many healings going on, or your re-adjusted energy body still re-adjusting, or an often-higher frequency of energy you have been attuned to and how this new frequency vibrates with your previous disharmonious state, or the process may become relevant to your life-healing needs, or there may be a development of your soul pathway progression.

In physics we are taught that different objects are not solid or liquid or gaseous - they simply vibrate at different frequencies. And we are taught it is possible to change matter from one frequency to another, e.g. ice to water, to steam.

When you are attuned to a higher frequency, there may similarly be an automatic release from your negative lower frequency energy to a more appropriate higher frequency.

The 21-Day Healing Process If ...

There are no certain rules as to what or how long any particular healing process should be. The following are guidelines only.

1. If You Have Had A Very Happy, Healthy Life

If you have had few or no problems in your life, and are in complete harmonious balance, you may not experience any changes. You may also not experience changes if you are already healed on the energy level that the attunement provides; or if you are so spiritually advanced that a healing need becomes irrelevant to your path.

2. If You Have Had A Relatively Good Life

If you have already done much work on yourself, probably you will not have much of a noticeable healing process, and maybe you will not experience much during your healing period.

During this period you are likely to feel only a gentle healing, and it should not take too long.

3. If There Are Current Difficult Areas In Your Life

If you have current problems, changes may occur gradually. Over some weeks, even if the problem still exists, you may find it easier to cope with or accept current ongoing negatives in your life.

4. If You Had A Very Traumatic Or Difficult Life

If you have had many past or continuous problems in your life and have experienced little or no previous therapy or healing on yourself you may have a difficult healing period.

395

Occasionally this may last for many weeks or even months. This period may not be nice, since so many issues could rise to be healed.

But rest assured. Every person I have heard about who has gone through that period has been immensely grateful after, becoming a healed and happier and better being.

5. If You Need Emergency Repairs

Some people have acute physical or other problems. Maybe the issue has not yet materialised into a conscious issue, but is 'evolving' within, growing into what may soon become a health problem.

It is common in cases like this that there is a fairly dramatic, but normally short, healing period.

6. There Are No Hard And Fast Rules!

In general, it seems that the more you need to heal from your life, the longer or more difficult will be your healing process. This means that, depending on how much you need to cleanse from your life, your healing period may be 21 seconds. Or 21 minutes, hours, days, or weeks. Indeed, the healing period does not have to be 21 anything! The period will last according to the individual healing need.

Two Reikis A Day
Help Keep Illness At Bay

More about 'The 21-Day Healing Process'

1. The First Half Hour

During or within the half hour immediately after an attunement is when the majority of people feel most inner healing. It is a time when the attunement energy is flowing through negative issues inside and outside the student. It is a time when reiki is working to push out or dissolve less positive energies. It is a time of rebalancing and reintegration for wholeness and wellness.

The feelings for some students are quite substantial. Whatever happens, you should <u>not</u> try to understand the issues arising but to accept them.

And do <u>not</u> try to heal away anything you don't like, such as a pain – you'll probably heal away the healing process! If necessary, seek a quiet space after the attunement to allow the energies to integrate within you.

If in doubt, ask your reiki master for an interpretation. Or see chapter 9, '*Biofeedback*'.

2. The First Three Days

The three-day period after attunements often holds big reactions. After the first half hour, the next three days are when the majority of attunement energies integrate with the student's energy body.

It is also the time period when you may feel chakras realign themselves, and also when the majority of other healing works take place, such as in the aura, and in the etheric and other energy bodies. Do not question 'unusual' experiences. They are without doubt perfectly normal experiences that you are not used to!

You should take life slowly during these three days. Still be busy, if you lead a busy life. But be busy slowly. Give the energies a chance to work.

3. Healing During The Next Weeks And Months

Although the following points are appropriate at other times of your healing process, they are particularly relevant during this period.

a.   A release of negative energy
Some students experience a release of 'negativity.' This could mean a positive change in previous problems with the physical body, emotional being, mental attitude, psychic nature, or spiritual awareness.

b.   Releases from the unconscious
You may have 'unusual' feelings, as old issues rise to the surface from your unconscious mind. These old issues may have been buried, perhaps because they were thought of unconsciously as being impossible to heal.

But when you have reiki, unconsciously you now know that it is potentially possible to heal anything. So you can release 'old stuff', naturally and gently, and then reiki yourself better.

c.   Dreams
You may have 'good' or 'bad' dreams. Such dreams are simply symbolic healing of your past, or release of bad habits or prejudices.

So it is with 'nightmares'. They are there to release old or deep-seated problems. They are not a problem in themselves. For example, it is common to have a 'nightmare' of being chased and murdered. In healing, not dream, symbology, this could mean a deep healing of severe guilt!

Simply accept all dreams and continue to reiki and heal yourself. If necessary, contact your reiki master or another professional for support as you progress.

d.   Diary
For those who experience a healing period, this may be an exceptionally important time in your life.

<u>Exercise 93 - Diary Logs</u>
**Keep a diary on what happens in your healing
period, your thought patterns, relevant
dreams.
Log this time in your life and one day in the
future look back at your records and wonder
at the amazing healing effects of reiki.
You never know; it may start your reiki book.**

e. Self-help

During your healing period, do practise reiki self-healing first
thing each morning before you get up, and last thing at night after you
go to bed. Give extra daily sessions if needed. This will continue the
process, and help raise your vibratory rate. And if you feel the need,
think about taking the next course or a reiki-sharing circle that will
have other healing tools and another attunement to help you progress.

4. Support

In rare circumstances, usually when a student has had a terrible
life with little or no previous healing of any kind, it may be necessary
to contact the reiki master for support through the healing processes.

Or, seek out other therapies, therapists, or medical professionals
to help heal and guide you through to the end of the healing process.

5. Acceptance

Above all, whether you actually feel change within or not, accept
that the highest universal source is working within you to help you
evolve to a better, even more wonderful person.

Accept whatever occurs, even if it seems nothing. Accept
everything, even if changes seem negative, or are hard to understand.
In fact, do not try to understand. Trust that this healing process will
ultimately work in your life for your highest God and goodness.

After The Healing Period

Life is a seesaw of good and bad events. It is natural that, as you go through life, different issues and situations will affect you adversely. The important thing is to keep self-healing or seek 'top-up' attunements, reattunements, or progression attunements so that, even in very difficult circumstances, you will stay reasonably in balance…

1. Keeping Up Your Self-Healing

No matter how long or short the healing period is, after, you may be adjusted, balanced, in wholeness and contentment.

Regular self-healing should be adhered to. Once a day if you now feel good, twice a day if you feel off-peak, and three times a day or more when ill. This will help you stay at your newfound higher, happier frequency.

Exercise 94 - Awareness Of Self-Healing Need
This is a long-term exercise.
Reiki yourself twice a day for one year.
Remember that reiki is not a religion, so part of the exercise is not to feel guilty if you cannot do reiki one or more days.
The next part of the exercise is that if you miss sessions, you give your self another self-healing treatment as soon as possible. It is easy to lapse into laziness.
If you become ill during the year, find time for an extra treatment or two each day. It has been proved by many practitioners that colds and flu's last less than one third of their

normal time when reiki is given three times daily.

2. Does An Attunement Last Forever?

Many students ask whether they need another attunement. The short answer is, 'Almost certainly, yes.'

The reason is that, although the memory of the attunement will be with the student for every lifetime, the energy of it probably will not be. For example, if you argue with the cashier in a supermarket, the memory of that argument will be with you potentially for every lifetime. But the energy of the argument will probably dissolve, or be resolved.

So it is with attunements. You have free will. You can choose good or bad paths in this world. If you choose a path that is not so good, or if you interact on your path in ways that create disharmony, positive effects of the attunement could be overridden by your negative ways.

This demonstrates one example of why reattunements, top-up attunements, or progression attunements are needed.

3. Top-Up Attunements - Reiju

In Japan, regular 'top-up' attunements are available. Japanese senseis give the Reiju attunements to all students at every meeting, or gathering, regardless of whether the meetings are daily, weekly or monthly. This helps keep their energy bodies balanced, in a higher frequency, and on the path of LOve and Light.

Many reiki masters around the world now also offer regular Reiju attunements to their students, especially in reiki sharing groups.

4. Reattunements

As stated in 2 above, nothing lasts forever, and free will means that attunement energy may not last. If the student has lapsed away from reiki for some time, practising again may be all that is needed. However, some students may need to 'kick-start' their reiki by retaking the course and having reattunements.

This is almost always extremely empowering because reiki knowledge will be refreshed (memory of knowledge clouds and fades over time). And the reattunements will help regain appropriate reiki flow.

5.   Progression Attunements

The next level of reiki is taken for many reasons. For some students, it is enough to take the next level just to have the next level attunement. This is because each attunement process can potentially help your inner and outer energies to heal in a different way, and your unconscious mind to allow reiki healing to be directed more forcefully or more appropriately for your self-healing and treatments for others.

Attunements are designed to be different on different levels to ensure the potential growth of each student is maximised.

WORKBOOK NOTES
On The 21 Day Healing Process

WORKBOOK NOTES
On 'The 21-Day Healing Process'

<u>(If Relevant)</u>

WORKBOOK NOTES
On Personal Healing Process

<u>FIRST 3 DAYS (If Relevant)</u>

WORKBOOK NOTES
On Personal Healing Process

4TH TO 21ST DAY (If Relevant)

WORKBOOK NOTES
On Personal Healing Process

MONTH AFTER 21 DAYS (If Relevant)

WORKBOOK NOTES
On Personal Healing Process

<u>(OTHER TIMESCALE)</u>

CHAPTER 24

CAVEATS, CONTRAINDICATIONS, DANGERS

Specific Rei Spiritual Healing – Caveats, Contraindications, Dangers

For caveats etc. relevant to any reiki energy, please see the section after this. The following are caveats, contraindications and dangers specifically appropriate <u>only to the use of rei energy</u>. As with all things there are issues to be aware of when using rei spiritual healing if we are only ever to do good and Godly works.

The following are the main issues I am aware of at present. However, spiritual healing and reiki are young therapies - so not all issues will yet have risen to the surface in enough numbers to be understood. Despite that, I am confident that there are few other caveats, contraindications and dangers of using rei that will be discovered over and above the following. (If any reader does discover an issue that has repeated at least three times, or the problem seems a certainty and should be included in this section, please write to me directly so that it may be included in the next edition.)

1. Craving For LOve

This is a rare possibility, but it is sad that some souls miss the connection of when their soul was with the LOve of God so much that they crave it, seeking LOve at every opportunity.

If this occurs, rei may make their hunger for LOve stronger and create more craving for the drug of rei. This could make them dissatisfied with their lot on earth, even to the extent of wishing suicide in order to 'go home', and be with LOve permanently.

If this happens, explain that it may take a long time – often two years – before rei may rebalance their craving of LOve.

In an extreme case wait until you take Reiki 2 to give this type of person healing with the more grounded Reiki 2 symbols. These lower frequency energies should not provoke a craving for LOve.

Exercise 95 - Being in Your Body
This exercise is not needed for most people. If needed, if you often crave LOve, consider the times when you felt 'normal', when you were happy with your lot in life. Meditate on the circumstances.   Try to recreate those situations in your life and stay happy.

2. Manic Conditions

Similar to the above, persons in a manic state of being may already be too high in the frequency of their energy body. If you give them rei healing when in the manic phase, it could take them higher still and make them extremely ill.

As above, this type of person needs low frequency energy only, to try to lower their frequencies to a more manageable earthly level.

3. Manic-Depressives

Treat manic-depressives in the manic phase the same as 1. and 2. above. Do not give them rei. Eventually take Reiki 2 and give low frequency Reiki 2 energies.

However, when in the depressed phase, they need spiritual rei healing to bring them back up again.

This treatment may work as a rebalancing aid over a medium to long-term period of time.

4. Schizophrenia

Some people diagnosed with schizophrenia may be affected adversely by spiritual rei healing. If the healee has been hospitalised with schizophrenia, ask permission from *the patient to ask* the nurse in charge of the case at the hospital if it is acceptable to provide rei healing. The nurse in charge may know that the person has been previously affected adversely by rei and ended up in hospital the next day each time they have received spiritual rei healing.

Respect the hospital professional's judgement.

5. Hallucinatory

Some healees may have been hospitalised due to seeing visions they cannot cope with. Indeed, these visions are then termed hallucinations, and because they cannot cope with them, they have to be on medication and perhaps have regular periods in hospital.

Spiritual rei healing, with its potentially high frequency connecting into the worlds of spirit, spiritual and Godly, may provoke visions that this type of person cannot cope with.

As above, if the person has been hospitalised, permission or advice should be sought from the nurse in charge of the case, and their opinion respected.

6. Grounding

Occasionally a person who gives or receives rei finds it difficult or even impossible to stay grounded. If this occurs, please read section in chapter 16, 'Grounding'.

In a very severe case where someone finds it impossible to stay grounded, consider taking Reiki 2 to use symbols that are already more grounded, lower frequencies.

General Reiki – Caveats, Contraindications, Dangers

Although the previous section is specific to caveats, contraindications and dangers of the use of rei or spiritual healing energy, the following general caveats etc apply to any of the reiki energies. Caveats and contraindications, whilst not being a part of any code or law at present, are all included together in the same section because some of them are so potentially dangerous, they may one day be enshrined in a law or code.

Many books state that healing and reiki energies are intelligent energy. This is often true. But some books go further and state that healing and reiki energies are SO intelligent that it is impossible for there ever to be any negative side effect. Whilst this is strictly true, there are contra-indications. In other words, whilst reiki in itself can only ever have good effects, there are certain conditions, illnesses and drugs that make giving reiki potentially dangerous. So although some of the following caveats are considered 'potentially highly dangerous', others are just a 'warning to be careful.'

Doctors, surgeons, nurses, and other medical healthcare professionals are taught that the treatments they give patients can have bad side effects. In fact, in training school, they are taught that sometimes a patient will be hurt or even die because the medical professional can 'get things wrong'. This is a realistic approach. But medical professionals have had the past 300 years to understand their caveats. And only in this last half-century have the medical professions been open enough to admit their caveats in advance.

Healers are just beginning their own 300-year progression. In England in 1944, Helen Duncan was imprisoned as a witch. It was only in 1951 that the Witches Act of 1735 was repealed. Previously, healing was an offence that could be punished by death. So it is early days for healers to understand their profession, and to understand if negatives may occur. I believe that, as did medical professions, healers should develop, and be open enough to admit their caveats.

412

If we healers are to work in the National Health Service of our countries, in surgeries and hospitals etc, we must be aware not only of the good effects of our therapy. We must also be aware and open about potential caveats and dangers. Currently, the UK, European, USA, and other governments are asking for research into various complementary and alternative therapies. Research is not just about how effective each therapy is. The research is also for proving any negatives and dangers of each therapy – and in particular the negatives, caveats, contra-indications and dangers of each therapy's reaction with each illness and condition and the drugs that each illness may need. To governments, the discovery of dangers is a positive step. If they then accept a therapy into the Health Service for a particular illness or condition, they can be assured that these dangers can be avoided where possible. Only good and goodness should then come from the therapy.

Except for the following, I am not aware of other possible dangerous reiki contra-indications, or caveats, but it should be noted that the list is not definitive. There have been recent suggestions about a possible danger of overdosing on thyroid medication if the thyroid is cured and the person does not realise it, and they continue taking thyroid medication (consult on this with a doctor to be certain about this!) And there could be more problems yet to be discovered. If you find a caveat, danger, or contra-indication not listed here, please first confirm your finding with three medical professionals. If they agree, write to me and I will be pleased to include it in the next edition of this book.

Over 23 years, I have consulted many medical people, and taught many Health Service doctors, hypnotists, psychotherapists, psychologists, and psychiatrists. One lady was a professor, a true expert in her field, who has written more than 20 books. So far, she and every other legal and medical professional have said that, as far as they understand, there are no more possible issues.

So please do not be concerned about the following list. The important thing is to <u>understand</u> any possible negative reactions so that we only ever do goodness!!

413

General Reiki – Caveats, Contraindications, Dangers (Continued)

Please read the previous pages before reading these caveats. Note that although these pages contain serious dangers, slight risks, and practical problems, in the whole healing field there are not many.

1. Diabetics Who Are On Insulin

It is sad that although all illnesses may be potentially healed with reiki, there are some dangers that make it almost impossible to heal certain conditions with the assurance of safety. This caveat is highly dangerous, but only relevant if the diabetic is <u>on insulin</u>. If he or she is <u>not</u> on insulin there is <u>not</u> a problem. Please give as much reiki as you like to someone who is <u>not</u> on insulin.

Many people ask the same question, 'What about diabetics not on insulin?' The answer is as above. Some words are underlined to emphasise that this section only applies to diabetics <u>on insulin</u>.

a. The danger
Usually it feels 'lucky' if we get a cure in one session. However, if the person is <u>on insulin</u>, you may have a severe problem - it may be <u>unlucky</u> to get a cure in one session! Because, if you are unlucky enough to cure the insulin-dependent diabetic in one session, and he or she does not realise there has been a cure, the person could die from the next insulin dose.

The reason insulin-dependent diabetics may die is, if they are suddenly cured, they will not need insulin because their own natural insulin has returned. The next insulin dose may be a fatal overdose.

b. Can we give reiki if insulin-dependent diabetics test themselves before and after reiki or an insulin dose?
It is true that diabetics on insulin can test their level of insulin need before or after their insulin intake or reiki. Theoretically

therefore, it should be safe to give reiki because diabetics should be able to adjust their insulin level if a cure has occurred.

However, hospital wards are full of diabetics on insulin who do not test themselves correctly! (If you are in doubt about this, ask a nurse or doctor.) Therefore, if you cannot trust a diabetic to test correctly, you cannot reiki the person, because a cure could kill.

c. Is there a way that is not dangerous?
Sadly, the safe answer is, 'probably not'.

i.   There are suggestions that people who have been on insulin for many years and never been in hospital with diabetic problems must be intelligent and motivated enough to test correctly.

   But are you willing to take that risk? I wouldn't...

ii. It has also been suggested that distant healing – say from your house to the diabetic's house – may be safer because distant healing works more on the etheric body, and less on the physical, and therefore there is less chance of a problem. This is possibly true. In my 23 years of experience, I have never heard of distant healing harming a diabetic.

   But are you willing to take that risk? I wouldn't deliberately give distant healing to a diabetic on insulin.

iii. In 1999, a student studying reiki with me for the first time gasped loudly when she heard of this caveat.

   He exclaimed, 'Oh! My previous reiki master gave reiki to his father who was a diabetic on insulin, and his father died the next day! He thinks he helped his father move on to the next world!'

   Maybe he had helped his father move on, but not in the way he thought. Not all things are 'meant to be'...

iv. Many people in Denmark have told me over the past five years that it is against Danish law for anyone except a

415

doctor to touch a diabetic on insulin. If this is true, I agree with the law. In fact, I would like there to be a similar law in every country to protect diabetics from the danger as in 1a above.

d.   What about reikiing other illnesses of a diabetic?

This may depend on what energy you will use. This manual only explains how to use spiritual or rei energy. However, after taking the Reiki 2 course, students will have the option of using lower level frequencies such as the first and second symbols.

i.   Certainly you should not use the first symbol for any other illness a diabetic may have. There may be an accidental knock-on effect from the low frequency of the first symbol that could cure the diabetes.

ii.   It may be OK to use spiritual rei healing or the second symbol because these energies vibrate at a much higher rate, and are thus unlikely to cure the low frequency problem of diabetes. However, do be certain that you stay focused to try to ensure that you really do only channel the energy of the rei or second symbol. Personally, I would not take the risk, and I ask all healers not to risk a life either. You never know.

e.   Safety first

When giving reiki to a diabetic on insulin, the advice is simple. You may be able to help or even cure that diabetic person. But a small risk of death is an unacceptable risk. Go by this simple rule. 'When in doubt, leave it out!'

Or go by the saying, 'better safe than sorry', and put safety first.

I remember that in 1998 a man arrived at my Reiki Healing Centre unexpectedly. He had driven about 5 hours from the other side of England. His problem was physical, a severe back pain. But during the initial interview he wrote that he was diabetic, and was having insulin. I explained gently about the problem, and that I would rather he drove home again, and was not driven back in a hearse! After he understood the problem, he was most grateful, and thanked me profusely for the honesty. He respected the honesty, and has since referred other people to me for healing. Honesty really is the best policy.

2. Pacemakers

It may be highly dangerous to reiki someone who is fitted with a pacemaker. Certainly most good healing organisations during the 1990s asked their healers to avoid patients who had pacemakers.

a. The danger

Pacemakers can be affected by electrical or magnetic energy. And reiki healing can be electrical or magnetic in nature. Therefore, reiki or healing can affect a pacemaker. Healing energy may make the pacemaker go much faster or slower – and I do not think your intention would be to speed it up or slow it down too much. Either too fast or too slow may be dangerous to that person's life.

b. Is there a way that is not dangerous?

Yes, possibly.

It depends on the frequency and amplitude of the healing provided. Rei healing at any amplitude should not affect a pacemaker, as the frequency is probably not low enough to have an effect. However, remember that many healers do not always channel rei when they intend to, as discussed in chapter 7 in the section *'Do All Spiritual/Rei Healers Channel Love?'*. Medtronic,[111] one of the world's largest producers of pacemakers, states that although low frequency fields such as those generated by usual household equipment such as microwaves will not harm the functioning of a

---

[111] This reference is from Medtronic at www.medtronic.com. Alternatively, you can also visit www.americanheart.org/presenter.jhtml?identifier=32 for similar information.

pacemaker, arc-welding equipment is still dangerous. This suggests that intense and relevant energies of a healer (more likely to be channelled on Reiki 2) could also be dangerous.

c. What about reikiing other illnesses of a person with a pacemaker?

These issues are identical to those of a diabetic on insulin. So please see 1.d. above.

d. Safety first

See 1.e. above. The maxim 'better safe than sorry' should always be borne in mind.

3. Hypocortisolism

Hypocortisolism is a condition where the adrenal glands have substantially or totally collapsed. This then causes a very inadequate flow of adrenaline. When there is minimal adrenal function, the patient could die within four days if the condition were not discovered. If the patient is 'lucky' enough to have the problem diagnosed, he or she must then take a high dose of steroids, as replacement therapy, to keep them alive.

a. The danger

The danger is similar to a diabetic on insulin. If someone is suddenly cured of hypocortisolism, the next dose, or doses, of the steroid replacement may be an overdose. And then the person may die. Because they will suddenly have the return of their normal adrenaline, and the steroid intake could give them 'way over the dose' needed.

b. Is there a way that is not dangerous?

Unfortunately, almost certainly there is NOT a safe way to heal this condition. At least with an insulin-dependent diabetic, they can potentially test regularly. Hypocortisolism cannot be tested regularly.

i.   A synacthen test can be done at a hospital. But the test is expensive, so hospitals will not give it often. Depending on the hospital, it may be every few months at the most - usually to see if the adrenal function is worse and extra steroids are needed. And it takes about two weeks to get the results.

ii. The delay in getting a test, and in getting the test results, means that you really cannot risk giving reiki to someone with this condition, because they will not know if they have been cured, and can overdose and die.

iii. As in orthodox medicine, healers face moral dilemmas. In the case of hypocortisolism, the excessive but necessary dose of steroid may kill the person anyway. And in the last stages before death, because the high dose of steroids can take calcium from the bones, there may be excruciating pain from bones fracturing as the person breathes.

Often, the moral dilemma is, 'When the final stage comes, do we allow that person to die, or risk giving reiki that may help or cure but that may also cause death?'

Medical professionals have serious concerns over their own moral dilemmas. I do not give an answer here.

I simply pose the question.

c.   A little of my health history

Many years ago I suffered from hypocortisolism. The high dose of steroids needed took much of the calcium from the bones, and caused severe osteoporosis. After a scan of my bones I was advised that within two years I would be in a wheelchair, if not dead. While writing this book, an astrologer looked at my chart and exclaimed, 'Why are you alive? You should be dead!'

In brief, after having a cataclysmic realisation that my soul purpose was to heal and teach full-time, I was cured in one session by a guided meeting - and incredible healing - from a 'Born Again

Christian' healer I had never met before. I have been psychically aware all my life, and that evening after I took my steroid dose, it felt as if every atom in my being was filled with steroids, as if I could vomit steroids from every pore. At that moment it felt psychically obvious I had been cured.

I have never taken steroids since, and the next synacthen test at the hospital confirmed the cure.

The problem is that if I had been wrong and had not been cured, without steroids I could have died within four days, because of the lack of replacement adrenaline.

Due to my psychic intuition, I was lucky. But many of your patients may not be so psychic, and as stated above, a sudden cure could result in death by overdose.

d. What about reikiing other illnesses of a person with hypocortisolism?

These issues are identical to those of a diabetic on insulin, so please see 1.d. above.

e. Steroids for other illnesses

Some students, when hearing the above, become concerned about a risk of giving reiki to patients taking steroids for other conditions such as asthma. As far as I understand from medical professionals, all other illnesses that need steroids are not a problem.

The point to remember is this: if the asthma or whatever else is suddenly cured, there is probably nothing that can suddenly be produced in the body like extra adrenaline. Therefore if the patient continues taking steroids for asthma after being cured, there should be no dangerous overdose.

4. Epilepsy

Epilepsy is not a danger in the same way as the above. Epilepsy is a 'practical problem'. Please carefully consider the following before treating an epileptic person.

420

a.   The practical problem

Reiki will not cause an epileptic fit.

However, if you give a normal reiki treatment to an epileptic, the person could have a fit by coincidence. And if they injure themselves during the fit, and at the same time as you are giving them hands-on reiki, you could be blamed for the injury and taken to Court for compensation.

b.   Is there a way to heal epileptics?

Thankfully, the answer is a definite 'Yes.'

As stated by the great English healer of the 1950s, Harry Edwards, any form of healing for an epileptic can and should be sent from a distance. This does not mean from a distance across the same room, but from, say, your home to their home. (Distant healing is normally considered a Reiki 2 subject so is described and discussed in depth in the Reiki 2 Manual.)

Then if the person has a fit by coincidence whilst you are sending reiki from a distance, you cannot be blamed and sued. It is unlikely that any court would take distant healing seriously, even if someone tried to suggest that the distant healing had caused the fit.

5.   Pain

Pain is one of the conditions that are relatively easy for most healers to relieve. However, there are dangers that should be understood by all professional reiki practitioners to ensure that you always do the very best for your healees.

a.   Pain healing

Pain is relatively easy to relieve for two main reasons.

i.   Higher level reiki classes teach techniques that have an exceptionally high success rate, even on students practising on each other during the course.

ii.   And there is a natural reason why most healers find pains relatively easy to relieve.

It is because, according to a 1992 tape from a conference by Valerie Hunt, some pains have a frequency of about 900 cycles per second; and by pure chance, it just so happens that most healers' natural frequency may also be about 900 cycles per second.

You may know that when two identical frequencies touch, one of the things that may happen is that they cancel each other out.

In the case of pain, the healer's 900-cps self-created frequency will disappear, and the healer will simply change to a combination of other frequencies within themselves. But the pain frequency of the healee will also disappear so that the pain is relieved.

b.   The danger of healing pain
There are two issues to remember.

i.   There is no problem whatsoever in healing pain if the healee has been to the doctor and the cause of the pain has been, or cannot be, identified. In these cases, please give reiki as often as needed for both the pain and, if known, the deeper cause.

ii.   The danger is if the healee has <u>not</u> had their pain diagnosed, or attempted to be diagnosed, by a medical professional. This is because it is relatively easy to heal pain, but relatively difficult to cure some of the causes of pain such as bacteria, or viruses. So if you reiki the pain away, the person may think that he or she is cured, but the bacteria or virus may spread unnoticed and do even worse damage inside the person. Please do not give reiki until <u>after</u> the cause has been identified.

iii.   A case example

One of my student reiki masters had a terrifying phobia about going to the dentist. So when she had pain in a tooth, she took no notice of the above teaching, but gave reiki to the tooth instead. The pain disappeared.

And when another pain appeared in a nearby tooth, she gave reiki to that pain as well. Again the pain disappeared.

Until eventually she had such an excruciating pain in her mouth she decided to brave a visit to the dentist.

The dentist discovered that the bacteria in the first painful tooth had spread. Now it was not just one tooth infected. The infection had spread throughout most of her teeth, gums, and mouth.

Please do not make the same mistake about the healing of pain.

6. Drinking Water Before Or After A Reiki Treatment

You will read in many books that, after a healing or reiki treatment, you should offer your healee a glass of water or some other drink. Please <u>don't</u>. Consider this:

a.   The danger
Thank goodness this danger is very, very small. Candy Gregory B.Sc., a nurse in the UK, described to me a rare kidney condition called hydronephrosis where drinking water may cause death. Ask any doctor you know if you wish to confirm this.

There could still be a problem whether they know they have the kidney condition or not. (See c. below)

A person can lose up to 90% of kidney function and not really know until they had a routine blood test. However, if someone were to slip below that level of functioning, which can happen for many reasons, there is a certainty of a coma within days to a week if it goes untreated. Giving water to someone in that condition would put him or her in the hospital or kill him or her for having too much fluid in the blood. The UK National Kidney Federation recommends that healers never offer water to their clients for this reason.[112]

b.   Why do so many books say to drink water?
Because they have simply repeated the healing Codes of Practice started by spiritualist churches.

In spiritualist churches, it is generally accepted that the energy body of a spirit is made from a substance called ectoplasm. (Photographs can be and have been taken of ectoplasm.) When a spirit enters a healer or healee, the spirit's ectoplasm will absorb much moisture from the physical bodies it enters. So in spiritualist churches it is essential for the healer and the healee to drink water after healing in order to replenish the moisture absorbed by the spirit.

---

[112] National Kidney Federation, www.kidney.org

In the usual way reiki is taught by most reiki masters, there should be no spirit guide entering the practitioner, nor the patient. So therefore there is no need to ever drink or offer water – unless you are thirsty!

c. If they do not know they have any kidney problem

Remember that any illness has to start at some point in time. It will of course be extremely rare, but someone could have slipped below that 10% threshold that day and the person will discover the problem very soon.

So do not offer anyone a drink of any sort.

At least if they discover the kidney problem at their own home, you will not have a crisis on your hands.

d. If they know they have this kidney problem

Of course, if people know that a glass of water may kill them, they should not accept a drink of water, or any other drink, from you. But some people are so weak-willed they may feel obliged to accept a drink if you offer it.

Remember that hospital wards are full of diabetics who know what will harm them, yet still they do not eat or test correctly. And they end up in hospital.

You cannot trust healees to do what is best for themselves. So never offer a drink to anyone.

e. Is there a way around this problem?

Yes. It is perfectly acceptable for you to have a jug of water and glasses in a prominent position for healees to see. If they are thirsty they are welcome to ask for a drink, or to help themselves – but please never offer one.

7. Hearing Aids

This is not dangerous – it is more of a practical problem. But care must be taken, for the comfort of your healee. If you give healing energies to someone wearing a hearing aid or deaf-aid, please do not hold your hands to provide reiki near the hearing aid whilst it is being worn.

If you do, the hearing aid is likely to make a loud rising, whining sound, similar to an air-raid siren going off!

It will not only potentially shock the healee. The unfortunate person may leave even deafer than when they arrived!

There are two simple but needed practical points to remember.

a.   Before giving reiki to the ears

Ask the healee to take out their deaf-aids so as to prevent the above problem.

b.   If the person is very deaf

Before the deaf aid is taken out, agree a signal such as three light taps on the left shoulder so the deaf person will know you have finished. If you do not agree a signal, if you tap them on the shoulder at the end when they may be extremely relaxed, they will 'come back' with a jolt or even a shock.

8.   Using More Than One Frequency At A Time

Although this is not a caveat, contraindication or danger relevant to spiritual or rei healing, it is mentioned here in order to keep all caveats in one section.

In the case of reiki, using one single frequency only at all times will have a purer energy force. Similar to homeopathy, if you use one frequency only, you will be more likely to work on the illness and get a cure; and using one single frequency means that two or more energies cannot fight each other (Greene, Benor v2).

9.   Healing From The Head Down Or The Feet Up

See section, 'Stress Versus Low Energy' in chapter 14.

Remember that if you heal all people by starting the treatment at the head, and finishing at the feet, someone whose main problem is low energy will probably feel worse after you have finished.

10. Chakra Balancing

Please see section on '*Chakras*' in chapter 20.

Chakra balancing can make someone ill to the point of being physically sick if you consciously decide to balance or put a certain colour in a chakra.

The classic example is of a spiritual person such as a nun or a monk. Please <u>never</u> with your ego put red in the base chakra area of such a holy person.

They do not need red. In order to stay on their chosen spiritual path they probably need violet, or white, or even gold in each chakra. Putting red in the base chakra of a spiritual nun or monk could give them feelings they do not want nor need! In a worst-case scenario, the spiritual destiny of the nun or monk could be destroyed.

11. Reiki Or Chakra Massage

Chakra massage should be avoided, as there are so many difficulties.

a.   Soul path
The healees may need certain forces in the chakras for their soul paths, and as with chakra balancing, doing something out of your egotistical conscious choice could be very harmful, and potentially take them off their soul path.

b.   Quality controlled massage
In any case, a reiki practitioner should not undertake chakra or any other type of massage unless a professional massage course has been taken. Because only then will you learn about the dangers of massage such as fracturing weak osteoporitic bones. And only then,

because reiki insurance does not cover massage, will you be able to insure yourself against such possible problems.

c. Chakra massage and sexual abuse

Most healers are professional and honourable people, but please beware... A court case for misunderstood sexual abuse is possible.

d. Better safe than sorry

I firmly believe that we will one day scientifically accept how complex the chakra system is. And when that day comes, healers will understand the problems and never do chakra massage again.

12. Bones With Plates, Pins, Or Bolts

Philosophically, this should not be a problem for Reiki 1 students because it is extremely unlikely that Reiki 1 high frequency spiritual rei healing could have the ability to become low frequency energy in the quantity needed to create this problem. There is further explanation of this, in the Reiki 2 Manual because of the low frequency from symbol one.

13. Third Eye Healing Of A Person With Schizophrenia

Many healers believe that they should heal the third eye of a person with schizophrenia, despite the fact that there are many medical causes.

In any case, the problem with healing the third eye of some types of schizophrenia is that it is too open. If you 'get things wrong' you could open it even more and the patient could be in hospital the next day.

Persons with schizophrenia could also end up in hospital if, for example, their frequency is too high and you use a spiritual energy and raise their frequency higher.

Be very wary of healing someone with schizophrenia – especially if they have been hospitalised with the condition. You could make the condition worse.

14. Can't Cope With Hot Or Electric Etc. Feelings

Although quite a rarity, some people when feeling reiki entering them become afraid. They are afraid of the power, or of the heat or of whatever other feeling rei may induce. The normal reasons for this are that the healer or teacher did not explain adequately prior to the session about the potential biofeedback of reiki energy. If explanations had been given, the person would have been more mentally prepared for the sudden changes of feelings and energy flows within their being.

In extreme cases where the person truly cannot cope with the biofeedback of energies, they need to stay away from further healing, meditation, yoga, prayer, or anything else that could give them their unwanted biofeedback response.

Very, very rarely a de-attunement may be needed.

WORKBOOK NOTES
On Caveats, Contraindications, Dangers

CHAPTER 25

CODES AND LAWS

The following are codes and laws from the UK. When they were introduced, they applied to spiritual and other healing forms. Reiki was almost unknown at that time. Therefore they do not mention reiki specifically. However, reiki in the UK is classed as a healing method similar to spiritual or other healing forms, so the codes and laws will therefore almost certainly apply to reiki as well.

There may be other UK codes or laws etc. that are not included here.

In the mid-1990s, Commander David Repard of the Confederation of Healing Organisations believed that all laws for healers were known. That is, until a lady took a healer to Court under the Cancer Act 1939.

So the list of laws and codes may not be definitive, and it cannot be guaranteed. It is your responsibility as a professional spiritual rei healer to act ethically, morally and within the law and codes as far as is known, to double-check these and check for other laws, codes, caveats, and contraindications.

There are also laws and codes for UK healers. The codes were introduced with suggestions from the Royal Colleges. The law is enshrined within a series of acts or statutes mainly concerned with the medical and paramedical professions.

If you heal in another country, please check local and national laws and codes before you start.

Codes And Laws

1. Psychic Or Clairvoyant Diagnosis

There seems to be a natural tendency that healers believe they can develop psychic 'gifts', such as clairvoyance, clairsentience, and clairaudience. To some extent this is true. I have been psychic since childhood, and nowadays teach most psychic subjects. However, when it comes to diagnosing an illness, I am most careful only ever to use information received 'from above' for my own reference as to how to heal the presenting issues.

It is a standard UK code of Conduct that healers should never give a clairvoyant reading, nor refer to guides or spirits or religious beliefs, as these issues could upset some people.

a.   The first lesson for psychic development

Many health problems are currently exacerbated by psychic misdiagnosis. It usually goes back to one thing – inadequate psychic training. Many psychics at present seem to think that they are completely accurate. Many are without any training whatsoever. Perhaps this little story may help the understanding.

i.   I remember about 23 years ago, before I started my proper healing path, I watched a brilliant psychic and healer, Jeanne Murton, also known as 'Jeanne of Kent', give healing to a lady for her negative emotions. I respect Jeanne's knowledge and ability very much – she had her own weekly phone-in clairvoyant programme on Kent County Radio.

During this particular healing, silent tears flowed down Jeanne's face. She said nothing of the tears, and when the lady left, I asked, 'Why did you have the tears?'

433

Jeanne replied, ' I saw a lot of terrible black energy inside her. She has very badly advanced cancer and doesn't have long to live.'

I asked, 'Why didn't you tell her?'

Jeanne's reply showed her true understanding of her psychic and healing professions. She said, 'Well, the first thing is I could be wrong. And if I were wrong, what would that have done to her health? She may have collapsed.

'And the second thing is, I could be right. And if I were right, what would that have done to her health? She may have collapsed.'

What Jeanne very cleverly did do was to ask the lady in a very relaxed way, 'have you had a thorough well-person check-up with your doctor recently?' Most people will answer 'no', as did this lady. Jeanne then added that she often recommends that her patients seek a thorough medical check-up, and gained the lady's promise that she would book an appointment with her doctor the next day.

ii.   So the first lesson for psychic development is that you can be wrong, and to admit that openly and humbly within.

iii.   Please do use any information 'from above you' to try to cure the person. But please keep it to yourself. Never impart that 'information' to a healee because you could be very wrong - and what would that do to their health?

b.   Is it OK to diagnose causes of simple pains or illnesses psychically?

As already explained, the answer is a simple, one hundred per cent, 'No!' Even truly brilliant psychics say they can be wrong about 10% of the time, such as the famous Sylvia Brown in the USA who has stated such on television.

And how much medical training does the average psychic have? Doctors have trained for many years.

If someone arrives in the casualty department of a hospital with a chest pain or stomach pain, the doctor is trained to look for over 15 emergency causes of each of those pains. Other symptoms are also looked at in conjunction with the pain in order to determine a final diagnosis; for instance, vomiting may mean the chest pain problem is a heart attack, not indigestion.[113]

How many causes, and combinations of causes could most psychics come up with? Probably not many.

Because most psychics could not come up with obscure illnesses, it means that if they diagnose, they could get it wrong, and someone could become very ill, or even die.

Of course doctors sometimes diagnose incorrectly. But psychics are much, much more likely to get the diagnosis wrong.

If we reiki healers are to become accepted in the health services of our countries, we must:

i.   Become professional healers, and just provide reiki energy.

ii.   Only work with the doctor's diagnosis.

Anyway, if something happened to the person due to your wrong diagnosis, and you were sued, you would not be covered by normal reiki insurance, and Court costs would come from your pocket.

c.   If you think you are a wonderful psychic

May I suggest that you have two different business cards? One card will be for your reiki healing, and one for your psychic work. Then ask your healees and clients whether they have come for your reiki healing or for your psychic work.

Explain that you have two different jobs, and that even if they choose to have your psychic diagnosis and not your reiki, they still should see a medical professional.

Make it perfectly plain that reiki practitioners will not diagnose. We must work with doctors, not against them.

---

[113] Nurse from NHS Direct, tel 0845 46 47 48

2. Change Of Intake Of Any Substance

Many healers recommend that the healee takes, or does not take, something because the healer 'knows it will help'. Recommendations like this may be dangerous.

a. Can you suggest dietary changes e.g. vegetarianism?

Vegetarianism has only become a big philosophical way of life in most Western countries within the past 50 years. Vegetarianism truly is a wonderful philosophy. Not eating meat may help your spiritual evolution. Being vegetarian may also help you improve on other levels, including karma, and release of toxins.

But has vegetarianism been around long enough in our modern Western scientific society to prove all of its benefits and possible drawbacks?

The following is not necessarily correct, but it attempts to explain some recent research. If this research is accurate, by understanding it you may not only help others, but also protect yourself against a possible court case.

i. In 1997, a book was published explaining research into different blood types (D'Adamo). It explained that some vegetarians would be completely at ease not eating meat ever again, whilst others would crave meat.

The research showed that those who became vegetarians easily, and never had a second thought about eating meat again were of a certain blood type.

However the other group of vegetarians who tried to be vegetarian but always craved meat were of a different blood type.

The research also showed if the latter blood group that desperately wanted to eat meat didn't eat meat, they could become ill with diseases such as arthritis within two years.

ii. One of my students in Denmark first showed me the research, stating that she had given up meat, and become ill with arthritis two years after. She said that after discovering the book and eating meat again, she is back to full health.

Since then I have heard of other similar examples of arthritically ill vegetarians eating meat and returning to good health.

iii. As stated, I am not suggesting the above is correct. The example of vegetarianism is taken as a model to work with to represent the potential issues of any dietary change.

iv. Please remember, what may be good for you, may not be good for someone else. If your suggestion causes illness, you could be taken to court. Not good if you are a well-meaning dietary amateur and you have no insurance cover.

v. Until these issues are completely proven one way or the other, may I suggest a 'better safe than sorry' approach? Unless you are a qualified dietary therapist, and have a certificate to prove it, and you are backed up by specialist insurance cover, please do NOT suggest a healee should, or should not eat meat, nor indeed change any other aspect of their diet. Leave it to his or her conscience and deep inner understanding.

b. Vitamins, minerals, dietary supplements, herbs etc.

These issues are similar to the issues of vegetarianism. In general, vitamins, minerals, and herbs have only become popular in most Western countries in the past 50 years. The original research was undertaken mainly to prove their effectiveness. Current research is showing the dangers of too much of certain vitamins, minerals and herbs, and also their contraindications. For example, the wrong combination of certain herbs etc. may not be good.

i. Nutrition and dietary supplements are extremely deep and complex subjects. Please do not think that because something worked for you, it will always work for everyone without any side effects.

ii.   Unless you are a qualified expert in this field, with insurance to cover you if something goes wrong, please do not suggest any dietary supplement.

iii.   If you really do believe a vitamin, mineral or herb may help a healee, please be professional and refer on to a professional person in that area of expertise.

iv.   Do not provide herbs or herbal medicines unless they are legally permissible.

c.   Can healers suggest changes to prescribed medicines?

The answer to this is an absolute 'No'. As with the above two points, unless you are a qualified medical person, you should accept a doctor's recommendation for a healee.

i.   You may disagree with a particular treatment or prescribed medicine, but doctors have trained in their field for many years. If you suggest changes against a doctor's advice, it is possible that your advised changes may be highly dangerous – even more dangerous than the danger you perceive.

ii.   Recently I heard of a complementary or alternative therapist who suggests to patients not to take antibiotics. And I have heard of a patient who took a therapist's advice and ended up as a hospital in-patient, seriously ill. They needed the antibiotic. I pray that I do not hear of a case where a patient dies because they listened to bad advice...

This example is relevant to other prescribed medicines.

iii. If healers are to be accepted by governments and work in doctors' surgeries, hospitals and other medical establishments, it is important that healers and doctors respect each other's opinions. Perhaps we could make the first move. Respect a doctor's decision.

iv. If we are to move closer to an integrated Health Service, we
should allow the doctor to be in overall control. So if you
think you have cured someone, do <u>not</u> suggest they come
off their medication. Instead, ask them to consult with their
doctor to check whether their condition has improved
enough to reduce or eliminate their medicine.

v. There may be an occasional case where the healee considers
that the doctor is not prescribing correctly.

Never agree or disagree. Instead suggest carefully that the
healee should refer himself or herself on to another medical
doctor for a second opinion.

3. Exploring 'Visions' Of This Or A Previous Life

See 'Biofeedback Through Your Seven Senses' in chapter 9.
Please also remember the main warning caveat that someone
who has a vision of an experience in the past of this or a previous life
may have had a simple unconscious release. They do not have to
know 'what happened next', or anything else about the memory
through their conscious understanding, because the healing will have
taken place <u>un</u>consciously.

Anyway, unless you are a qualified psychologist or other
relevant medical professional, you may do more harm than good and
uncover a 'can of worms' you will find difficult to heal.

Your reiki insurance may not cover you for exploring-style
counselling. Just allow reiki energy to heal naturally. And only if
needed, refer on to a medical professional.

4. Counselling

From information given above it should be clear that you should
not give counselling to a healee unless you are a properly qualified
counsellor, covered by a counsellor's insurance policy.

If a healee comes for reiki healing that is all you give. If you
consider the person needs counselling, if you are not a qualified

counsellor with insurance, please do not provide counselling yourself in any way. Be professional and refer on.

5.   Referring On

Develop the professional insight and humility to know when to refer on to any other professional therapist or medical person.

a.   Suicidal persons
A classic case is someone who is suicidal. If you are not trained in this type of counselling, and think you can help all suicidal people, you may have a shock when one takes their life. Referral means being sensible.

b.   Conditions that may threaten you, a healee or others
The guiding principle is that if you feel your healee could affect the health of someone, even the health of their own self, they probably need extra help.

Ask the person delicately about whether they could or would seek others' professional help. Then encourage them gently to seek and accept this extra help.

6.   Drug / Alcohol Addicts, Clinically Mentally Ill, Hallucinatory Or Violent People

a.   The problem
If you have one of these types of healees, you may experience one of two problems. Either the healee may become violent and you may have to take that person to Court; or their unstable nature may lead them to accuse you of something you have not done and they will take you to Court!

b.   Have a third party in the same room
In the UK, there is a guideline for healers working with these types of healees. It is simply to insist on having someone else,

someone you know, in the room at the same time. That friend will then be able to first help protect you in case of violence, and second be a witness in case of an unjust accusation.

c.   What about the first appointment

This is a possible problem, because often it will not be until you have seen the healee that you will realise that a third person may be needed.

d.   Tapes - the solution for the first appointments

I have friends who are National Health Service psychologists. Some of these have converted a part of their home into a space where they can see private clients. These professionals always use a tape recorder for the first few sessions, quite openly.

i.   Explain to the client that the conversation is being taped because you can play it back later to see if there was a way you could help the client that you had not previously thought of.

ii.   Ask permission before, and just after, pressing the record button.

iii.   Explain whilst the tape is recording that the information is confidential unless anything bad happens - and that in certain circumstances you are obliged to inform the police or other authorities.

iv.   Of course, the client may not agree that the session is taped. The psychologist then makes a quick decision on the basis of the appearance and mannerisms of the client whether or not to calmly and gently show him or her the door.

v.   There are naturally still dangers.

A tape will not record everything, such as sexual abuse. And the client can steal a tape after physical abuse.

But the knowledge of the presence of the tape in the room usually has a dramatic calming effect on the client.

vi.   Usually after three or four sessions it will be apparent whether you can be safe in the patient's presence and you may be able to say that the tape is no longer needed.

7.   Mentally Ill Hospitalised By Their Illness

This UK code does not mean conditions such as depression or a breakdown.

The code relates to healees <u>who have been in hospital</u> with conditions such as schizophrenia, paranoia, psychoses, or hallucination, all of which may be made worse by healing energies.

Some of the reasons are given in the previous code.

a.   More dangers of healing these types of mental illness

i.   If healees hallucinate, they may well have visions during a treatment that they would not be able to cope with.

ii.   If they have paranoia, their illness may make them think that you have done something you haven't.

And so on. With these illnesses there is always a risk that the person could be affected adversely by healing energy, and be admitted to hospital.

b.   Is there a way to heal these mentally ill patients?

i.   Yes, if you are able to liaise with the hospital nurse in charge of the case. In the UK this is the guideline for healers, and I have always found the staff helpful. After all, they want to help that patient as well.

ii.   Do keep to any guidelines the hospital nurse may suggest. Remember that it is the hospital you need to work with usually, not the patient's regular doctor, because the hospital will be in overall control of the case, and probably have huge wads of notes for many patients.

iii. If it is not possible to liaise with medical people, then always have a third party present.

iv. If in doubt, refer on.

8. Notifiable Diseases

In UK it is statutory law that certain infectious diseases are notified to the Medical Officer for the Health Authority in which the patient was living when the diagnosis was discovered. The doctor in charge of the case is responsible for notification.

If a reiki practitioner identifies a Notifiable Disease, it is law that a doctor <u>must</u> be called. And the patient must not be allowed to come into contact with any other person.

The following list is probably accepted in all Health Authorities; although check with your local Health Authorities for descriptions of the illnesses below, local additions or differences.

Acute Encephalitis	Measles
Acute Meningitis	Ophthalmia Neonatorum
Anthrax	Paratyphoid Fever
Acute Poliomyelitis	Plague
Cholera	Relapsing Fever
Diphtheria	Scarlet Fever
Dysentery	Tetanus
Food Poisoning	Tuberculosis
Infective Jaundice	Typhoid Fever
Leprosy	Typhus
Leptospirosis	Whooping Cough
Malaria	Yellow Fever

9. The Healing Of Teeth And Gums

It is against UK law for anyone to touch teeth or gums except a dentist. Even a doctor cannot touch a problem with teeth or gums.

This law does NOT protect dentists' jobs! It safeguards patients. Because it is only a dentist who has the appropriate instruments – and training – to see exactly what is happening inside the mouth.

So the advice is simple. If someone comes to you with a tooth or gum problem, refer on to a dentist immediately.

10. Pregnancy And Childbirth

a.   Reiki during pregnancy

i.   It is perfectly acceptable within UK law to give reiki to a lady who is in any stage of pregnancy.

ii.   Most healers find that a baby who is kicking within the womb absolutely loves feeling the beautiful healing energies. When the healer places hands near the baby, usually the baby will go into absolute peace, or kick in a manner that the mothers-to-be commonly describe as 'glee.'

iii. I have known many babies who have received reiki whilst in the womb, and all except one have become remarkably peaceful children.

It is as if they have had pre-birth healing, and that many of the problems they may have had as children cannot exist because of the pre-healing.

b.   Reiki births

In the UK it is against the Codes healers have with the Royal College of Midwives to give healing during childbirth or for 10 days after, <u>unless</u> the midwife gives permission and is present. (For reasoning behind this, see *'How The Codes Of Practice Originated'* below.) However, reiki births are becoming not only popular, but also often desirable because:

i. A reiki birth may help prevent the birth traumas that can cause emotional and mental problems for the baby – and/or mother - later in life, and

ii. A reiki birth can be a pain-lessening birth.

One of my students in Malaysia received reiki from her husband during the birth of her second child. Apparently she had absolutely no pain or difficulties whatsoever. Yet, according to the midwife, she should have needed painkillers. The midwife asked to learn reiki.

iii. I have heard of reiki friends being present at the birth, and giving reiki to help a painless, or pain-lessening birth.

From all the many reports received so far, a reiki birth seems to be a beautiful birth.

c. Attunements during pregnancy

The question is often asked whether it is OK for a lady who is pregnant to take a reiki course, and more pertinently, to also receive attunements. The answers are that in the UK, there is no law or code that suggests this should not be done. And anecdotal evidence gives positive support that both mother and unborn child can benefit enormously from the healing and bonding processes of attunements.

11. Trance Healing

Quite simply, trance healing is dangerous. In trance, the healer is not aware of his or her actions. Therefore the healer may fall, push the healee over, or even commit unconscious sexual abuse.

Trance healing is not acceptable to any insurance policy, so if, whilst in trance, a healer inadvertently damages someone, the healer would be liable for any damages.

Also, trance healing is not allowed for reiki or spiritual healing research projects, or for healing provided to the National Health Service, nor at a reiki or spiritual healing public demonstration.

In brief, stay sensibly in control of your senses.

12. Giving Healing To Children Under Age of 18

If a parent or guardian does not provide adequate medical aid for a child under the age of 18, they have committed a criminal offence, and can be prosecuted.

Reiki is not a medical aid as defined in law, so a healer who gives reiki to a child whose parents or guardians refuse medical aid and who is consequently ill, may be considered as aiding and abetting the offence, and be taken to Court.

a.   The form to help protect you and the child

Because of the above, it is advisable to secure the signature of the parent or guardian of every child under the age of 18, using a form such as the following.

Ensure the form is completed prior to the first session of treatment. The signed form should then be kept with the healing records in case you become involved in Court hearings. Suggested wording is below:

'I have been warned by

....

(Full name of healer)

that according to law I should consult a doctor regarding the health of my child

....

(Full name of child)

Signed..

(Full name of parent or guardian)...............................

Date..

Signed by witness ....

(Full name of witness, e.g. the healer)...........................,'

b.   Reikiing children of friends or family members

Giving reiki to a child under the age of 18 without their receiving adequate medical care is a criminal offence in the UK even

446

if it is your own child! Although you or your friend or family member may think reiki is better than drugs, you will have committed a criminal offence if the child does not see a doctor – because a simple operation could perhaps have saved the child's life.

And what would happen if the child does not see a doctor, and you give reiki instead, and he or she dies that night from an undiagnosed internal problem? It only needs one 'nosy neighbour' or 'busy body' to report you, for you to be taken to Court.

For both your own and the child's protection, even your friends and family should sign the above form!

c. Reikiing a 16 or 17 year old child who left home

In the UK, children are entitled to leave home at age 16 and receive Housing Benefit to pay for a room or flat, and Income Support for their food and necessity expenses. This poses a dilemma if the child has fallen out with the parents, and is not speaking to them, or has even lost contact – and the child requests reiki.

It is suggested that, unless there is adequate written proof that the child has seen a doctor, you

i.   Ensure the child gets that written proof before you give reiki, and

ii.   If the written proof is not forthcoming that you do not give reiki so as to keep within the law.

iii. If hands-on healing cannot be given within the law concerning children, some healers prefer to send distant healing, believing that something is better than nothing, and that no one will ever be able to prove or disprove distant healing in a court of law.

I cannot comment on this, and leave it to your discretion. But I urge you to urge the child to see a doctor, to ask the child to gain the needed written proof, and then give hands-on reiki.

d. On having an adult in the healing room whilst giving a reiki treatment to a child

It is advisable for a parent or guardian or adult friend or relation to be in the healing room with the child. This will often:

i.   Relax and calm the child,

ii.   Allow better information about the child's illness, general condition and biofeedback response, and

iii. Ensure that you have a witness in case of any fears or untruths of the child.

e. If a child needs to speak privately

Private chats with children will not be common, but are valuable if used with discretion, care, and common sense. In any event, a private chat with a child should not be undertaken unless you are a trained counsellor, because you never know what you may uncover.

f. Practicalities when giving reiki to babies or children

As stated above, there are no UK regulations against this. The main points to remember are:

i.   Preferably heal babies or young children when they are asleep. Often they will unconsciously and automatically turn over in the cot to a position that allows easier access for your healing hand position. Whereas, when awake, they will often wriggle and writhe and make the healing session almost impossible!

It is often suggested that babies and young children need less reiki healing energy than adults. Although there is no scientific evidence for this, the assertion is probably true because they are much smaller, so logically they would need less energy.

They are also likely to need less energy because they probably will not have the huge emotional and mental attachments to their problems that adults have – therefore child healing is often easier.

ii.   However, be aware that some inherited conditions may take a long time to rebalance.

13. Animals And Pets

a.   The law

UK laws regarding provision of healing to animals are much more restrictive than laws for the healing of humans.

The Protection of Animals Act 1911 states that anyone who is aware that an animal needs a vet must inform the owner of the animal.

The Animals (Scientific Procedures) Act 1986 must be adhered to.

The Veterinary Surgeons Act 1966 allows for the administration of first aid in an emergency in order to save the life of an animal or to save it suffering from pain.

The Veterinary Surgeons Act 1966 also prohibits anyone who is not a registered vet from helping animals by:

i.   Diagnosing the conditions and illnesses,

ii.   Performing tests of any kind in order to make a diagnosis,

iii. Giving advice based on a healer's diagnosis, and

iv.   Providing treatment.

Therefore, in the strictest interpretation of UK law, healing should not normally be given to an animal. However, in a letter dated 16th August 2000, the Royal College of Veterinary Surgeons stated:

'The Veterinary Surgery (Exemptions) Order 1962 does permit the treatment of animals 'by physiotherapy' provided that the animal has first been seen by a veterinary surgeon who has diagnosed the condition and referred it to

an appropriate therapist. Since the order refers to 'physiotherapy' rather than to a 'physiotherapist', the RCVS in consultation with other interested bodies, agreed that it should be interpreted as encompassing all kinds of manipulative therapy which would clearly include osteopathy and chiropractic, Bowen therapy, and reiki, but not, for example, aromatherapy where the general consensus appears to be that the choice of oils to be used in aromatherapy is in itself a diagnostic process, and thus an act of veterinary surgery.'

Since the acts were passed, the following has become 'accepted' practice according to the Codes of Practice healers have with the Royal College of Veterinary Surgeons.

b.   Responsibilities of healers

Providing these guidelines are followed, healers will probably be allowed to give energy to an animal. If these guidelines are not adhered to, the healer may become liable to prosecution under one of the above acts.

i.   Before giving reiki (unless it is an emergency) the healer must ensure that the animal has previously seen a vet.

  To protect the healer from potential prosecution, it is best if the assurance that the animal has already seen a vet is given in writing by the vet, and that the letter from the vet includes agreement that the animal can receive reiki.

ii.   The vet must stay in overall charge of the case.

iii.   A healer must not contradict any advice given by a vet, nor suggest any change to any medication, nor change to the intake of any substance.

iv.   A healer must also not give 'veterinary advice or treatment.'

v.   A healer should not suggest a medical diagnosis.

Remember that these guidelines are not to protect the income of vets. They are to protect the health of innocent animals that cannot speak up for themselves. A vet has had many years training.

A simple operation could save the animal's life.

c.   The Royal College of Veterinary Surgeons

In the UK, the Royal College of Veterinary Surgeons recognises healing as being ethically acceptable within the terms and spirit of the Code of Conduct that healers abide by, and all of the above laws and guidelines.

Under these circumstances, the RCVS accepts in terms of the act the complementary treatment of animals by contact healing, laying on of hands, thought transference or prayer.

14. Working In Hospitals With Healing

There are common-sense Codes of Practice guidelines about giving healing energies to patients in hospital. Although these guidelines were agreed in the UK, they would probably be sensible and relevant for most other countries:

i.   Patients in hospital must ask for healing. You must never offer it. This is to stop lots of healers going into hospitals and offering their services to patients who know nothing about healing - and perhaps upsetting some patients such as disbelievers or religious patients.

ii.   When going into a hospital to give healing, you must never wear a white coat – or whatever colours and uniforms are worn in the hospital. This is to stop you being confused with a doctor or nurse.

iii. On each and every visit to give healing to a patient you must ask permission from the nurse in charge of the ward at that time. Not the consultant or doctor, because it is only the duty nurse who really should understand the up-to-the-

451

minute condition of the patient. For example, if the patient is about to undergo a test or examination, or if a patient has entered a critical stage, the nurse may request that you leave the person in peace.

The nurse must also be informed that the patient has requested healing, and written evidence given if needed, as well as the healer's credentials.

iv. When providing healing, the guidelines suggest you can heal by holding hands or by saying prayers without fuss. They do not say you can give a full all-over hands-on body treatment whilst chanting or shaking! This is because other patients who watch, may be disturbed by what they see.

v. If a patient on another bed also asks for healing, the healer should go through the same procedure as above.

vi. Healers must not undermine patients' faith in hospital treatment or regime.

Most healers agree the above guidelines are sound common sense. Please abide by them. This will help keep the good name and practice of healers in the forefront of the minds of hospital staff.

15. Reikiing Someone With HIV Or AIDS

Guidelines vary between different organisations.

a. No risk

Some UK organisations such as the Department of Health and Social Security say that there is 'no risk' of you contracting the virus. Perhaps this is true. However, there are differences of opinion.

b. Minimal risk

Other UK organisations such as The British Medical Association state that providing cuts, grazes and sores are covered, contracting HIV or AIDS from hand healing has 'minimal risk.'

'Minimal risk' means that there is almost no chance of contracting HIV or AIDS from a healee – but that it is possible.

It is generally accepted that the virus can be passed to another person through contact with their bodily fluids.

'Minimal risk' suggests, for example, that someone with AIDS could sneeze into the eye or mouth of a healer and pass on the virus through 'bodily fluid contact.'

Or, because the virus can live outside the body for about four minutes, drinking from the same cup can be potentially lethal.

These are extremely unlikely scenarios, but ones that should be considered by responsible, professional healers.

c. Recommendations
Each healer must decide for him or her self whether to give reiki to an AIDS patient. However, most organisations agree that:

i. Cuts, grazes and sores on both persons should be covered.

ii. If there is a real, perceived danger, protective breathing masks and glasses should be worn.

d. Concerns
Please do not worry about risks too much. Maintain a balanced approach. Remember that, at worst, there is only a 'minimal' risk, and that some organisations say there is no risk. But if in doubt it is probably wise to take the precautions as described above.

16. The Venereal Diseases Act 1917

This is an old UK law that probably, due to wartime prostitution, was quite valid in its day. Although it does not seem appropriate nowadays, the law is still in force and can therefore still be applied.

The law states healers must not accept payment of any kind if they are healing syphilis, gonorrhoea, or soft chancre (an almost extinct form of syphilis). So, if you are healing one of these three venereal diseases, you cannot accept gifts like a cake or a new car.

It is perfectly OK to heal these three conditions if your healing is completely free. Note that AIDS and herpes were not around at that time and so do not come under this law.

17. The Cancer Act 1939

"Clause 4. -(1) No person shall take any part in the publication of any advertisement –

(a) containing an offer to treat any person for cancer, or to prescribe any remedy therefore, or to give any advice in connection with the treatment of…"

Healers only discovered this old UK law in 1996 when a lady who knew about the law took a healer to court. Strangely, the year after, she actually came to my exhibition stand in London, explaining how she had 'done her duty to society.' It just shows that you cannot be too careful in abiding by the law of the country you are in!

Another interpretation of UK law is this: if you believe that you have healed someone of cancer, and you write an article about it, if the healee had chemotherapy as well, you MUST mention the chemotherapy in the article. If you do not mention that the healee had chemotherapy as well as healing, you have broken the law, and could be taken to Court. Of course, if the healee has not had chemotherapy, you do not have to mention it.

18. Confidentiality

All healers must comply with the Data Protection Act.

No third party such as a friend or even another healer should be present without the express permission of the healee.

Records must be kept and are only for the healee, practitioners concerned and office staff. Disclosure is not allowed even to a healee's family unless the healee gives permission.

The only occasion when this does not apply is when disclosure may be needed as required by the legal process of law.

Laws Of Other Countries

Most countries have unique laws about healing, and many that do not have laws or codes at present are considering bringing them in. The following are a few that students and others from around the world have mentioned. They are not stated as true and correct though I have no reason to believe otherwise.

1. Germany

The brilliant English healer, Matthew Manning, often tells a story about giving a healing demonstration on stage in Germany. The essence of the story is that just before he started his demonstration he was told that there were police in the audience. And that it was against German law to touch a healee.

Even if the person gave consent to be touched, it is no excuse in German law and the healer would be arrested for 'common assault.'

So Matthew Manning healed through the aura. He did not touch the person, so the police could not 'touch' him!

2. Austria

I have been told that it is perfectly OK to heal in Austria – but only if the healing is free. If money passes hands, then Austrian law has been broken, and the healer may be taken to court and even imprisoned.

3. France

Some French reiki healers have said that it is almost impossible to advertise and practise healing in France because under Napoleonic Law, because there is not a law stating that healing has been allowed, it is therefore banned. Local authorities will often try to close down healing centres.

4. USA, State Of Florida

Complementary and Alternative Medicine practitioners in the United States must be very careful only to practise what they are licensed to practice.

In one case, Stetina v State, a nutritionist who also practised iridology, prescribed colonic irrigation and additional nutritional remedies. Even though the court acknowledged that she was well-intentioned in her advice, which was aimed at getting people to feel better, she was barred from practice. She also lost an appeal. The upheld verdict was that she was acting outside of her remit and was therefore practising medicine without a license (Ernst).

At the time of writing and according to a friend in Florida, there is a 'practice act interpretation' in that State that says a reiki healer must be licensed as a massage therapist. If the reiki practitioner is not licensed, and is reported to the Unlicensed Division of the State, the healer could be fined or jailed.

In Florida, reiki comes under the laws for massage, and the American Massage Therapy Association hired a lawyer to say that, since hands could be considered electrical devices, you could interpret this to mean that hands of reiki practitioners are doing massage and lightly touching a body is manipulation of the superficial tissues of the body. Appeals are currently underway.[114]

In the meantime, it seems as if it is acceptable to teach reiki, and to offer free treatments, whether by hands on, hands off, or over a distance. Free in Florida means not only accepting no money - it also means no donations or gifts of love or payments in kind no matter how big or small.

Alternatively, you can heal with reiki and accept payment if you are a Licensed Massage Therapist, or licensed to touch patients, such as also being a doctor or a nurse.

---

[114] Information from the American-based Reiki Plus Institute (+1 305 451 9881)

5. Others

Because of the global upsurge in grassroots interest in having or learning healing, many countries around the world are now introducing their own version of laws and codes. These currently include Australia, Denmark, and Malaysia. Please check the laws and codes of the country you live or heal in.

Exercise 96 - Researching Laws And Codes In Your Country

Whatever country you live in, or intend to heal in, write to the country's government to ask for a list of laws and codes about reiki and healing. Then abide by them.

(Although correspondence cannot be entered into, the author would be most interested to see a copy of reiki and healing laws and codes of any country. Thank you.)

How The Codes of Practice Originated

In the UK in the 1980s, Codes of Practice between healers and the various medical professions were introduced. They became the foundation for the codes still used by most healing professions today.

It is an interesting story how these codes came about. In fact, because the story includes a potential rule of how to enter the corridors of government, the story could be a blueprint for healers in other countries to follow.

A top Civil Servant, Dennis Haviland,[115] had to retire from his job in Whitehall, the bastion of Civil Service Government, due to ill health – severe arthritis. Not even the country's best doctors could help him.

After some time in retirement his brother-in-law, Commander David Repard, introduced him to healing. Like many people hearing of healing for the first time, he was initially sceptical about the potential for healing to help him. But, to his surprise, the healing cured him completely. He then began to wonder why the National Health Service – that had been completely unable to help his arthritis – did not have this healing cure available to everyone in similar distress. Having been a top civil servant, he asked in the corridors of government why this miraculous therapy should not be available to everyone. Most people he spoke to politely shunned him. All normal doors to acceptance of healing were slammed firmly shut.

But some friends told him why. It was because there were no commonly accepted healer Codes of Conduct or Codes of Practice. And even if there were, there would also need to be a Disciplinary Procedure in place so 'bad' healers could be thrown out of the organisation. Further, if healers were to work with doctors, there would need to be a standard insurance policy for healers to cover potential claims against them.

---

[115] This information is from verbal conversations with Cmdr David Repard, who was the chairman for the Confederation of Healing Organizations in the 1980's and 1990's.

Because he had been a top civil servant, this did not daunt him. Instead he used his knowledge of how the corridors of government worked.

This is the clever bit!

He helped devise everything asked for, including the Codes of Practice! Then he sent it to all of the Royal Colleges in the UK – the top bodies for each medical subject such as Doctors, Veterinary Surgeons, Dentists, and Midwives – asking for their opinion.

They all wrote back with their opinion.

He did not argue with any point.

He accepted their comments and started The Confederation of Healing Organisations, a UK body that represented healers from all healing disciplines who agreed to abide by the codes, disciplinary procedures, and pay for the standard insurance policy.

Thus the codes were formed 'in consultation with' the medical authorities, and are part of the reason why England and the UK has been leading the world in the integration of medicine and healing.

__Keeping To The Codes And Laws__

There are healers who do not agree with some of the laws. And some laws do seem inappropriate or at least outdated. But, whether we agree with them or not, the laws of a country are there to be enforced. So please abide by them. I teach reiki in prisons, and do not want to see you there!

In any case, if we hope to get reiki and healing accepted by governments for their health services, it would not do our case any good if healers breaking the law kept appearing in the news!

In this manual are current UK laws and codes that should be adhered to by healers. However, remember that laws and codes can be misunderstood, changed, repealed, or extra ones can be passed.

It is your responsibility to see that all regulation information is correct at the time you read and need to use it. You must also keep yourself updated with changes to any regulation that may affect you as a reiki practitioner, and ensure that there are no other regulations, or interpretation of regulations, currently in force.

Then, for the highest good of all, keep to the letter of each law and code and promote professionalism in healing to its highest value.

WORKBOOK NOTES
On Codes And Laws

CHAPTER 26

FINAL SUMMARIES

The Five Foundation Rei Treatment Options

After a Reiki 1 course, it is expected that the student can practise rei healing (spiritual healing) with the following five healing options.

When understanding of these five healing processes has been reached, it is possible to progress on to the next level – providing that:

1.   *The student also has adequate common sense to apply the understanding, and*

2.   *The student has adequate enthusiasm for the next stage.*

1. To Reiki Dis-ease Or All-Over Problems, Give All-Over Treatment And Back To Worst Area

Diseases should be healed differently, as a disease's cause could originate or manifest throughout a body, or in many areas of a body.

Therefore, any treatment for disease, whether self-healing or for healing others, should consist of an all-over treatment as outlined in chapter 19, *'The Complete Reiki 1 Method'*.

At the end of the standard hand positions, you should return to the worst area of the condition. For example, in the case of arthritis, you could return to the worst arthritic joint, or in the case of osteoporitic bone pain, return to the worst bone pain area.

2. To Reiki Injury Or Localised Problem, Give Treatment To Injury Or Local Site Only

In chapter 4, Dr Usui said,

'if the patient suffers pain in the chest, the practitioner of this therapy considers the patient's chest, if the stomach gives pain then the stomach, and if there is something wrong with the eyes, then the practitioner must be concerned with the patient's eyes themselves.'

If there is a local problem with a local cause, like an injury, the healer should only heal that local area. In this case healers should heal the presenting issue, and not try to give an all over treatment or some other healing unless it may help the localised problem.

3. Be Guided In Time

Beginners should practise the standard *'Healer Hand And Healee Body positions'* in chapter 18, and the section on *'The Complete Reiki 1 Method'* in chapter 19. The more you practise the greater will be your understanding. The more you practise, the more you may realise that the energy seems to turn off sometimes after only a very short while. And yet at other times it seems as if the energy flows more forcefully and for longer. Ultimately you may realise that you need more or less time in each hand position. After some practice with the standard 3-5 minutes in each position, you can progress.

If you feel little energy in one hand position move your hands on quickly to the next. It is probably the intelligent nature of the reiki energy knowing that not so much was needed there.

If you feel extra energy in another hand position, stay there for longer. It is probably the nature of the energy knowing that much healing is needed there.

4. Be Guided In Space

It is important to first practise, *'Healer Hand And Healee Body Positions'*, in chapter 18, and, *'The Complete Reiki 1 Method'* in chapter 19. The more you practise, the more you may realise the standard hand positions might not heal every need.

Eventually you may realise that there are countless hand positions, depending on the illness/condition, the presenting symptoms, and the individual healee.

Let yourself be guided to 'new' hand positions that are not 'standard' positions. Maybe you are being guided by the reiki energy, or by your or your healees' higher consciousness, or by your or your healees' guides. If guidance comes, simply accept. These 'new' hand positions may be very relevant for the healee.

5. Scan

Practise according to chapter 21, *'Scanning'*.

Exercise 97 - The Five Foundation Rei Spiritual Healing Treatments

Before each self-healing or before healing others, consider which approach you will take from the above 5 methods.

Analyse records of each treatment to see which seems to get the best result for which condition.

Practising Foundation Treatment Options

After the course, do not practise on a person, animal, or living thing. First, ensure you understand the five treatment options and how to channel rei healing properly. Progress your understanding.

1. Teddy Bear

First, practise on a teddy bear. If you haven't got one, buy one. It will come in useful when practising methods and techniques taught on Reiki 2, Reiki 3 and above, or if you need a toy for a child to hold when you eventually become a practitioner.

2. Self-Healing

Next, practise on yourself. Keep reading this manual to help understanding. See how reiki and the different day-to-day energies feel. Know you are on a learning curve, and if questions arise, find the answer from your reiki master.

3. Trusted Friend

Only when you feel able to answer questions should you practise on a friend. But do not practise on just any friend. Choose someone you trust to give you positive constructive criticism. Do not choose someone overly critical who could destroy the little confidence you may have built up.

4. Other Friends And Family Members

When you feel ready, it will be a natural progression to heal other friends and family members. Go for it. Create a pocket of healed happiness around you.

Accept Your Fears – Just Do It!

There are many fears that beginner healers commonly go through, often thinking that the fears are normal and acceptable. The fears may be common, but they are not normal or acceptable, because the fears will stop them becoming full practitioners.

Reiki, as Dr Usui said in different ways in Chapter 4, can be used by reiki healers for self-healing and healing their family and their friends and therefore has the potential to create pockets of happiness around the world.

If we allow fears to become reality, and this stops us sharing reiki, these pockets of healed happiness may not exist. We will not spread Light. Rather, we will allow pockets of darkness to exist.

Free will exists. If someone does not want to do reiki, that is OK. If one of the following fears prevents them spreading Light and allows darkness to exist, this is not OK.

1.   Fear Of Being Laughed At

a.   Problem

This is a common, and perhaps a realistic fear. Certain friends and family members, let alone members of the general public, may scoff at you, pick holes in your reiki, or even laugh at you.

If this happens it is easy to become demoralised.

b.   Solution

Reiki 1 beginners should initially only talk about reiki to trusted people who may provide constructive appraisal. Continue with this until confidence is gained. Remember Dr Usui's words in Chapter 4:

'We practitioners of Usui Reiki Therapy do not mind however much our practices are doubted, held in contempt, or rejected.'

Reiki it. Just do it!

2.   Fear Of Having Too Much Ego

a.   Problem

Having too much ego is not the main problem.

Personally I quite like those with too much ego because at least those with too much ego will go out and spread the love and healing and beauty of reiki.   And in the process, the energies will naturally knock their ego back a little.

Too much ego is a rarely reached limit.   The main problem with ego is having too little, because this type of person is less likely to do reiki to begin with.

Trying to eradicate ego can bring the fear of being thought of as having ego.

b.   Solution

Understand that our culture and society dictate that we do not boast of our gifts, and do not become precocious.

But then know that we need to stand up and admit, 'I am a reiki healer.'

These words are difficult to say for this type of person, (it took me many years) but are very empowering when said with meaning.

Reiki it.   Just do it!

3.   Fear Of The Power Of The Energy

a.   Problem

For some people, the vast energy force rushing through them is scary.   They feel the power and are in awe of its potential.

b.   Solution

Study chapter 9, '*Biofeedback*', and then discuss the energy responses with other reiki practitioners.

Reiki it.   Just do it!

4. Fear Of Not Getting Results

a. Problem
Many beginners are afraid of not being able to help their healees. They fear people arriving, and leaving the same as when they arrived.

b. Solution
Healers must develop the dual attitude as doctors. Accept some people may never be helped. But then do the very best to try to help. Reiki it. Just do it!

5. Fear Of Change

a. Problem
To become a healer means change. Change of job, change of colleagues, and change of income, all can create fear because the future is unknown.

b. Solution
Accept that nothing in life is forever. Accept that whatever you are doing now will change one day anyway. So, if you feel the calling, you might as well try reiki and see what happens. Reiki it. Just do it!

Exercise 98 - Advance Anyway
Take Reiki 2. There is a symbol that you will learn to help with mental or emotional issues in general. Many healers have found they help specifically with their fears, including the fear of change.
You are more likely to get quicker self-healing results after Reiki 2 than with Reiki 1 rei energies.

6.   Fear Of Working With Difficult Cases

a.   Problem
Some potential healers do not even begin their reiki practice from fear of having healees coming who have cancer, schizophrenia, or some other emotive illness.

b.   Solution
If a particular illness presents itself for the third time, even if you have said 'No' on the first two occasions, see this as synchronicity. Perhaps you should have 'just done it' on the first occasion. You should now see it as your God or guides putting cases in front of you so that you can learn your healing lessons.

It is quite common for healers to be 'sent' groups of certain illnesses, and only when the healer has little left to learn – or is deemed by the guides to be unable to learn that lesson - will another group of a different illness be 'sent'.

Fulfil your soul destiny.

Reiki it. Just do it!

7.   Fear Of Not Being Good Enough

a.   Problem
This is the only potentially realistic fear – because, of course, you will not be good enough until you have practised for a long time to understand what you are doing. Only then will you gain Reiki 1 wisdom to know how good you are.

b.   Solution
The only way to gain Reiki 1 wisdom is to practise, practise, and practise whilst keeping records of the scores of each symptom. If, over seven sessions, the scores of all conditions come down by at least 35%, you are good enough. See the section '*Simple Record Keeping Form*' in chapter 19.

However, the 7-level system of reiki is a progression of knowledge and on other levels the scores should come down even quicker!

Reiki it. Just do it!

Exercise 99 - LOving Your Fear Away
As in chapter 8, spiritual rei healing will have an eventual ripple effect on the fear, providing it is not a genetically inherited issue.

Give yourself regular rei healing over a period of 9 to 18 months and record any differences in your fears.

8. Fear Of Commitment

a.   Problem
Providing reiki or spiritual healing is a commitment. It demands time – time away from other work, and time away from family and friends.

b.   Solution
To start with, see reiki as a new hobby. And, to give them understanding of your hobby, invite some of your friends and family to join in.

Reiki it. Just do it!

Exercise 100 -Releasing Fear
There are many advanced techniques available now in books, tapes, and courses that can help you release fear in a matter of minutes, if it is not a genetic issue. Also, if necessary, seek support from your reiki master.

9.   Your Reiki Master

Whatever your reason for taking reiki, your reiki master should give post-course help. In an emergency, contact your reiki master by phone immediately. If it is not an emergency, write, fax, or email your reiki master's office with your query so that you have the written response for your reference.

Your reiki master is there to help you. Always ask him or her for advice. If they cannot provide an adequate answer to your query, they should be able to refer you to someone who can help.

Lineages of reiki can be likened to the guru lineages in India. If one guru cannot answer a question, the disciple can go up to ten gurus up-line until an adequate answer is found. Respect is still held for all gurus. So it should be in reiki.

If you have studied all your reiki courses with the author, regardless of how recent or how long ago, please send me any query you have on any reiki, healing, psychic, or spiritual subject. Otherwise, please stay with your reiki master and his or her lineage. Send your questions to them. Have respect.

However, many people choose to study with more than one master for a broader range of esoteric knowledge.

> **Exercise 101 -Let Our Own Light Shine**
> **If you have any of the fears above, understand that they will prevent healing of those in need around you. List your personal fears.**
> **Then recognise your potential as a light to be shone into the darkness of people's health and of our world.**
> **Take this exercise as a project for goodness.**
> **Read and understand the poem below by Marianne Williamson, 1992, and used in 1994 by Nelson Mandela in his inaugural address. And then just do it!**

Nelson Mandela
Let Our Own Light Shine

Our deepest fear is not that we are inadequate.
Our deepest fear is that we are powerful beyond measure.
It is our light, not our darkness, that most frightens us.
We ask ourselves, 'who am I to be brilliant, gorgeous,
talented and fabulous?'
Actually, who are you not to be?
You are a child of God.
Your playing small doesn't serve the world.
There is nothing enlightened about shrinking so that other
people won't feel insecure around you.
We are born to manifest the glory of God that is within us.
It's not just in some of us; it's in everyone.
And as we let our own light shine, we give other people
permission to do the same.
As we are liberated from our own fear, our presence
automatically liberates others.

Nelson Mandela
1994 Inaugural Speech

Further Reading List

Please note that there are many reiki books on the market. The ones chosen for this short list are by people with direct access to Dr Usui's original teachings and should therefore be highly respected.

Avid readers who scrutinise the texts will notice differences of opinion and teaching. However, in general terms, the differences are less vast than most other reiki books.

Please also note that the 7-level system of Dr Usui's reiki has still to be portrayed properly in any book.

Benor, Daniel J. *Healing Research: Volume 1*
www.wholistichealingresearch.com
(Summaries of scientific healing studies)

** Brennan, Barbara. *Hands of Light.* New York: Bantam Books, 1988.
(Auras, chakras etc.)

** Buzan, Tony. *Use Your Head.* London: BBC Worldwide Ltd, 1974.
(Vital thinking and learning skills)

* Doi, Hiroshi. *Modern Reiki Method for Healing.* Canada: Fraser Journal Publishing, 2000.
(Student of 6th President of Usui's Society)

Gawain, Shakti. *Creative Visualisation.* USA: Bantam Books, 1982.
(Visualisation)

Harris, Thomas. *I'm OK - You're OK.* London: Pan Books Ltd, 1970.
(Basic psychology)

Jeffers, Susan. *Feel the Fear and Do It Anyway*. UK: Arrow Books, 1991.
(Taking control of your fears)

** Krieger, Dolores. *The Therapeutic Touch*. Prentice. New York: Hall Press, 1989.
(USA healing method for nurses)

Macbeth, Jessica. *Moon Over Water*. UK: Gateway Books, 1990.
(Meditation)

** Peale, Norman. *The Power of Positive Thinking*. UK: Vermillion, 1998.
(Bestseller by the 'father' of positive thinking)

Peck, M Scott. *The Road Less Travelled*. USA: Hutchinson & Co, 1983.
(Love, traditional values, and spiritual growth)

* Ray, Barbara. *The Reiki Factor*. USA: Associates, 1983.
(Radiance Technique, and perhaps Mrs Takata's main student)

** Redfield James. *The Celestine Prophesy*. UK: Bantam Books, 1994.
(Novel of awakening)

Taylor, Ross. *Confidence in Just 7 Days*. London: Vermillion, 2000.
(Practical strategies to transform your life)

* Yeshe, Lama. *Medicine Dharma Reiki*. Delhi: Full Circle Publishing, 2001.
(Usui's memoirs by son of discoverer)

* = Direct access to some of Usui's teachings
** = Highly Recommended

WORKBOOK NOTES
On Final Summaries

WORKBOOK NOTES
On Further Reading And Courses Needed

References

Astin J.A., E. Harkness & E. Ernst. (2000) "The Efficacy of Distant Healing: A Systematic Review of Randomised Trials", *Annals of Internal Medicine*, 132: 903-910.

D'Adamo, P. J., C. Whitney. (1997) *Eat Right 4 Your Type.* London: Putnam Publishing Group.

Bacup: http:/www.cancerbacup.org.uk/questions/living/genetics/cancer-inherit-risk.htm. 2nd August 2002.

Beecher, HK. (1995) "The Powerful Placebo." *J Am Med Assoc,* 159(17): 1602-1606.

Benor, D, MD. (1993) *Healing Research: Holistic Energy medicine and spirituality Volume 1 and II – Research in Healing.* UK: Helix Editions Ltd.

Burbeck, R et al. (2002) "Occupational Stress in Consultants in Accident and Emergency Medicine: a National Survey of Levels of Stress at Work", *Emergency Medicine Journal* 19: 234-238.

Byrd, R.C. (1988) "Positive Therapeutic Effects of Intercessory Prayer in a Coronary Care Unit Population", *Southern Medical Journal,* 81: 826-829.

Brown, C.K. (1995) "Spiritual Healing in a General Practice: Using a Quality-of-Life Questionnaire to Measure Outcome", *Complementary Therapies in Alternative Medicine*, 3: 230-233.

Dixon, M, Dr. (1998) "Does 'Healing' Benefit Patients with Chronic Symptoms? A Quasi-Randomised Trial in General Practice", *Journal of the Royal Society of Medicine,* 91: 183-188.

Dodes, J. (1997) "The Mysterious Placebo", *Skeptical Inquirer.* (Jan/Feb)

Doi, H. (2000) *Modern Reiki Method for Healing.* British Columbia: Fraser Journal Publishing

Doi, H. (1999) *Modern Reiki Method for Healing*. Earlier version of book presented at his "Hiroshi Doi Reiki Master Workshop", Vancouver Canada, 20-22 August 1999.

Edwards, H. (1987) *A Guide to Spiritual Healing*. UK: Books Print.

Ehrenreich, B., D. English. (1989) *For Her Own Good: 150 Years of Expert's Advice to Women*. 2nd Ed. New York: Anchor Books.

Ellyard, L. (2001) *The Tao of Reiki*. Delhi: Full Circle Publishing.

Ernst, E. MD. (2001) *The Desktop Guide to Complementary and Alternative Medicine*. China: Harcourt Publishers.

Goleman, D. (1996) *Emotional Intelligence: Why it Can Matter More Than IQ*. London: Bloomsbury Publishing.

Greene, B. (2000) *The Elegant Universe*. London: Vintage.

Hammond, S. (1973) *We Are All Healers*. London: Turnstone Books.

Harding, OG. (2001) "The Healing Power of Intercessory Prayer", *West Indian Medical Journal*, Dec, 50: 269-272.

Hart, C. (1999) "The Mysterious Placebo Effect" *Modern Drug Discovery* 2(4), 30-40.

Hunt, V. (1996) *Infinite Mind*. USA: Malibu Publishing Company.

Kelly, S. and J Bunting. (1998) "Trends in Suicide in England and Wales, 1982-1996". *Office for National Statistics - Population Trends* (92), 29-41.

Kienle GS, Kienle H. (1996) "Placebo Effect and Placebo Concept: a Critical Methodological and Conceptual Analysis of Reports on the Magnitude of the Placebo Effect." *Alter Ther Health Med,* Nov, 2(6): 39-54.

Lübeck, W., F. Arjava Petter, W. Lee Rand. (2001) *The Spirit of Reiki: The Complete Handbook of the Reiki System*. Wisconsin: Lotus Press

McTaggart, L. (2001) *The Field: The Quest for the Secret of the Universe*. London: HarperCollins Publishers:

Pearsall, PK. (2001) "On a Wish and a Prayer: Healing Through Distant Intentionality", *Hawaii Medical Journal,* 60 (10): 255-6.

References

Pert, C. (1999) *Molecules of Emotion: Why You Feel the Way You Feel.* London: Simon & Schuster.

Rudebeck, C. (2002) "If the Spirit Moves You", *The Independent Review, Health.* 31 July: 13.

Schneider, M., M. Larkin & D. Schneider. (1994) *The Handbook of Self-Healing: Your Personal Program for Better Health and Increased Vitality.* London: Penguin Books.

Targ, E. (1997) "Evaluating Distant Healing: a Research Review", *Alternative Therapies,* 3(6), 74-78.

Williamson, M. (1992) *A Return to Love.* London: Thorsons.

Yeshe, L. (2001) *Medicine Dharma Reiki: An Introduction to the Secret Inner Practices.* Delhi: Full Circle Publishing.

Index

7

7-level path. See 7 level system
7-level system, 4, 27, 107, 109,
110–31, 471, 474
Barbara Ray, 76

A

Acceptance, 214, 235, 239, 399
of impermanence, 253
of own gifts, 210
Active healing. See Chapter 17
Active reiki, 300–301
dangers, 301
Acupuncture, 39, 97, 188, 226,
Acute conditions, healing of, 174
Adam's apple, 324
Addiction, 248, 440. *See also*
Clients, addicted
Aesclepius, 196
Affirmations
Benedictine, 232
AIDS, 452
Akasha. See Ki
Akashic Records, 280
Alpha waves, 251, 295
Amplitude, 171, 172, 187, 269,
448
low, 208
Angels, 196, 197, 219, 241, 347
human, 197
Anger, 134, 135, 171, 172, 248,
380, 495
Animals, healing of, 26, 377, 449

Antibiotics, 41, 438
Anxiety, 169, 198, 237, 248
Appointments, 351
Archetypal images, 192
Arms
strained, 314
Arthritis, 91, 314, 436, 437, 458,
463
Asthma, 91, 420, 497
steroids, 420
Attunement
blessing of Master, 233
heat, 241
high frequency, 207
longevity of, 401
Attunements. *See Chapter 11*
benefits of, 221
distant, 27
during pregnancy, 445
in Christianity, 219
in Islam, 220
in Japan, 217
on-going, 400
progression, 401, 402
re-attunements, 402
universality of, 220
Aura, 43, 186, 362–65
balancing, 226
illness through. See Ripple
effect
knots in, 379
release from, 208
scanning, 383
weakness in, 370
Australia, 457

Austria, laws in, 455

B

Back pain, 188, 238, 358
Bacteria, 40, 213, 422, 423
Bacterial infection, 184
Bad habits, 398
BBC, 42
Beaming, 314
Beams of light, attuning, 65
Bear, 357
Beech wood, scent of, 196
Benedictine
  affirmations, 232
  attunements, 219
  monastery, 219
Benor, Daniel, Dr, 40
Beta waves, 300
Bioenergy, 39
Biofeedback, 28, 34, 179–203,
  228, 242, 243, 244, 245, 287,
  348, 350, 386, 397, 439
  beaming, 183
  circular motion, 185
  cold, 184, 357, 359
  colour, 357, 358, 359
  distant healing, 183
  explanation of, 180
  falling over, 185
  fear of, 429
  from hibiki, 371
  heat, 184, 239, 356, 358
  importance of explaining, 179
  movement outside, 358
  nausea, 357
  nothing, 371. See Chapter 10
  pain, 239, 356
  pain relief, 149, 356, 358

  peace, 359
  pushing or pulling, 185
  scanning, 183
  self-healing, 181
  tingling, 185, 357
  touch, 184
  vibration or shaking, 185
  visible, 350
  within healee, 181
  within healer, 182
Bioplasma, 39
Birth, 444
Birth issues, 269
Blackwell, Captain, 64
Blocks, energy, 25, 39, 185, 207,
  213, 225, 226, 247, 254, 257,
  261, 316
Bone fracture, 180, 182, 184,
  188, 351
  pins, plates or bolts, 428
Breath, 254–57
Brown, Ray, 371
Brown, Sylvia, 434
Buddha, 231
Buddhism, 55–59, 63, 316
Burns, 347
Byosen, 369–82, 387, 388, 389,
  390
  cord connection, 388
  difficulty, 388

C

Cancer, 153, 158–60, 163, 179,
  206, 434, 454, 470
Cancer Act, The, 431, 454
Caveats, 34. *See Chapter 24*
Chakra, 43, 366
  balancing, 366

blocks in, 225
closing, 225
crown, 188, 223, 238, 241, 302, 358
in hands, 189, 225
opening, 225
realignment, 397
self-healing, 250
third eye, 188, 224, 428
throat, 186
Change, fear of, 469
Channelling, 39, 140, 149, 153, 156, 320, 353
symbols, 223, 238
Chemotherapy, 454
Chi. See Ki
Chicago University, 62
Children, healing of, 377, 446–49
Chopra, Depak M.D., 253
Christ, 150, 196, 231, 239, 241
scent of, 196
Christian, 62, 67
Christianity, 62, 219
Chronic condtions, healing of, 173
Chronic fatigue, 227, 265
Circular sensation. See Biofeedback
Clairaudience, 149, 195
Clairgustation, 196
Clairolfaction, 196
Clairsentience, 149, 184, 185
Clairvoyance, 149, 182, 189, 194, 240
Claustrophobia, 321
Cleansing process. See Healing process
Clients
mentally ill, 442

Codes of Practice, 458
Cold. See Biofeedback
Collective mind, 177
Colour, 189, 238
Commitment, fear of, 471
Complementary or Alternative Medicine (CAM), 29
Concentration, lack of, 300
Conditions, how to treat. See hand positions, Chapter 18
Confederation of Healing Organisations, 431
Connecting meridians. See Meridians
Conscious choice, 306
Contraindications. See Chapter 24. See Caveats
Counselling, 190, 191, 202, 389, 390, 439, 440
Cure, 85–100
Sweeney, Allan, Dr, 419
Cure, Reiki, 227
Cure, Takata, 74
Cure, The Reiki, 42
Cure, Usui, 51

D

Dangers. See Chapter 24. See Caveats
Dangers to healer
safeguards against, 440
Data Protection Act, 454
Death, healing into, 152–54
Denmark, 457
Depression, 239
Desire
ego dangers, 427
ego of, 221, 231, 235

false, 301
of gifts of others, 210
of healing outcome, 296
Detachment, 252
Development as healer, 466
Development of own gifts, 211
Diabetes, 414–17, 425
Diagnosis, 372, 422, 433, 434–35
Diary, 398
Dietery supplements, 437
Difficult cases, fear of, 470
Disease, 370
Diseases, general
healing strategy, 463
Distant healing, 26, 29, 43, 183,
273, 415, 421, 447
Dixon, Michael Dr, 42
Dizzy sensation. See Biofeedback
Doi, Sensei, 81, 109
Doshisha, 62
Dreams, 192, 359, 398
Drink, after treatment, 424–25
Duncan, Helen, 412
Dying, 152

E

Ecstasy, 197, 233
Ectoplasm, 304, 424
Edwards, Harry, 173, 421
Ego. See Desire
Ego, too much, 468
Electromagnetic energy, 179
Energy
blocks. *See Blocks, energy*
bodies, 227, 229, 288, 363
body, 397
fear of, 468
fear of release, 389

flow, 315
flow differentials, 306
loss of. See Biofeedback
*movement sensation. See
Biofeedback*
negative attachment, 388
negative attachment to, 390
plus and minus, 315
projection, 381
resolution, 401
Energy blocks
release of, 226
Enlightenment, 4, 26, 33, 217,
231, 253, 316, 492
Epilepsy, 420
Etheric body, 186, 304, 415
Exoteric subjects, 99, 100, 107
Expertise development, 466
Eyes
open or closed during healing,
348
Eyesight, 186

F

Failure, fear of, 469
Faith healing, 42, 419
*Falling over sensation. See
Biofeedback*
Fear, 152, 169, 203, 227, 229,
248, 389, 467–73, 496
Field, human, 223
Florida, laws in, 456
Forms, 353. See Scores
France, laws in, 455
Frankincense, scent of, 196
Free will, 401, 467
Frequency, 148
interactions, 46

of ki, 44
of matter, 394
of rei, 44
raising, 228, 399, 428
Frustration, 248
Furumoto, Phyllis Lei, 76, 80

G

Gakkai, Usui, 52, 81, 108, 109
Ganesh, 231
Geopathic stress, 230
Germany, laws in, 455
Gokai. See Reiki Ideals
Grecian Reiki, 194
Gregory, Candy, 424
Grounding, 177, 287–91, 320, 411
    customisation, 288
    during a treatment, 289
Guides, 150, 195, 230, 239, 240, 241, 270, 284, 304, 347
    animals, 193, 357
    hearing them, 195
    scent of, 196
Guilt, 248, 398
Gums, 443

H

Hallucinations, 177, 411, 440
Hand positions, 308–14
    difficulties, 314
    guidance in, 464
    specialist, 309
    starting position, 265, 347
    thumbs, 308
    time in each, 463
Hands
    energy from, 374

stuck, 350
Happiness, 135, 175, 229
Haviland, Dennis, 458
Hayashi, Chijiro, Dr, 56, 66, 68, 70, 71, 72, 74, 80, 124, 218, 347, 393
Headache, 188, 356
Healee position, 315–20
    couch, 318
    couch advantages, 319
    couch disadvantages, 319
    Egyptian position, 315
    sitting advantages, 316
    sitting disadvantages, 317
Healer
    dangers to, 440, 453
Healing
    animals, 26
    credit for, 304
    development in, 466
    end of a session, 350
    eyes, open or closed, 348
    family members, 26
    friends, 26
    from attunements, 227
    in hospitals, 451
    in trance, 445
    inappropriate touch, 320, 325, 328
    into death, 152–54
    magnetic, 297, 301
    payment for, 453, 455
    persistence, 173
    pets, 26
    pre-agreements, 426
    professionalism in, 460
    recording sessions, 441
    responsibility, 306
    third party present, 448

third person present, 440
time in positions, 350
timing, 165, 173
touch or no touch, 346, 455
who can, 25
with eyes, difficulty, 380
with toys, 466
Healing process, 393–99
afterwards, 400–402
first half hour, 397
first three days, 397
length of, 395–96
next weeks and months, 398
old issues, 398
Healing process, 21 day. See
Healing process
Hearing aid, 322, 426
Heat. See Biofeedback
Herpes, 454
Hibiki, 369–82, 384, 387, 390,
391
Higher consciousness, 347
Highest good. See Intention
HIV, 452
Homeopathy, 46, 275, 426
Hospital, healing in, 451
Hui yin, 268–71
Hunt, Valerie, 44, 148, 149, 223
Hydronephrosis, 424
Hypocortisolism, 418–20

I

Ideals, Reiki, 66, 134
Illness
how to treat. See hand
positions, Chapter 18
secondary benefits, 389, 390
smells of, 196

taste of, 196
Inadequacy, fear of, 470
Infection, 423
Injuries
healing strategy, 463
Insecurity, 248
Insulin, 414–17
Insurance, 33, 182, 194, 257, 372,
428, 435, 437, 438, 439, 445,
458, 459, 494
specialist, 437
Intention, 150, 157, 158, 159, 347
Irritability, 248
Itaki. See Ki
Itami, Watanabe, Dr, 66
Iyashi No Gendai Reiki Ho, 312

J

Jakikiri Joka-ho, 389. See
Chapter 22
when not to use, 389
Japanese techniques, 110–31
Jealousy, 248

K

Kanji, 272–82, 348
combinations, 273
meditation, 272
thumb position, 279
unconsicous use, 272
when to use, 273
Karma, 230
Karuna Reiki

uses of, 39
Kidney condition, 424
Knowledge
  seeking of, 32
Krishna, 150, 196, 231

L

Laughed at, 467
Laughter, 197
Letting go, 200
*Light-headed sensation. See
  Biofeedback*
Localised problems
  healing strategy, 463
Loneliness, 248
Love, 145
LOve, 155, 45, 154–60, 175, 225,
  233, 248, 285, 305, 401
  addiction to, 177, 409
  crime reduction, 156
  explanation of, 145
  ill from, 287
  teaching, 30, 38
Low energy, 187, 265
  caveats, 427

M

*Magnetic healing. See Healing -
  magnetic*
Malaysia, 457
Mana. See Ki
Mandela, Nelson, 473
Manic depression, 177, 224, 410
Manning, Matthew, 206, 371,
  455
Manual, 30
Martial arts, 39
Marxism, 347

Mary, 150, 196, 231, 239
  scent of, 196
Massage, 427
Mastership Pathway, 25
Matter, nature of, 394
Mecca, 231
Medication dosage
  changes, 436, 438
Meditation, 45, 185, 260, 295,
  429, 500
  peace through, 259
Meridians, 226, 250, 268, 270,
  271
  to mouth, 268
  to perineum, 269
Midwives, 444
Milner, Kathleen, 77
Mind
  emptying, 373
Monads, 39
Moral dilemmas, 417, 418, 419,
  420, 447
Mount Kurama, 52, 63, 64, 65,
  93, 393
Moxa Cautery, 97
Mudra. See Kanji
Murton, Jeanne, 78, 433
Music
  during treatment, 350
Mystic subjects, 52, 100, 107

N

National Health Service, 413,
  441, 445, 458
Natural healing, 148–51
*Nausea sensation. See
  Biofeedback*
Neck pain, 257

Negative Energy Spot, 369, 370, 376, 377, 378, 380, 383, 391
Nightmares, 398
Notifiable diseases, 443
Nutritional advice, 436–39
Nuwati. See Ki

O

Od, 39
Odic, 39
Odyle, 39
Okajima, Sensei, 82
Old injury, 187. *See Reiki - old injuries*
Orendo. See Ki
Orgon, 39
Orgone, 39
Orthodox medicine, 412

P

Pacemakers, 417–18
Pain, 397
    caveats, 421–23
    during healing. See Biofeedback
    frequency of, 422
    undiagnosed, 422
Passive healing. See Chapter 17
Passive reiki, 295–99
    dangers of, 299
Past life, 190–92, 228, 324, 439
Payment for healing, 453
Peace, 234, 238, 239, 249, 295
Peaceful, 172
Permission, 446, 450, 452
Persistence, 206
Pert, Candice, 223
Pets, healing of, 26, 377

Phobia, 227, 248, 316, 346, 423
Placebo, 41, 209, 353
Plus and minus energies, 373
Possessions, 278
Power. See Amplitude
Practice strategy, 466
Prana. See Ki
Pregnancy, 444
Prejudices, 398
Protection, 230, 284–86
    caveat, 286
    from negative energy, 285
    in spiritual healing, 284
Psychic. See Chapter 9 for section on Biofeedback from the Seven Senses
Psychic abilities, 26, 221, 224, 237, 240
    inaccuracy of, 433
    misuse of, 434
Pulling sensation. See Biofeedback
Pushing sensation. See Biofeedback

Q

Quality assurance, 29, 33
Quality times, 75
Quan Yin, 196

R

Radiance Technique, 76
Rand, William, 77
Ray, Barbara, 76
Ready-made reiki course manual, 30
Record form, 353
Record keeping, 208

Recording outcome. See also Scores

Records, 215

Referring on, 43, 199, 389, 399, 439, 440

Rei, 33, 38, 165, 200. *See LOve*
    frequency, 46, 44–47, 146, 148
    healing acute conditions, 174
    healing chronic conditions, 173
    limitations, 146, 165, 169, 170, 172, 177
    mental healing, 168–70
    on continuously, 345
    quick healing with, 148

Reiju, 401

Reiki, 409
    discovery of, 393
    escaping, 269, 270
    history of, 51–83
    how it heals, 40
    Ideals, 133–41
    intelligence of, 146, 185, 263, 412
    lack of flow, 254
    lineages, 472
    nature of, 417
    old injuries, 263, 297
    reference information, 31
    regulation of, 29
    specialities, 28

Reiki 2, 33, 43, 45, 46, 139, 143, 150, 154, 160, 168, 174, 183, 185, 192, 195, 273, 275, 285, 286, 287, 294, 297, 298, 305, 306, 314, 350, 351, 353, 410, 411, 416, 421, 428, 466, 469, 496, 502

Reiki 3A, 43, 225

Reiki 3A - Healing Mastership, 115

Reiki 3B – Intuitive Mastership, 117

Reiki 3C – Spiritual Mastership, 119

Reiki 3D – Self-Development Mastership, 120

Reiki 4, 120, 121

Reiki 5, 122

Reiki 6, 123

Reiki 7, 124

Relaxation, physical, 257

Release, healing signs, 350

Repard, Cmdr David, 431

Replacement Therapy, 169, 171, 175

Respect, 389

Re-training, 31

Ripple effect, 147
    timing, 162

Roses, scent of, 196

Royal Colleges, 432

S

Sadness, 171, 172, 199, 200, 229, 238, 239, 248, 301, 495

Scanning, 369–82, 464
    aura, 383
    plus and minus energies, 373
    use of information from, 372
    which hand to use, 373
    with eyes, 379

Sceptic, 42

Sceptics, 42, 212, 458, 499

Schizophrenia, 170, 177, 224, 225, 411, 428, 429, 442, 470

Schneider, Meir, 269

Sciatica, 226, 250
Scientific research
  cancer, 206
  flow, 279
  who can heal, 25
Scientific studies, 413
  distant healing, 43
  frequency of rei, 45
Scoliosis, 318
Scores, 180, 181, 199, 266, 351, 353
Scream, primal, 202–3
Seichem, 77
Self-healing, 26, 33, 222, 234, 241, 466. See Chapter 19
  aura, 250
  biofeedback, 181
  development, 251
  difficulties, 261
  emotions, 248
  how to practice, 343
  mental, 248
  meridians, 250
  missing treatments, 343
  necessity for, 342
  physical, 247
  regularity, 343, 344, 400
  reports of, 356
  scanning, 378
  sleep during, 343, 358
  soul, 249
  spirituality, 248
  timeline, 247, 250
Shaking. See Biofeedback
Shintoism, 60–61
Shoden, 109, 110, 111
Shoulder pain, 257
Solar plexus, 167, 358
Soul, 38, 105, 166, 168, 249, 394

Soul path, 26, 229, 230, 427
Special needs, 28
Spiralling sensation. See Biofeedback
Spirit, 166
Spirit body, 165
Spiritual healing, 143–60, 409, 462. *See Rei or Love*
Spiritualist healing, 304, 305
Spirituality, 248
St Teresa, 239
Star of David, 192
Steroids, 418
Stress, 187, 316
  grounding, 266
  release of, 254
  test for, 257
Stressed energy
  earthing, 265
Suicide, 440
Super Radiance Groups, 156
Support, from reiki master, 209, 472
Sutras, 63
Sweeney, Allan, Dr, 78–83
  biography of, 32
  cure, 79
Symbols, 46, 240, 241
  channelling, 223, 238
  first, 416
  one time use of, 193
  second, 416
  visions of, 193
Synacthen test, 419, 420

T

Takata, Hawayo, Mrs, 38, 73, 71–75, 347, 393

fees, 74
Tantra of the Lightening Flash, 52, 63
Tears, 198–201
Techniques, Japanese, 110–31
Teeth, 423, 443
Therapeutic Touch, 300
Thyroid conditions, 413
Ti. See Ki
Tibet, 67
Tingling. See Biofeedback
Tinnitis, 195
Touch or no touch in healing, 346, 455
Traditional Usui Reiki, 75, 109, 112
Trance healing, 445
Trauma
  emotional, 165
  energy of, 165
  manifestation, 163
  mental, 164
  physical, 165
  spiritual, 164
Tumours, 184

U

Unconscious mind, 222
USA, laws in, 456
Usui Reiki Therapy, 86
Usui, Mikao, Dr, 68, 50–70, 218, 229, 240, 253, 312, 365, 369, 379, 393, 474
  enlightenment, 65
  fasting, 65
  manuals, 27
  quotes, 105, 145, 154, 467
  scent of, 196

V

Vegetarianism, 228, 436
  arthritis from, 437
Venereal Diseases Act, 453
Veterinary Surgeons Act 1966, 449
Veterinary Surgery (Exemptions) Order 1962, 449
Vibration. See Biofeedback
Violence, 440
Viruses, 422
  frequency of, 46
Visions, 192, 194

W

Waiting times, 75
Waka poetry, 133–41
Water. See Drink
White light, 197
Wholeness, 30, 43, 229, 233, 358
Witches Act, 412, 431
Wolf, 193
Work, 39
Workbook
  explanation of, 31

Y

Yamaguchi, Chiyoko, Mrs, 72
Yeshe, Lama, 52, 64, 66, 475, 480
Yoga, 45, 185, 296, 358, 429

Our International Reiki & Healing Training Centre

A key issue that has haunted people in our field over the centuries is the dichotomy between taught knowledge and mystical experiences. For example, in 601AD Saint Augustine built a healing and spiritual university at Canterbury, and taught to view healing from both taught knowledge AND mystic experience perspectives.

Some in-dependent healers who just "tune in and trust", seem to tune in and trust their lower consciousness! But of course, they would never dream it was their lower consciousness, because they "get results". They do not realise that most of their "healings" could be accounted for by placebo response! This in-dependence simply leads to many healers having many opinions that cause confusion and opinionated conflict.

Beautiful feelings experienced by healers and healees from healing with Universal LOve cannot be underestimated. However, the experience within this book comes from almost 25 years of teaching psychic, healing and spiritual subjects to 1000s of students.

The way forwards is to not to trust our in-dependant inner ego, which is likely to be wrong and lead to conflict with others of a different opinion; but to work with many others inter-dependently to explore both scientific knowledge, and mystic experience. We need to stop being in-dependant and become inter-dependant.

In this context inter-dependant can mean

a. Spiritual / psychic / intuitive healers sharing systematically observed knowledge to discover repeatable processes to increase quality success rates.

b. Science being encouraged to help prove the case for healing especially by using current equipment within labs, and research methodologies within hospitals and surgeries.

My reason for being with the UK's Doctor-Healer Network is to help medical professions and governments accept that healing is a valid therapy, proven to be significantly effective and cost-effective, with minimal researched contraindications, and with techniques that have quality-assured repeatability.

So, we teach we are most likely to be accepted by governments and orthodox medicine if we take an inter-dependently responsible approach, backed up where possible by scientifically based knowledge.

Yours with LOve

Allan Sweeney

Reiki & Healing

Products & Services

Including Discounts
For Reiki Masters,
& Distributors

Order Form
On Pages 505-506

OR ORDER VIA WEBSITE
www.reiki-healing.com

Reiki Healers
and Teachers Society

**Started in 1998 by Allan Sweeney as The International Reiki Healers,
the organisation has been upgraded and expanded to include teachers**

Are you studying,
practicing, or teaching
reiki?

Then join the Reiki Healers
and Teachers Society. We
offer:
- Insurance
- Regular newsletters
  and information
- Study Days
- Codes of Conduct and
  Practice
- Referral Register

To become part of our society, or to find
out more, please see
www.reikihealersandteachers.net

or call 020 8776 0546

or 01843 230377

Reiki Healers
and Teachers Society

'SYMBOLS IN SOUND'

For Healers To Heal By And Masters To Attune With

This remarkable CD is not really flute music - it is healing, spiritual sounds, played by Paul Cheneour, a clairaudient flutist who hears music in all he looks at. When I taught reiki to therapists in prisons, Paul, a therapist, heard and played the healing energy of Reiki symbols.

Free Booklet Included Inside

The booklet explains what the 18 tracks may help. E.g., different tracks may help to heal physical, mental, emotional, past life, reality awareness, psychic attack, bad habits, fear, and many other health problems.

From Letter Received

'Although I am only Reiki level 1, the CD had an incredible effect on my self-healing. I was expecting good results but was completely unprepared for the healing intensity - it was similar to when I received reiki healing from a master – I could feel into areas of my body and energy field with a depth and precision I have never previously experienced – thank you! The CD is truly a blessing and indescribably beautiful. My little six year old daughter also loves it, and it now accompanies her bed-time story each night.' FH

Four Ways To Benefit From This CD

1. In daily self-reiki treatments, play tracks relevant to your main healing needs
2. Continuously play a track specific to a patient's needs in a healing session.
3. Play the complete CD to cleanse your body, emotions, mind, etheric body and soul. (A track played after another may cancel the frequency of the previous track safely. See the Reiki 2 Manual for full explanation.)
4. Play loud with interior doors open and exterior doors closed to cleanse homes of bad energy, or to improve a bad atmosphere.

CD Comment

"I bought the 'Healing Symbols in Sound' CD from my local shop in Norfolk, and found it superb. So much so I have several friends who want it. Hence my enclosed order for 10 copies." CS

Only £14.00 each + p&p
30% discount for 5 (or multiples of 5) copies
Please see Order Form on pages 505-506

STRESS MANAGEMENT CD

"Highly Recommended For All"
"Brilliantly Relaxing Voice"
"The Complete Stress Management Programme"

Do you suffer from stress?

Do you know someone with stress? If so, this should help!

This CD is for Stressed Individuals and
Clinics, Surgeries, Healers, Hospitals & Medical Professionals

RELAXATION FROM USING THIS CD may help relieve symptoms of migraine, pain, phobia, excema, tension, fear, asthma or bereavement. The techniques may also help relieve symptoms of high blood pressure, increase skin resistance, quiet the autonomic nervous system, decrease anxiety, reduce hypertension, decrease addictions, insomnia, and reduce emotions you don't want any more such as anger, hate, revenge, or sadness.

Benefits are
better all-round health, greater inner peace,
and more happiness in the soul.

"Brilliant. A great help!" GG

One lady even phoned UK from Australia

saying how much the CD helped.

Only £14.00 each + p&p

30% discount for 5 (or multiples of 5) copies

Please see Order Form on pages 505-506.

Healing Cassette Tape for
'Emotional & Psyche Healing Release'

As many of you know, for 24 years I have sought the quickest, easiest, and best ways to heal. These Emotional and Psyche Release methods are gentle, but highly successful. Some of you have experienced the wonderful healing ability of these techniques in my Harley Street Reiki Clinic. Now they are on cassette to heal yourself and your healees.

Side A – Emotional Release
A special technique with a high success rate - maybe 75% are cured! The technique may release emotional issues such as sadness, anger, hate and some phases of bereavement.

Side B – Psyche Release
A similarly successful method – maybe 75% are cured to relieve psyche problems such as fear, negativity, or phobia.

"Thank you. Through your tape I have been able to let go of my sadness, regret, fear, and anger." J F

A respected psychiatrist gave success rates in his practice as about 75% in one session.

Only £10 each + p&p

30% discount
for 5 (or multiples of 5) copies.

Please see Order Form on pages 505-506

PRE-ENERGISED MASTER REIKI QUARTZ CRYSTALS
For Reiki Crystal Grid

These natural crystal pieces are pre-energised
with a Reiki Master Symbol
via a Special Reiki Attunement
The crystals' energy has high loving frequency.

Crystals' electrons retain memory information, so the Master Reiki Crystals have many possible beautiful uses. E.g., you may keep them:

1. On your person for self-healing,
2. Under the pillow at night for better sleep,
3. By your work desk or in the car for stress reduction,
4. On a pain or problem area for relief,
5. In your hands during a meditation to raise the vibrations,
6. On written goals or plans for clarity,
7. Clusters of 8-16 Master Reiki Crystals are used to form loving, healing energy circles. Explanatory leaflet sent with order,
8. For protection use crystal circles around a bed, healing chair, room, window, door or object,
9. Each crystal is quartz. Be creative. Gain the full benefits from nature's marvellous source of pure energy,
10. Give energised crystals to those who need reiki healing, or LOve,
11. Use for distant or other healing with a Reiki Crystal Grid, (leaflet given free when ordering 8 or more crystals).

CRYSTAL PRICE LIST
Use 8 small, medium or large crystals
to make Reiki Crystal Grid – 16 crystals makes two grids

Small (approximate size - 2" i.e.5cm)

8   Energised 2" master Reiki Crystals @ £20.00 per 8
+ £5.00 p&p
16 Energised 2" master Reiki Crystals @ £35.00 per 16
+ £10.00 p&p

Medium (approximate size - 21/2" i.e. 6cm)

8   Energised 2_" master Reiki Crystals @ £25.00 per 8
+ £7.50 p&p
16 Energised 2_" master Reiki Crystal @ £45.00 pr 16
+ £15.00 p&p

Large (approximate size - 3" i.e. 7cm)

8   Energised 3" master Reiki Crystals @ £30.00 per 8
+ £10.00 p&p
16 Energised 3" master Reiki Crystals @ £55.00 per 16
+ £20.00 p&p

**Half-price Special Offer – 5kg bag of mixed-sized crystals
£100 postage free**

VIDEO OF REIKI 1& 2 ON TV

SHOWS A BBC REPRESENTATIVE,
A SELF-CONFESSED SCEPTIC, BECOMING A HEALER

How this Short Film was made

A BBC film crew spent **two days** at my Reiki Healing Centre. **With great care and beauty the film was edited to a 10-minute synopsis capturing the essence of the Reiki class.**

Comments about this Video

After the TV broadcast,
telephone calls flooded in.
Callers said that the film portrayed
**a powerful and genuinely
unbiased opinion,
and that sceptical friends
or family now believe
that reiki works!**

Suggested Uses for this Video

1. Show sceptical people that reiki works
2. Promote reiki to medical & other professionals
3. Aid to teaching for lectures, workshops, and demonstrations
4. Show patients reiki may help
5. Play in reiki shares groups and to other organisations
6. Appetiser before each reiki class
7. Enjoy with friends.

Only £15.00 each + p&p
30% discount for 5 copies

Email
mastershippathway@reiki-healing.com

Please use Order Form
on pages 505-506

Silver and Gold Pendants

Reiki Living Symbols

See <u>www.reiki-healing.com</u> for pictures and prices

Produced as **pendants**, these profound symbols are attuned to frequencies designed to provide **prescribed benefits** when kept within your aura.

They can therefore be worn around your neck, kept in a purse or pocket, or beneath your pillow at night.

Each symbol is finished in **silver** using energy of **24 carat gold** to enhance its high frequency and spiritual properties.

10 different symbols provide 10 different energies to help different needs, including emotional healing, universal love, positive energy, awakening to reality, and loving relationships.

For full information,
Pictures of the Reiki Living Symbols jewellery and prices

see **www.reiki-healing.com**

Retail price between £10 and £20

30% Discount

for distributors buying 2 or more sets.

10% Royalty on every item purchased
is donated to charitable works.

The Future Of Reiki In Your Hands

Many national governments are currently exploring
options for voluntary controls for reiki,
both in taught knowledge
and in ethics.

At the time of going to press, plans are well under way
for a complete system of ethics and knowledge,
based on this series of reiki manuals,
so that reiki healers and teachers
can be recognised as being
quality registered
or accredited.

If you are interested in joining
our world wide systems,
integrating extensive
knowledge and
abilities,

Please contact

By email: registration@reiki-healing.com

Fax: 01843 230378

Write: Reiki Registration, Box 368, Margate Kent CT9 5YQ

Products Due by End of 2004

The Reiki 2 Manual – over 500 pages

The Reiki 3 Manual

The Reiki Video Series

Reiki 1 video

Reiki 2 video

Reiki 3 video

Reiki 4 video

Psychic Development video

Spiritual Development video

Psychic   Surgery   video

**For 2004 New Product Availability And Prices
please see website www.reiki-healing.com**

Order Form For Manuals And Products
(Note that postage prices apply to the UK and EUROPE only – see post and pack prices for REST OF WORLD)

Reiki 1 Manual (Extra copies of this 504-page manual)
1 @ £18 each plus £3 p&p   £..........
5 (or 5 multiples) @ 30% discount - £12.60 plus £16 p&p £..........
Rest of world post and pack 1@£8 or 5@£31   £...........

Reiki 2 Manual – prices as Reiki 1 Manual above   £..........

Insurance – Reiki Healers and Teachers Society Membership
Tick for application form and prices, or add from website £.........

Reiki Registration and Accreditation
Tick for application form and prices, or add from website £.........

CD, (Flutes) – Reiki Symbols in Sound
1 @ £14 each plus £2 p&p   £..........
5 (or 5 Multiples) @ 30% discount £9.80 plus £7 p&p   £...........
Rest of world post and pack 1@£4 or 5@£8   £...........

CD, (Voice) – Complete Stress Management Programme
1 @ £14 each plus £2 p&p   £..........
5 (or 5 multiples) @ 30% discount £9.80 plus £7 p&p   £...........
Rest of world post and pack 1@£4 or 5@£8   £..........

Tape, (Voice) – Healing for Emotional & Psyche Release
1 @ £10 each plus £2 p&p   £..........
5 (or 5 multiples) @ 30% discount £7 plus £7 p&p   £..........
Rest of world post and pack 1@£4 or 5@£8   £..........

Crystals – Pre-energised Master Reiki Quartz Crystals
Size (2", 2_", or 3") …Quantity (8 or 16)...@ £......   £..........
See crystals description for postage costs   £..........
Half-Price 5kg – Quantity...@ £100 (post free)   £..........
Rest of world add post and pack twice the UK p&p   £..........

Video – Reiki 1 & 2 on BBC 1 Television

1 @ £15 each plus £3 p&p   £........

5 (or 5 multiples) @ 30% discount £10.50 plus £9 p&p   £........

Rest of world post and pack 1@£5 or 5@£15   £........

Reiki Jewellery

Add types required ....and prices ....from website £.........

Total Amount Payable..   **£........**

Paid by cheque / credit card / cash / bankers order other ....

Please state which ....

Type of card e.g. VISA..

Name on card ....

Card number...

Expiry date ....

Issue number (if relevant) ....

Total amount to be taken in UK pounds (£'s)..............................

Your name ....

Delivery address. ....

....

Date of order ....

Signed ....

All payments in Pounds Stirling (£'s)

All Major Credit Card Payments

Email to mastershippathway@reiki-healing.com

Phone 01843 230377

Fax 01843 230378

Cheques please to: 'Mastership Pathway UK Ltd'

PO Box 368 Margate Kent

CT9 5YQ England

PLEASE ALLOW 28 DAYS DELIVERY
GOODS USUALLY SENT BY RETURN

WORKBOOK NOTES
On Reiki Products Needed

Notes

Notes

Notes

Notes

Notes